19/5

COAST to COAST
with Janet Street-Porter

COAST to COAST

with Janet Street-Porter

BBC BOOKS

Thanks
For research, Helen Littleboy and Elizabeth McIntyre.
For typing, Susan Proctor.
For walking with me, Janet Cristea and Darryl Burton,
and all my guides and companions en route.
For suggesting the *Coast to Coast* routes,
Alan Mattingley of the Ramblers' Association.

Acknowledgements
My route through England was based on *Channel to Channel* by Ian and Kay Sayer, published by
Kimberley Publishing, 68 Kings Avenue, Christchurch, Dorset BH23 1NB (tel: 01202 484523).
I departed from their route at times and also walked it the other way round.

My route through Wales was based on *The Cambrian Way*, written and published by
A. J. Drake. Enquiries to 2 Beech Lodge, 67 The Park, Cheltenham GL50 2RX
(tel: 01242 232131).

Picture Credits
All photographs are the copyright of Janet Street-Porter
with the exception of the following:
Those on pages 12, 15, 16, 38, 86–7, 89, 92, 96–7, 98–9, 102, 103, 169, 172–3,
178–9, 180, 183, 186–7, 201, 204, 206, 210, 212–13, 214, 220 and 223
were specially taken by Ray Wood, © BBC Worldwide Limited;
pages 32, 42–3 and 61 (David Woodfall) and
pages 34–5, 54–5 and 82–3 (Bob Gibbons) from Woodfall Wild Images;
pages 79, 113, 124–5, 129 and 130 from J. Allen Cash Limited

This book accompanies the television series *Coast to Coast with Janet Street-Porter*
which was produced by Screaming Productions in association with the BBC.
Executive Producer: Janet Street-Porter · Producer: John Bush
Associate Producers: Helen Littleboy and Elizabeth McIntyre

Commissioning Editor: Sheila Ableman
Project Editor: Charlotte Lochhead · Copy Editor: Kelly Davis
Designer: Linda Blakemore
Maps: Line & Line

ISBN 0 563 38424 7

First published in Great Britain in 1998
Published by BBC Books, BBC Worldwide Limited,
Woodlands, 80 Wood Lane, London W12 0TT

Set in Gill and Ellington by BBC Books
Printed and bound in Great Britain by Butler and Tanner Limited, Frome and London
Colour separations by Radstock Reproductions Limited, Midsomer Norton
Jacket printed by Lawrence Allen Limited, Weston-super-Mare

For Lucy

Contents

Introduction 10

West to East
Dungeness to Weston-super-Mare
Day 1 Dungeness to Rye 12
Day 2 Rye to Battle 19
Day 3 Battle to Gun Hill 21
Day 4 Gun Hill to Ringmer 25
Day 5 Ringmer to Lewes to Steyning Bowl 28
Day 6 Steyning to Amberley 36
Day 7 Amberley to Cocking 40
Day 8 Cocking to South Harting 40
Day 9 South Harting to Buriton to Warnford 44

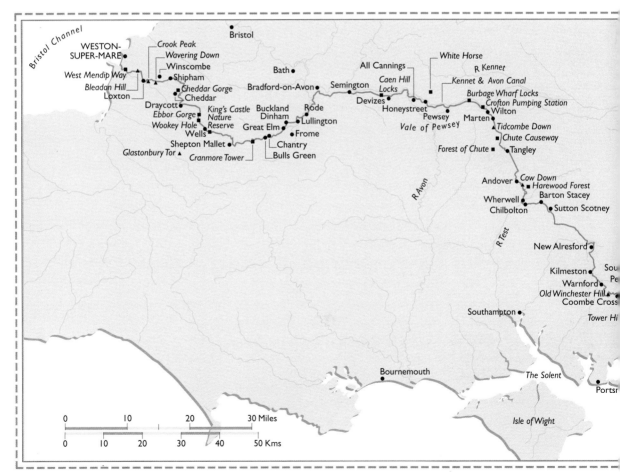

Day 10 Warnford to Sutton Scotney 50
Day 11 Sutton Scotney to Andover 52
Day 12 Andover to Chute Causeway 57
Day 13 Chute Causeway to Pewsey 59
Day 14 Pewsey to Devizes 64
Day 15 Devizes to Bradford-on-Avon 68
Day 16 Bradford-on-Avon to Great Elm 72
Day 17 Great Elm to Shepton Mallet 75
Day 18 Shepton Mallet to Wells to Draycott 78
Day 19 From Draycott via Cheddar Gorge to the M5 85
Day 20 M5 to Weston-super-Mare 93

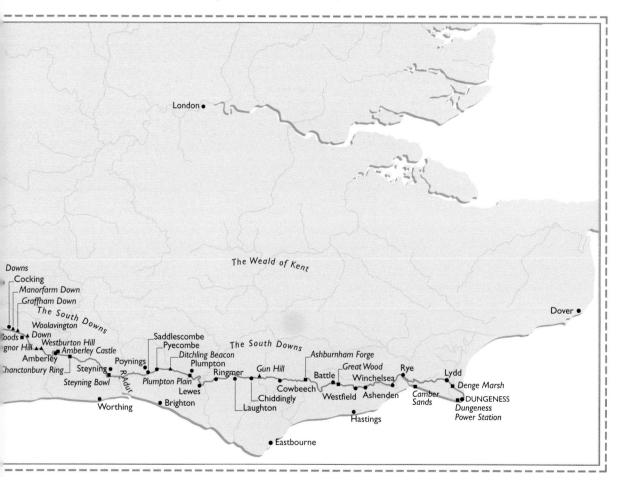

South to North
Cardiff to Conwy

Day 21 Cardiff Harbour to Castell Coch 100
Day 22 Castell Coch to Machen 104
Day 23 Machen to Pontypool 105
Day 24 Pontypool to Forest Coal Pit 110
Day 25 Forest Coal Pit to Capel-y-ffin 114
Day 26 Capel-y-ffin to Crickhowell 117
Day 27 Crickhowell to the Torpantau Pass 122
Day 28 Torpantau Pass to the Storey Arms (Pen y Fan) 127
Day 29 Storey Arms to Fan Gyhirych 132
Day 30 Fan Gyhirych to Llyn y Fan Fach 136
Day 31 Blaenau to Llandovery 138
Day 32 Llandovery to past Rhandirmwyn 141
Day 33 Llandovery 143
Day 34 Dinas fawr to Nantymaen 145
Day 35 Nantymaen to Teifi Pools 150
Day 36 Teifi Pools to Devil's Bridge 153
Day 37 Devil's Bridge to Dyffryn Castell 157
Day 38 Plynlimon: Dyffryn Castell to Dylife 161
Day 39 Dylife to Commins Coch 165
Day 40 Commins Coch to Dinas Mawddwy 168
Day 41 Dinas Mawddwy to Cadair Idris 174
Day 42 Cadair Idris to Barmouth 176
Day 43 Barmouth to Cwm Nantcol 188
Day 44 Rhinogs to Maentwrog 190
Day 45 Maentwrog to Croesor 195
Day 46 Croesor to Bethania to Beddgelert 200
Day 47 Snowdon 202
Day 48 The Glyders: Pen-y-Pass to Ogwen 207
Day 49 Llyn Ogwen to Drum 215
Day 50 Drum to Conwy 218

Places and People 224

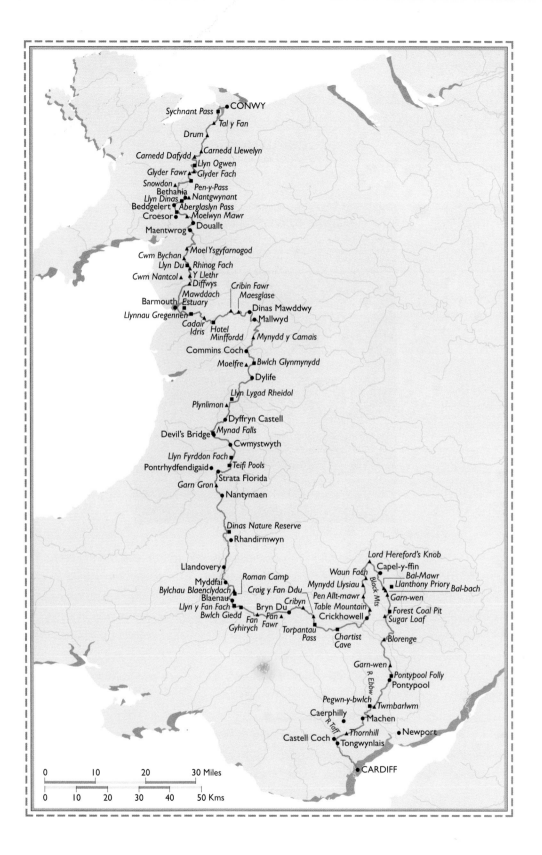

Introduction

How did it all begin? I suppose when my mother took me up into the mountains above Llanfairfechan in North Wales to pick bilberries as a child. How I hated that task – it meant spending hours on my knees collecting tiny purple berries in jam jars which my granny turned into jam. For my Welsh relatives walking meant collecting – firewood in shopping bags from the banks of the three streams above the village; blackberries up the lanes in the autumn; and the biggest horror of all – bilberries on the high moors above Carreg Fawr. I did acquire a taste for the loneliness of the ritual though, drinking ice-cold spring water interspersed with lukewarm tea from a thermos.

In the sixties I walked in Mid-Wales, around Tregaron, and in the seventies my love affair with the Yorkshire Moors began. In the last decade I have walked in Ireland, the Himalayas, the Canary Islands and the Pyrenees. I even made a television series following the some-what unpredictable long-distance walker Ffyona Campbell as she completed her walk around the world, from Southern Spain to John O'Groats. When Ffyona rounded on me and claimed that ramblers weren't somehow 'real' walkers, I secretly felt wounded and

angry. How dare this woman who had reduced such a pleasurable activity to mile-chasing along roads, trash my passion? Through the Ramblers' Association I have met hundreds of happy walkers who found her remarks crass and ill-considered.

I generally prefer to walk alone but I began to see that by undertaking a really long walk, going from coast to coast, I would have the chance to experience the post-election mood in Britain in a unique way. I suggested six routes crossing the country to the Controller of BBC2 and he cunningly put two together to create a marathon that started in Dungeness in Kent and crossed Southern England diagonally, ending at Weston-super-Mare. Then I would cross the Bristol Channel and walk through Wales from south to north – from Cardiff to Conwy. My journey would take me across Romney Marsh, along the South Downs, through Hampshire and the Vale of Pewsey. I'd follow the Kennet and Avon Canal, and pass through the Mendips and Cheddar Gorge. In Wales I'd dip into the Brecon Beacons and the Black Mountains, climb in Snowdonia, and emerge just a few miles from where I used to pick bilberries over 40 years ago.

I decided to meet some people en route and walk with them for a few hours – it's always good to have an entertaining companion in small doses to drag one away from the seductive solitude of walking alone. They were to range from comedians Vic Reeves and Bill Bailey, to Government Minister Chris Smith and Welsh pop star Donna Lewis. Some, like Vic and Bill, had connections with the area they walked through; others, like author Nick Albery, are fanatical walkers with strong opinions. All added to my enjoyment of the project enormously.

My route was loosely based on two little books for the serious hiker: *Channel to Channel* by Ian and Kay Sayer; and *The Cambrian Way* by Anthony Drake. Throughout my walk I used Ordnance Survey maps, but *The Cambrian Way* is indispensable, with its detailed maps and route information. *Channel to Channel* covers the journey from Weston-super-Mare to Dungeness, with very vague directions and sketchy maps. It was also written quite a few years ago and is out of date in places. Nevertheless, it's a starting point. I've given the broad details of the route I followed, but anyone wishing to follow my route through England needs to be a good map-reader, and extremely adaptable. Time after time, when you leave a recognized long-distance path you will find few signs and lots of nettles! My ideal walk combines both kinds of path – from the South Downs Way to the little tracks used by locals – but patience is a definite necessity.

Finally, the best thing about embarking on a walk of this length is the sheer enjoyment to be gained from its unpredictability. Travelling on foot, you not only experience our land-scape in a unique way, but you are also able to meet an extraordinary mix of people, from farmers to fishermen, walkers to shopkeepers. They've all added their imprint to this story.

Opposite: With my younger sister and my nain *(Welsh granny) at Menai Bridge.*

West to East

Dungeness to Weston-super-Mare

The longest walk of my life started on a blazing hot June day in 1997, by Dungeness Power Station at 8 a.m. The wind was howling as I set off up the beach to Prospect Cottage, where the artist and film-maker Derek Jarman used to live until his death. His companion Keith Collins has become a fisherman and gets up each day at 4 to go out on a local boat.

He has lovingly kept up Jarman's extraordinary garden with its melange of driftwood, sea pinks, poppies and circles of round stones. The cottage is surrounded by a motley collection of shacks and fishermen's huts, but its fame has driven up property prices in the area. Outside one shack was a wooden tree for drying sheets festooned with a new kind of fruit – plastic sandals.

Dungeness, like Cape Canaveral on the coast of Florida, is one of the largest shingle formations in the world and is home to rare birds, plants and insects. The nuclear power station is promoted as a free tourist attraction, with its visitor centre (over 40,000 trippers a year) and information leaflets. The fact is, it's a pretty depressing sight, with non-stop winds and plenty of rubbish strewn around the perimeter fence. I hadn't made any special plans or purchases for my route, but as I walked the quarter of a mile to Prospect Cottage I thought it might have been a good idea to pack a hat as my hair ferociously whipped across my face. The light was dazzling and the road was deserted.

Derek Jarman bought Prospect Cottage ten years ago and made his garden from the flotsam and jetsam of the beach. He made trellises for climbing plants from the anti-tank fencing which had covered the beaches in readiness for the German invasion, and sculptures from the empty cases of mines which had riddled the area.

Keith, an actor and vegetarian, explained to me that his new career as a fisherman was part of integrating himself into the neighbourhood. The process would finally be complete when he married a local girl. He enjoyed the teamwork on the boats, the extraordinary cloud formations and the exotic creatures that found their way into the nets: 'I've waited a whole year to see a stingray and we had two in one week. They were small but astonishing – battleship grey but round the edge is a colour that is the opposite of fluorescent, a deep indigo. It's the colour Isaac Newton meant when he invented the word indigo and it just absorbs all colours – an immense purple.'

The flowers in the garden bent in the wind. They were an equally intense blue, deeper and more electric than the sky. Keith told me that the local fishing industry was threatened by plans to extract gravel from the sea bed which would affect access to a spawning ground. Seventeen local boats were fighting a multinational company – an industry where nothing was written down, and fathers showed their sons where to fish, was in danger of having its traditions destroyed.

Opposite: In front of the nuclear power station before setting off on my longest walk to date.

We walked together into Lydd, so Keith could go to the bank and I could cross Denge Marsh to get to Camber Sands. The road crossed the private railway line which takes the nuclear waste from the power station to Sellafield. There were several freight containers inside an ugly chain-link compound. To our left a ribbon of pylons stretched across the marsh as far as you could see. The power station land was surrounded by more fencing and keep-out signs. And on the other side of Lydd was the Army firing range with more keep-out signs and fencing.

Above: Saying goodbye to Keith outside Prospect Cottage.
Opposite: The cottage and some of Derek Jarman's garden sculpture.

The marshes were dry land until the thirteenth century when storms destroyed old Winchelsea and breached the shoreline. Salt water then flowed over the land, forming mud flats. The 'inning' or draining of the marshes was a haphazard affair, and was completed by the 1830s. As the land rose – with the silting up of the Rye and Winchelsea harbours – farmers would spy a plot and annex it, building an embankment to keep out the salt water. There were no roads on the marsh before the beginning of the twentieth century and locals who lived on the beaches crossed it wearing 'backslays', a kind of snow shoe for marshes – little pieces of wood braced with leather.

The approach to Lydd isn't particularly auspicious. Luckily, like all marsh villages, its church gives the place some distinction, with its square, sturdy flint tower. I crossed over the road in front of the church and walked a short way down the lane. Turning left by a deserted playground, I searched for a footpath sign. The crew had gone to get lunch, and I was confidently expecting to meet them in the car park at Camber Sands 6 miles away in an hour and a half. How wrong I was!

According to the OS map, a path headed almost due west. I found a couple of faded blue arrows on top of some fence posts, but then spent an hour getting more and more exasperated as I could not find a path that crossed the deep drainage ditches. Farmers had planted crops right up to the edge of them, making it impossible to see where any crossing points were. I counted the number of pylons on the map. Following the OS route

meant struggling through a field of rape over 4 feet high. It scratched my legs and I cursed and swore. Day One and I was lost within three hours! Above me circled little aircraft from Lydd Aerodrome and seagulls mocked my howling frustration.

Where once the marshes were grazed by sheep, they are now planted with potatoes for Tesco, rape and corn. Just to add to my misery, the rape I'd walked through had been sprayed with something that was making my legs itch furiously. I'd also forgotten my compass and spent five minutes belatedly rubbing sunblock on my face and arms. The sound of machine-gun fire drifted over from the firing range. I was boiling hot. It felt more like the bloody Sahara than East Kent.

Eventually I found the farm track to Scotney Court and followed it for a while. When it petered out I decided to cut my losses and head towards the road. Having crossed several fields with sheep in them, I joined a track leading down to Broomhill Farm. As I trudged despondently down it, a blond farmer emerged from a large barn, 'Do you know you're trespassing? This is a private road,' he said. I pointed out that I'd just spent almost two hours lost because all the footpaths had been ploughed up. 'Well, you can walk round the edge,' was his reply. 'Anyway no one's walked that footpath in ten years!'

I walked briskly along the road, past the caravan site and the holiday camp, and turned left down the beach road to the car park. Camber is exactly the same as when I visited it as a child. The hugeness of the beach never disappoints. The car park is approached via a gay avenue of pink lilos and green inflatable crocodiles flapping in the breeze. How I remember those family picnics where we barely managed to get our rug down and our tin of sandwiches open, only to taste mouthfuls of grit as the wind lifted half the dunes into our egg sandwiches. How embarrassed I was that my dad insisted on bringing a primus stove and brewing up a kettle so we could have fresh tea from a teapot when all I wanted was to sit in the café and look moody, drinking cups of coffee.

Vic Reeves was on the point of leaving in his pick-up truck when I dashed up, all hot and sweaty. He lives about 10 miles away and comes to Camber to surf. Like me, he adores the beach and tries to forget the wind and imagine he's living in an episode of *Baywatch*. We repaired to the wooden veranda of the Kit Kat Café and gazed out at Britain's answer to Malibu. Everywhere we looked there were overweight holiday-makers with varying degrees of sunburn. Dogs chased gulls, bottoms dropped out of bikinis and I wolfed down egg, chips, beans and a white roll unlike any bread I'd ever eaten – all light and foamy. I hadn't eaten since 7.30 a.m. and it was now 4. While we sat there I showed Vic some hilarious stills from movies shot on Camber Sands. My favourite was the *Carry On* film *Follow That Camel*, made in 1966, which *Halliwell's Film Guide* describes as 'direly unamusing'. It starred Phil Silvers and Kenneth Williams as well as the usual gang of regulars. The camel

Opposite: Camber Sands, exactly the same as when I was a child and a favourite for family holidays.

in the film was called Sheena and had spent all her life in Chessington Zoo – apparently she had to be specially trained to walk on sand.

Vic and I walked into Rye along the beach. The wind dropped and so did the temperature. In the evening sun we passed the golf course and then followed the riverbank up to the bridge at the edge of Rye, climbing from mud flat to mud flat. We turned into the town at the bottom of a cobbled street where the old timbered fishermen's huts have been turned into a wine bar and some bric-a-brac shops. I think Rye is at its best in winter when the streets are empty and the tourists have gone home. In the sunset, from a distance, it looks like a French hill town. Close up, you can see how it's being choked by cars and people in its attempt to market itself as a kind of twee English theme park (not helped by the sound of 50 bikers revving their engines outside the fish and chip shop).

With Vic Reeves, a fellow beach lover and my companion walking from Camber to Rye.

Being surrounded by marshland (until it was drained in the early nineteenth century), the town became very isolated as its only communication with the outside world was by sea. From Georgian times it became popular again with authors and actors – Edward Lear, Ellen Terry, E. F. Benson, Joseph Conrad and Henry James all visited or lived in Rye.

Nowadays three worlds collide at Rye: the day-trippers who eat and walk simultaneously; the middle-class literary acolytes with their trips round Charles Lamb's house and the churchyard; and the locals. I've always been interested in what the locals get up to when the tourists go home, and now I hoped I'd find out.

We walked up Mermaid Street, past timbered houses and elegant Georgian cottages, orange pantiles giving the place a warm glow in the evening sun. As we crossed the churchyard, we glimpsed the sea through the rooftops to the south, and headed down to the Community Centre where Mambo Jambo, a local salsa band, was playing. The hall was decorated with a local craft exhibition. We sat at a table covered with a gingham cloth, drank beer and watched Rye's local inhabitants – from babies to women with fringed scarves tied around their hips – letting their hair down. There was a lot of gyrating to a South American beat. It seemed like something out of the sixties – far more erotic and exotic than one would have expected from prim and proper Rye. After a giant curry from the Gandhi restaurant round the corner, I said goodbye to Vic (and Keith who had turned up to see the band, even though he was getting up to go fishing at 3.30) and fell into bed.

Day 1 – and so much had happened in 13 miles!

awoke at 7 a.m. to another clear blue sky. When I came in last night my legs were on fire. I had sunburnt legs and arms – even my nose was looking a bit red. I couldn't believe I'd been so stupid. I went to Boots in the High Street to get cold sore lotion for my lips, block-out cream for my legs and arms and headache pills. I forgot a knife as well which would have been useful for digging the mud out of my boots. (I'd had to clean my boots on the hotel towel, so they wouldn't have been too pleased.) I didn't ache, but annoyingly I had a blister on the sole of my foot.

I left Boots and walked down the main street of Rye for my real breakfast at the Fat Controller Café by the station. The hotel I stayed at – Rye Lodge – was a bit like Fawlty Towers. The hotel owner had a bellowing voice and I heard him explaining in very loud, fractured Franglais to some French people that a good thing to go and see might be the prison ship moored off Portsmouth. On another table four middle-aged people discussed me as if I was either dead or not there.

Over a cup of coffee and a bacon sandwich Dave, the owner of the Fat Controller Café, told me that several people commuted to London each day – a two-hour journey with a change of trains at Ashford. It seemed Rye was totally dependent on the tourist industry. People were already disgorging from the Marsh Link train, armed with luggage and heading for Camber. As the streets of Rye started to fill up with shoppers and holiday-makers, I stopped at the hat shop to buy something sensible to keep the sun off my hair and nose.

I headed out of town, past the fish and chip shop where bikers were already starting to congregate for the day (weren't they sweltering in those red and black leathers?), skirted the busy roundabout, and after a few yards turned right down a lane in the direction of Winchelsea, a route I have taken dozens of times over the last few years, usually with my friend Neil. I wear a rucksack and we make the journey on foot to buy meat from Jamie Wickens, the best butcher in the area.

On my left was the Royal Military Canal, dug around 1805 as a defence against Napoleon. But why would troops be put off by 30 feet of water after crossing the Channel? The fields en route to Winchelsea were cracked and very dry. In the middle of one I turned around and saw the farmer spraying peas with some vile chemical. My legs were still smarting from whatever I had walked through the day before.

I climbed up the hill into the prim and proper world of Winchelsea. It's one of those towns where every house is trying to outdo its neighbours. There was an abundance of hanging baskets, fresh white paint and chintz curtains. The history of this little town, laid out so perfectly on the grid-iron principle, is extraordinary. Like Rye, it sits on top of cliffs and looks out to sea.

The original town of Winchelsea was built on shingle and was badly damaged by

storms throughout the thirteenth century. Because this bit of coast was seen as crucial to national security, Edward I commissioned a new town, to be paid for by national funds, on the hilltop where it now stands, 6 miles from the sea. New Gate and the massive town ditch were built as defences against French attacks from the south.

These days Winchelsea is little more than a posh village, with a tea room, a post office and a shop, and of course my favourite butcher, Jamie Wickens. He knows how to make up to 50 varieties of sausage and people come from miles away to buy his local lamb. I bought a pork pie from Jamie and set out at midday to walk through the Brede River valley, heading west towards Battle.

As I left Winchelsea, it was like Clapham Junction for walkers – literally dozens of signs all saying 'To the 1066 Walk', and then I walked about 400 yards and there were no signs and then a mile further and I was lost. In the valley, trying to work out a route, someone had kindly stuck a few planks over the ditches so if you went wrong, as I did, you could attempt to cross back to the other side. I crossed over the railway line where the Marsh Link train went past every now and then, went about 100 yards and got lost. I counted pylons (that old trick), guessing which pylon I was supposed to be near. Anyway, I managed to get back to the right side of the river by crossing a ditch on a very, very rickety plank. I sat under the shade of a hawthorn bush and ate my lunch. I hadn't seen another person for a couple of hours.

My only companions on this sweltering June day were sheep and gulls. The River Brede wound lazily along the valley floor, and considering how close I was to Winchelsea, the sound of the motor car was mercifully absent.

The hamlet of Udimore lay half a mile away on the north ridge of the valley and Icklesham to the south; but down here by the river and ditches all was still and sleepy. I turned left up a track and walked through strips of intensively cultivated broad beans, strawberries and onions, climbing up a hill and turning left at Snailham Farm, along another track to Lower Snailham, and crossing fields to Lidham Hill.

I met farmer Jenny Farrant who grows hops nearby and we chatted about the plague of wild boar which is causing havoc in the area. She's heading a campaign to get the Ministry of Agriculture, Fisheries and Food to recognize the problem and try to get farmers EU grants to erect strong fences to keep these 300-pound monsters out. Jenny was a jolly, likeable woman in a white blouse and jaunty straw hat. According to her, the wild boar problem went back to the late eighties. They were being bred locally for restaurants in London, and escaped. Now, when cornered, they could kill a dog, and the adult males were charging through electric fences and damaging crops. The business of growing hops, which is such a strong tradition in Kent and East Sussex, was dying out: 'Once absolutely every village, every farm had hops, they all had a little oast house. Now we're down to five hop growers in the whole of Sussex. Someone else can grow them cheaper.'

To try and make some extra income, she had turned their farm into an educational tour about hops, to appeal to people who'd seen hop-picking on television series like *The Darling Buds of May*. Her farm once kept four families, and sent the boys to public school but now just earned enough to keep one family. The future was looking bleak. Like many farmers, she felt the Government did not understand their predicament.

I left Jenny and walked down the hill across a meadow to Ashenden, going across the valley floor again and emerging into the village of Westfield, crossing the busy A28. This marked the start of commuting country, being on the main line between London and Hastings. I began to feel the countryside change too, putting the serenity of the marshland of the Brede River behind me as I entered the rolling hills of East Sussex. Crossing the busy A21, my legs were feeling like lead weights, and then I entered the coolness of the Great Wood, to the east of Battle. I had originally planned to walk to Catsfield, but it was out of the question. The last half-mile into Battle was a slog along a B road, with the air heavy and thundery as I skirted the walls of Battle Abbey, coming to a full stop on the steps outside the entrance gate at 8 p.m. I'd left Rye at 10.15, but lots of path confusion had really delayed me, and the blisters under my right foot were slowing me down.

My arrival at the hotel was somewhat bizarre. It was a very beautiful house which had seen better days. The garden was a complete mess and my room had a primrose yellow theme with a canopy over the bed. The owner asked me if I'd like a hard bed or a normal bed. I said I just wanted a comfortable bed. Anyway, it turned out that I got the double bed which was the hard bed. (The normal bed was a single and I don't sleep in single beds as I'm six foot tall.) I was awake all night – it was like sleeping on a tombstone. The carpet had stains all over it as if someone had given birth on it. I resorted to my usual trick of putting a shower cap on each foot, using them as instant slippers. It was 8.30 and I popped the blisters on my right foot.

I was told that last orders for dinner at the restaurant down the road was at 9 o'clock, so I told Claire, the production manager, to order anything she liked for me and sank into bubbles in a very weird-shaped corner bath. I felt it was going to eject me sideways like in that film where they come out of the pods, *They Came From Outer Space*. Anyway, dinner was pleasant and I forgot about not liking my room.

It had rained during the night: really heavy, thundery showers. I popped my blisters again, put on thick socks and decided to walk in my trainers rather than the heavy leather walking boots I'd worn for the last two days. I didn't mind if my feet got wet in long grass; it was best to give them a bit of a rest.

DAY 3
Battle to Gun Hill

I started the day by meeting Norman Knight at Battle Abbey. It was 9.30 and the

hordes of tourists hadn't yet arrived. I walked through the impressive gates rather than the English Heritage official entrance (which is through a wooden hut, housing the inevitable gift shop, at the back of the car park).

Norman (real name Derrick) dresses up as a Norman knight and stands stock still in the ruins, suddenly springing to life as a piece of living history. Once an architectural draughtsman, he was made redundant and now spends his days researching Norman

With volunteer tourist attraction Norman (Derrick) Knight in the grounds of Battle Abbey.

England. Derrick remembers his school teacher pointing him out as a typical Norman. But he was ashamed that he didn't know anything about the Battle of Hastings. Once he started reading he was hooked and started researching armour and weaponry. It took him two years to finish his chainmail suit, which he made in the traditional way. It weighs 35 pounds and contains 15,200 rings, he told me proudly. At first he came as a volunteer to try and attract more tourists to the Abbey, but now he's employed by English Heritage at the weekends to talk to people about the battle, have his photograph taken and sign autographs as 'Norman Knight'. His helmet was made from old fridge panels, beaten and riveted together. He made his shield from wood, covered it with animal skin and made pockets in the back for his tourist library – his guide books and several scrapbooks containing his finely detailed pencil drawings of the stone carvings in the Abbey.

'I give you my salutations, my lady!' he warbled out at me in a rather quavering accent that sounded more South London than medieval French. Derrick was wildly enthusiastic about his subject and there was no stopping him on the subject of the Battle of Hastings!

'If you face this way, King Harold would have stood here, right on this very spot and all his Saxon front line would have been lined up each side and in front of him on this hill top. He would have commanded a wonderful view of the Norman front line and Duke William, coming up this hill. Showers and showers of

these nasty things would have been shot from the Norman archers in the front line just at the bottom of this hill.'

At this point Derrick brandished a home-made arrow taken from a pouch on a leather strap.

I looked past Derrick, down through the Abbey ruins and over Tower Hill to the south. The edge of the path was a mass of red and white roses, looking blousy and patriotic in the early morning sun. The first coachloads of tourists were trickling by, staring incredulously at Derrick as he swung his home-made sword about his head. Derrick has been filmed and photographed by visitors from all over the world; in fact he's probably appeared on more videos than I ever will do in my professional career.

I bade him farewell and walked down the wide bridleway past the car park, dropping down to the west of the battlefield – a most tranquil and enjoyable stroll after my struggles through the fields of the last two days. I could imagine people riding up this path into the town of Battle in their carriages a hundred years ago. The trees formed a cool canopy. Derrick was delightfully 100 per cent eccentric; no doubt about that. You'd have to be, to stand around in 35 pounds of chainmail for eight hours at a stretch. But his enthusiasm for making history a living rather than a dead subject had rubbed off on me and put me in a thoroughly good mood for the day, even if it was already ominously hot. At least the air was fresher as a result of the showers the previous night. I was pleased to be walking alone as well. After only two days I was worried we were falling behind schedule. Walking, meeting people and being filmed was taking far longer than I had anticipated.

I skirted round the village of Catsfield (according to our original schedule, I was meant to get here the night before!) and met the crew for lunch in a pub called the Squirrel Arms near Beechdown Wood. I asked the bloke behind the bar if I could have a squirrel burger and he didn't think it was very funny at all. After lunch the crew walked with me, and the weather, unfortunately, got really hot again. The scenery was sensational. We left the forest behind and walked over parkland. Once a huge estate, it had now been turned into rolling hills of corn, peas and barley with narrow footpaths through them.

We dropped down a steep hill towards Ashburnham Forge and the marshes seemed a long way away; the scenery was completely different now. We could see for 10 miles across the expensive East Sussex farmland. The houses changed too – a lot had very intimidating signs: 'Private Keep Out', 'Loose Dogs', 'Private Property Do Not Enter', or my favourite, 'You are under video surveillance'. Other houses were very, very run down. I walked past farms completely overgrown with nettles, and derelict barns. You wouldn't believe anyone was living there, but they were.

We were crossing what remained of the Weald – once a thick, impenetrable forest, 12 miles wide and 30 miles deep, which cut the Sussex coast off from the rest of England. It used to be the home of wolves, wild boar and bears. Now commuters have replaced

My path through farmland outside Ashburnham Forge.

these exotic inhabitants. The next few miles west took us through extremely isolated countryside. Our aim was to get to Cowbeech by 5 o'clock and have tea. But in this part of Sussex there are no shops, no villages, just lonely farms and commuter homes, and certainly no tea shops.

We went along a track and lost the cameraman who was on a mobile phone call. Ian, the soundman, and I struck out on our own. We got so very lost I can't begin to describe it. At one stage we went through a patch of land by two farms, Attwood Farm and Hole Farm. The *Channel to Channel* book was hopelessly out of date. The footpaths were consistently blocked up, ploughed over, and simply ignored by the farmers. We got lost in some woodland where all the trees had been allowed to fall across the path, and we had to climb around them. Then we battled through 5-foot-high nettles, and I tied my jacket round my legs but it fell off and I got completely stung all over.

Eventually the rest of the crew discovered us walking in the wrong direction along a tiny track. If they hadn't found us we would have ended up walking down to the bloody coast in completely the wrong direction. We got to Cowbeech at about 6.30 where, in the Merrie Harriers, I met the publican, Jim Conroy from County Mayo. I couldn't face drinking so he kindly made me two pots of tea, and I ate half a packet of chocolate Hob Nobs.

Jim told me that hardly any of the locals walked the footpaths in the area, which was why they were so overgrown. My good humour was restored by chatting for half an hour about walking in Ireland. I had also under-estimated how much I would need to eat and drink on the walk. After the tea and chocolate biscuits, I agreed to walk on to Gun Hill in the evening light so we would not fall behind schedule.

I set off across fields of hay and there was no way you could see where the footpath was because nobody ever walked it. By then, we'd got our jackets on. It was about 8 o'clock at night and pretty cold and it was pouring with rain. We ended up on the edge of a golf course near Gun Hill with a few snooty golfers looking at us as if we were insane. The sun was setting and we took a few shots of me stumbling off into the distance and that was it.

I had spent a day in Sussex, expecting it to be almost suburban, and discovered that between the commuting belt around Heathfield and the Downs and the south coast is an extremely lonely part of the country. I hadn't seen another walker all day.

I was exhausted, and it was 8.30. My hotel was miles away in Magham Down, near Hailsham. I asked for a quiet room as it was on a main road. Naturally, being England, food was not available after 9 o'clock. This was dormitory land, full of old people who eat at 6.30 p.m. A surprisingly tourist-free zone, too. In the end we drove into Hailsham and had a Chinese at 10.15 – it was actually really good. I was too tired to do any work when I got in, or even read and, before I fell asleep, I put my wet trainers on the towel rail in the bathroom, in the vain hope that they would be dry by the morning.

I woke up to grey, wet and windy weather. My quiet room turned out to be above the kitchen so my sleep was shattered by the sounds of the staff coming in at 7 to make breakfast. The smell of bacon wafted up through the waste pipe in my bath as I cleaned my teeth. I had already decided to write the 'bad hotel guide' and the 'bad pub guide' as companion books to this walk. As for food, well most British pubs were not proving to be gourmet experiences.

DAY 4
Gun Hill to Ringmer

I got a taxi to Gun Hill to start the walk. I had just started filming and the first two walkers I'd seen in four days came in the other direction. They were very nice, in their late fifties, and they were walking the Weald Way, from Gravesend to Eastbourne. They claimed they hadn't seen any blocked footpaths; of course if you walk along well-signposted, published, long-distance paths like the Weald Way, you won't have a problem. But this coast to coast route is a different proposition.

After they had gone, I crossed a couple of fields and went up to the church in Chiddingly which had a stylish wrought-iron lamp commemorating the coronation of

Elizabeth II in 1952, and a whopping 128-foot spire which had been built as a monument to Elizabeth I's Baron of the Exchequer.

I turned left along a minor road, and searched in vain for a footpath sign. Then I cut across a field to a corner by a wood and promptly got lost. I really did need a compass – because the alternative was carrying a lot of large-scale maps, and that would simply be too much paper. I hadn't been near any shops for days. We were thinking of sub-titling the walk, 'Where the hell are we?' Spending so much time searching for footpaths makes it hard to enjoy the views or the countryside and at this point I seemed to be spending most of my time squinting at a map.

I managed to find the right way out of the wood in the end, and headed across the fields to Whitesmith. Then it was a fast bit of power-walking along a broad track through woodland to Laughton Common. The only sound I heard was the squawking of the pheasants in the trees. The weather improved and so did my humour as I felt I was at last covering some distance. At a cross-roads I took a left-hand turning and then left the road, heading west along another track. I'd already been told by villagers from Laughton that the footpaths around here were some of the worst in East Sussex, and unfortunately that turned out to be true. After sitting in the shade in the grass on the edge of a field to eat my sandwiches, I decided to leave the route proposed in the *Channel to Channel* booklet and head slightly further south, approaching Ringmer from Rushy Green, because I wanted to see the women's stoolball match that was to take place on the village green that evening.

When I finally find a sign, what does it mean?

Near Broyle Place I got the shock of my life – I suddenly came out of some bushes and saw a figure standing stock still in the cornfield ahead. After a few seconds I realized it was an extremely life-like scarecrow – probably designed to scare off ramblers rather than birds!

Although the South Downs rose up majestically only a couple of miles away to the south and Lewes Bay lay 2 or 3 miles to the south-west, I had spent another day without seeing anyone else walking in my direction. The path skirted the edges of a couple of fields – the farmers had planted as near to the edge as possible, making it extremely uncomfortable walking on a 6-inch gap between nettles and corn. At the B2124 I turned right and headed westwards to the semi-detached housing estates of Rushy Green, emerging opposite Ringmer's village green, with its little sports pavilion and scoreboard.

The stoolball wasn't due to start for an hour and a half so I decided to get a lift into Lewes for a cup of tea. Halfway down the High Street, in a back alley, was a craft market. I wandered through inevitable displays of stained glass and candles and sat down in the café. People were walking through it en route to a parking lot (Lewes is a parking nightmare).

Halfway through my tea and toasted teacake, a voice boomed out: 'It's Janet, isn't it?' I looked up and saw a woman with short brown curly hair, lively eyes and a friendly face. She was wearing an extremely respectable navy blue linen suit to well below the knee, and yet I immediately realized that the outfit did not correspond to the personality of its wearer. It was Hilary Lane – my friend from the sixties, who I had not seen since about 1970! When I was a wild student at the Architectural Association in 1965, Hilary was studying painting at the Slade, with Derek Jarman. I owned one of her abstract paintings of multi-coloured squares, and it's hung in my cottage in Yorkshire. When we both got parts as extras in Antonioni's *Blow Up* I made silver PVC trousers for Hilary to wear. Now she was the Arts Officer for East Sussex County Council, and a magistrate, which explained the rather conventional suit.

I arranged to have supper with Hilary to catch up on the gossip of the missing decades. And, as we drove back to Ringmer, I reflected on how a walk like the one I was doing was a chance to reassess one's life and rearrange one's priorities. I felt that by walking across England and Wales I would be able to draw strands of my life together and try and make sense of where to go next. Perhaps being 50 had something to do with it. I had already made the decision the previous year to stop being an executive, to stop working in a routine for someone else, to try and live a freer, less structured existence. Seeing an old friend like Hilary reinforced this idea that our lives possess a divine symmetry, a pattern we may not be aware of. We choose our friends extremely carefully: they are a gift from God. When they reappear in our lives it is to teach us something, to place a thought or idea in the forefront of our consciousness.

Back at the Ringmer village green, women in white shorts were busily marking out the stoolball pitch. The pavilion was a hive of good-natured activity, with children running about, women changing and the scoreboard being prepared. Sharon Booth, the extremely jolly captain of the local team (top of the East Sussex league), sat with me on a white bench in front of the pavilion and explained the rules. Basically it was a female version of cricket, with underarm bowling, round wooden bats shaped a bit like omelette pans, and a red leather ball with red stitching. It is played with a square wicket and eight balls in each over. Sharon told me that stoolball was seen as a chance for ordinary women to get together and behave badly! It is ruthlessly competitive and no one in her team was allowed to take their holidays until the season was over. I could see how different Ringmer, with its new housing estates and preponderance of lower middle-class families, was to Lewes, with its manicured town centre and genteel atmosphere.

Stoolball is ample proof that local life is surviving: according to Sharon, there are 69 teams in Sussex (all women only – unlike other counties such as Kent and Surrey, who allow mixed teams). Tradition has it that the sport started as a milkmaids' game in the fifteenth century.

A chilly breeze had sprung up by the time the game started at 6.45, but there was plenty of activity on the pitch. Ringmer were batting first. I asked Sharon why stoolball was seen as a peculiarly female sport.

'Men do play,' she said, 'but we believe that it's a women's game because you need technique where men are using brawn. That's brains!'

I left while Sharon was giving her team a pep talk: it must have worked because Ringmer thrashed Ditchling. As the sun set over the pretty green, there was no love lost between the two teams – screams of encouragement came from the run-out players on the benches. The only spectators were locals walking their dogs and the odd husband who'd turned up to make the tea.

At the end of the road was a sign to Glyndebourne – only 5 miles away, over the Downs. The opera-lovers would be settling down for their posh picnics in full evening dress, unaware of the Clash of the Titans they were missing in Ringmer.

DAY 5
Ringmer to Lewes to Steyning Bowl

I walked along the main road from Ringmer into Lewes, over the bridge by the Brewery and up the High Street, where I met Hilary Lane for breakfast in a café run by a charming lady who fussed over us. According to Hilary, Lewes had all sorts of strange undercurrents beneath its prim and proper facade:

'On Bonfire Night it does feel very, very pagan. Have you been?'

I replied that I hadn't.

'It's incredible. It's a sort of health and safety nightmare. It's as if you're in Spain or something and there are people with flaming torches coming down the High Street which is just packed with people…'

I tried to imagine the scene outside as a pagan orgy – it seemed light years away from the sedate middle-aged couples entering the newsagent around the corner and emerging with their copies of the *Daily Telegraph*. Hilary explained that, although the locals were happy to participate in the pagan ritual of bonfires, there was a local element strongly opposed to anything that could be construed as witchcraft. A bookshop called Fallen Angel had just opened and there had been vociferous opposition to it in the local papers, implying that it was a centre for un-Christian activities. In fact, it was perfectly respectable, selling books on alternative medicines, philosophies and lifestyles. I decided to walk around the corner and check it out. As we left the café, I noticed a sign in the window that said: 'No

parties, no children, no smokers and no vegetarians'. Were they joking? I couldn't be sure.

We passed the blue-rinse set on the genteel High Street and crossed over, walking down a side street. Opposite a gents hairdressers was the Fallen Angel Bookshop. The manager was Richard, a friendly young man with a natty peroxide blond mohican haircut and pierced ears, nose, chin and eyebrows. In fact he had so much silver plugged into his face I wondered how heavy his head must feel. On the counter was a leaflet entitled *The Alternative Guide to the Sussex area for June, July and August '97.* Under regular events, Monday carried about 17 classes in the area, from Reiki healing to hypnotherapy, classical yoga and homeopathy. On Tuesday I could have studied aromatherapy, Tai Chi, Buddhist meditation or belly dancing. I could buy anything from Hopi Ear candles to vegan fruit bars with hemp. Lewes appeared to be the epicentre of alternative living.

Richard, it transpired, had married his partner in a gay pagan ceremony at the local King Arthur Leisure Centre. I bought a slim paperback entitled *Protect Yourself Against Psychic Attacks* for £1.99 and said my goodbyes. I hoped the book might offer some clues as to how to keep my mind unencumbered as I went forward on my journey. Nothing annoys me more when I'm walking than useless pieces of trivia clogging up my head. I needed it free, empty, receptive.

It was a sunny morning with fluffy white clouds scurrying across the sky and a light breeze. I walked back up the High Street, turned right up a cobbled street and went under the Castle Arch, past the Lewes Bowling Club green, down a steep hill of pretty Georgian houses and came to the main road. In the pub opposite, a group of morning drinkers cheerily directed me to the river path out of town, past Victorian terraces in the lower, more working-class part of Lewes to the River Ouse, where I followed a pleasant path through water meadows, jostled by cows with big white numbers stencilled on their bottoms.

I crossed under the railway line and climbed the hill to Offham, at the A275. I turned left after a short distance and then climbed up a steep chalk path up on to the exhilarating expanse of the South Downs, just past Offham Hill.

I had already walked about 55 miles, and could add on at least another 5 for all the times I'd been lost. My hairdresser Keith had given me a compass on a wristband. Perhaps I'd make better progress now. It was exciting to be in such a huge landscape after the stifling environment of Lewes, with its small-town politics. I was thoroughly looking forward to a couple of hours walking alone.

My path soon joined the South Downs Way, a long-distance path which opened in 1972 between Eastbourne and Winchester, only dropping to cross rivers. Rolling chalk downs, steep slopes and extensive views over the the Weald, with glimpses of the Channel, would be my reward for the next few days walking. The Way itself was probably an important Bronze Age trading route, as shown by the large numbers of hill forts, tumuli and cross-dykes.

Over 30 million people a year visit the 500 square miles of Downland between Eastbourne and Winchester. How to retain its beauty, prevent over-development and yet still maintain an arable landscape is a subject of hot debate. The Ramblers Association, environmentalists, and organizations like Friends of the Earth and the Council for the Protection of Rural England would like it to have National Park status.

However, many local farmers and landowners don't agree, and fear that National Park status will result in the area being run by outsiders rather than locals. Some farmers feel that National Park status will bring even more walkers and lead to further erosion of paths. Now a decision is urgently needed.

I'd walked the entire route in the late spring and early summer of 1996 with my friend Janet. Every Wednesday we caught a train down from London and then a taxi to where we'd finished the week before, returning to London at the end of the day feeling refreshed and recharged, seeing a tidal wave of commuters heading home in the opposite direction after a day spent cooped up in offices.

In my enthusiasm to pick the first wild mushrooms I'd seen on this walk, I didn't notice the darkening skies. The puffballs looked like white pearls spread out on the close-cropped grass around me, and I filled my pockets. Suddenly there was a torrential downpour and I discovered that my waterproof jacket was missing its hood. As the rain turned to hailstones I got wet through to the skin and up on Plumpton Plain there was no shelter of any description. My red hair dye began to run drastically down my forehead, irritating my eyes. I used a spare sock as a towel. If anyone had been walking towards me, they would have

Above: Plumpton Plain – soaked by a sudden downpour.
Opposite: Drying out with Brian at the Jack and Jill windmills.

seen a woman who seemed to have a serious head wound, but was also reminiscent of Dirk Bogarde in the final scene of *Death in Venice*, where he dies facing the beach with black hair dye streaming down his face. My glasses were spattered with hair dye and torrential rain, but visibility anyway was about 200 yards and the wide chalk path was as slippery as hell underfoot.

The next 2½ miles over the Downs is lonely in any weather, and I didn't see another soul. As I reached the road and car park at Ditchling Beacon the rain stopped. The crew weren't at the meeting point and I couldn't raise them on my mobile phone. I didn't want to stand and wait because a still breeze was chilling my wet limbs. Even my knickers felt

clammy and cold! I decided to walk on – two people passed me and said hello; they were carrying those Alpine walking sticks I once used to despise, but after nearly twisting my ankle again on the wet chalk I started to re-evaluate their usefulness.

The sun came out as I headed west towards the Jack and Jill windmills. Another walk-er had been caught in the downpour like me, and was drying his gear – coat, trousers, gaiters – on a bit of fencing. I stopped and talked to him. Brian was a mature sociology stu-dent (about 35, I'd guess) at Manchester University and was walking the South Downs Way in the same direction as me. Apparently the severe rainstorm had come from the east, and the walkers who'd passed us coming from the west were bone dry and had missed it entirely. We met the crew in the car park at the windmills and after I'd had a bit of a tantrum about getting wet and not meeting earlier, I gave Brian some of the cheese and pickle sandwiches they had brought me and we walked together for a couple of hours, sharing walking experiences.

At one point we dropped down onto the A273 by a golf course, then turned left into Pyecombe, crossed the extremely busy A23 by the Plough Inn, walked up a little lane by riding stables and climbed back up onto the Downs. During this stretch I was boasting to Brian about the efficiency of my compass watch when I smartly took us off in the wrong direction. Brian consulted his maps and after 50 yards we retraced our steps. We dropped down a steep slope past some farm cot-tages at Saddlescombe and Brian turned north towards Poynings and his bed-and-breakfast desti-nation.

I walked on to Devil's Dyke, passing through a gate where on 1 May last year I tripped on a plank that had been tied across between the gateposts (it was still there), fell heavily on my left elbow and grazed my legs badly. After my injury had been diagnosed (wrongly) as a hairline fracture I felt that I'd never get the strength back properly in that arm again. Perhaps that was the curse of Devil's Dyke? (The steepest of the South Down combes and an Iron Age fort, Devil's Dyke gets its name from the legend that the devil was digging a ditch to let in the sea and drown Sussex but was outwitted by a woman with a candle – who tricked him into thinking the sea had risen so that he fled before he could finish.)

It was getting late and, without Brian to talk to, I began to feel extremely tired. I crossed the River Adur and passed through the pretty village of Botolphs with its beautiful

flint-covered church. Then I turned onto a path which went up Annington Hill back to the top of the Downs.

Looking behind me, the view was sensational. I pressed on, as it was late and I had to meet an extraordinary group of locals up above Steyning Bowl. They were silhouetted against the skyline – about half a dozen men by their cars which were parked in the middle of a field. One stood apart, casting a fishing line using a long rod and a lead weight. After he'd completed his cast another man meticulously measured the length of it. This is long-distance casting and it's considered a serious sport by its participants who practise twice a week on the Downs. Each man – there are only men – casts and then they all retrace their lines, winding in, untangling, and then measuring the weight, to see who got the farthest. Casting has developed from beach fishing to become a sport in its own right, with the current distance record standing at 300 yards.

We filmed Adrian, who is apparently one of the best long-distance casters in the area, and he told me the international championships were to be held shortly in Kiel in Germany. It was all completely surreal. We finished filming at 8.30 p.m. It transpired that nowhere within a 20-mile radius was prepared to serve us any food after 9 o'clock. One of the men who ran the Casting Club eventually persuaded a place called the Tollgate to allow us to eat there. It was a very pretentious carvery full of people who looked like car dealers and night-club owners from the coast. By the time I got to the restaurant at 9.50 all I could get was a plate of over-cooked meat, mushy vegetables, and a very sickly pudding. But at least it was hot food. The fact that these places consider themselves to be providing some kind of culinary excellence is a complete joke.

We seemed to be in a bit of the country stuck between the seaside scroungers and the nightlife of Brighton, Worthing and Shoreham, and the commuter belt. And the people who run hotels here certainly aren't interested in the idea of looking after you. We stayed in Steyning; a pretty hotel, and there was nothing really wrong with the rooms. The problem was that the place seemed to be run by two school-leavers. I do think it's a bit odd that the hotels of Britain are, by and large, run by people who are about 18 years old, who've never stayed in an expensive hotel in their lives (let alone anything resembling what they're running). They've no idea what standard you might be expecting. The woman running the hotel told our production manager that she wanted to go home at 9.30 p.m. After a long debate she agreed to leave the key under a stone outside the front door.

Outside my room, on the landing, was a fridge with a display on it of tampax, tea bags and biscuits. For some reason it reduced me to hysterics. I fell into a deep sleep – but spent the whole night waking up fitfully with toothache.

Opposite: Devil's Dyke, South Downs, Sussex.
Overleaf: A view across the Downs near Steyning.

DAY 6
Steyning to Amberley

The school-leavers made my breakfast – fruit salad that looked as if it had been around for a week, mushy old banana and bits of apple that were all brown round the edges, two slices of thin white sliced bread, no offer of orange juice, black coffee so strong I had to put cold water in it. Fascinating, isn't it? No wonder everybody likes reading that 'Room Service' column in the *Daily Telegraph* on Saturdays, because when you're filming and you get to stay in a different hotel every night, you certainly see the British service industry in action. Well tonight I've rebelled and demanded that I stay in Amberley Castle. It's super-posh and we've done a major deal on a room rate (got £150 off). Apparently I'm booked into the hotel room of the year!

This morning my taxi driver tells me that this is a dead part of Sussex. According to him, there's lots of life along the coast, but 5 miles further in nothing happens, and some coastal towns like Brighton and Hastings have chronic drug problems. The southern part of Sussex and the Downs is a mixture of rural scenic beauty and seaside urban ugliness.

I met the crew on top of Steyning Bowl and we walked past Chanctonbury Ring (which marks an Iron Age fort and a Roman temple) where I sat and looked at the views. We dropped down through woodland and went into a pub in Washington to meet Nick Albery, who I was going to walk with that afternoon. Once again, we felt well equipped to write the 'bad pub guide'. This one managed to make a ploughman's lunch virtually inedible. How can people call 'bread' bread when it tastes exactly like fluffy, white foam pillow?

After Washington we crossed the busy A24 and climbed back up on to the South Downs Way where the weather took a turn for the worse. I wasn't going to make the same mistake I'd made the day before and get soaking wet, although I was wearing my shorts in the hope of getting wonderful tanned legs. Nick produced something extraordinary out of his pocket – it was a folding white cotton Chinese hat and it was very odd. He told me his walking boots cost £10 and he had a strange plastic raincoat. We must have looked an eccentric pair. Then it started to pour with rain. I still didn't have the hood to my water-proof jacket but this time I had a shower hat from last night's hotel, so I walked along wearing it, with all my hair tucked in to prevent the dye running. And I popped on my dark glasses so that I'd look like a stylish rapper rather than an unattractive wet walker. People coming in the other direction looked completely horrified.

Nick Albery is someone who comes up with lots of good ideas. One is to try and raise money to build an A to Z avenue of trees, where trees would be arranged in alphabetical order by their common name so that children could learn all about them. He's just published *The Time Out Book of Walks Around London*, and every Saturday he goes walking with different walking clubs he's set up (made up of people who've met through the book); he's scheduled walks right through to the end of next year so he's not going to have much time off.

Eccentricity in the rain on the South Downs Way – Nick Albery sports his strange Chinese hat while I model a shower cap from my last hotel as I've forgotten the hood to my jacket.

He set up a commune movement in the sixties, and helped to find empty houses for squatters. He lived in a squat himself till he was about 33, and then he and his wife travelled round Wales in a horse and cart. They slept rough and his first child was born in Caernarvon. Back in London he set up his own country – The Free and Independent Republic of Frestonia – in West Kensington. He declared it a republic, with its own ministers, stamp designs, national anthem and so on, and it had its own communal garden.

Then Nick set up a charity called The Institute for Social Inventions, a think tank for social entrepreneurs which collects non-technological ideas and projects from around the world. He's also set up the Natural Death Society, looking at alternative approaches to death and burial.

A few years ago I went to the Canary Islands and walked the route that he'd described in another book, *The Alternative La Gomera*. He's very entertaining to walk with and the time passed quickly. We followed the South Downs Way across Springhead Hill and then Rackham Hill. It was a well-walked, easy-to-follow bridle path.

We could see the sea and Worthing to the south, and to the north the lovely valley of the River Avon. Our only companions were sheep bleating aimlessly, and by Amberley Mount we dropped steeply down to the village itself, a charming backwater of thatched

Above: The medieval walls of Amberley Castle.
Opposite: With Gareth Hale and Norman Pace in the castle grounds.

cottages and perfect English gardens just off the B2139. Because the village is about half a mile from the station, and right off the road, it is unspoilt by traffic and extremely tranquil.

We encountered a jolly woman called Caroline Seaton who ran the Amberley Pottery. She was a bit like a 1950s Rank starlet, with masses of bright red hair and a very booming voice. She came to Sussex about 30 years ago, and she explained to me that, far from being

dead, villages like Amberley were really lively places and that they hadn't got people in them who'd lived there hundreds of years. Most of the houses in Amberley, she said, were occupied by people who'd lived there less than 10 years.

Suddenly seeing the big wall of Amberley Castle at the back of the village, I felt as if I was walking through one of those medieval French fortified towns. According to Nick, this wall of the castle was in fact a huge medieval toilet(!). He said that Amberley Castle had been built in the twelfth century as a country residence for the Bishop of Chichester and it was one of his favourite houses. We had tea, amongst the white peacocks and topiary, and Nick caught the train back to London.

I couldn't possibly eat dinner there because my hiking wardrobe didn't include anything suitable for the rather grand dining room. All I had to wear was a screwed-up knitted dress and a pair of trainers. But my bedroom put me in an extremely good mood. I was finally in the hotel bedroom of the year, complete with two bathrooms (one with jacuzzi and washbasin; the other with power shower, wash basin and loo and masses of free samples). I had a four-poster bed,

windows on two sides, tapestry blinds and a writing desk. I had a jacuzzi bath, which wasn't quite the exciting, sexy experience I'd expected. More like lying on top of rather scummy water, which was my fault for putting relaxing aromatherapy oil in the bath after the sign clearly told me not to. I slept really soundly.

The next day I got up early and persuaded the comedians Hale and Pace to be in my film, and we shot a sequence where I chased them round the courtyard. I asked them if they'd walk 15 miles with me and they more or less told me to bugger off. Then they went into my bedroom where the four-poster was being taken apart to turn into a collapsible bed for a London Weekend Television comedy moment in their new series.

DAY 7
Amberley to Cocking

I decided to walk this stretch with my friend Janet, as it wasn't being filmed. We set out from Amberley Castle on a blazing hot June day, walked down some little steps into the moat, turned to the west and retraced the route I'd entered by with Nick Albery.

At the back of the castle we turned west through a gate and then followed a path across the railway line and through parched water meadows full of flowers, down to the River Arun. On reaching the bank, we turned south along a raised path. Opposite, an angler was sitting under a large umbrella. We were envious, as it was sweltering (in the upper 70s). A glamorous new bridge over the river shortened our route. We passed near a farm outside Houghton and then took a broad chalky path that rose distressingly steeply up through a field of corn to the A29.

At the main road we turned right and then left, climbing even higher up Westburton Hill. Then, as we left all roads and traffic behind and entered the secret world of the South Downs, the path dipped down to some barns where the farmer was already storing hay. We climbed up the expanse of Bignor Hill, with the fine Roman Villa below us to the north. (If you've never visited, I promise you it is well worth it – the mosaics are first rate!) By a car park there was an extremely confusing set of paths and signs crossing our route, but luckily we remembered (from walking the route earlier in the year) that if you head due west you get back on to the South Downs Way. In spite of the blistering heat several elderly couples sat resolutely in their cars, munching on sandwiches. I give up on the British!

The next part of the walk was somewhat frustrating, views obscured by trees and a drop down through woodland to the A285. Skylarks were singing, though, and we were grateful for the shade. By Littleton Farm we climbed back up a hill (I had forgotten just how much up-and-down there was in this stretch of the walk!) and then a very long section through woods. Having eaten our sandwiches, we passed through Tegleaze Woods, Woolavington Down and Graffham Down – all easy, pretty level walking, the only irritant being the occasional mountain biker who appeared from nowhere and whooshed past us.

At last, as boredom was starting to set in, we emerged from the woods at Manorfarm Down, dropped down a steep hill and turned right on a track at Hill Barn, heading north into the village of Cocking. The path crossed a stream, turned up a narrow alley between houses and emerged by the village tea shop. Earl Grey and chocolate fudge cake beckoned.

DAY 8
*Cocking to
South Harting*

This was going to be a short day because I had to return to London before lunch. I'd spent the night before at Park House in Becton, which got my vote as the nicest hotel en route so far (apart from the sheer luxury of Amberley Castle, obviously!). It was owned and run by a family who couldn't have been nicer or friendlier, and my only complaint

was that I arrived too late to demolish the crew at croquet (and there was a fine drizzle) on the immaculate lawn. The small bar was full of pictures of polo teams receiving awards (some from Royalty) at Cowdray Park, just the other side of Midhurst. All around Becton was the Cowdray Estate, with its colour-coded paintwork on the houses: yellow for ordinary estate workers; green for managers; and black and white for the top toffs. Who says the English can't invent a class system for every occasion?

Above Cocking, I climbed the long chalk track heading west to the top of the Down. It was completely straight, passing a farmyard and emerging from the hedges into fields. At the top there was a parked van, one that converts into a kind of camper, with a huge radio mast up by the side of it. I was completely fascinated – perhaps it was a pirate radio station? No one was about. I peeped inside the van and it was empty. It must have been a brilliant place to spend the night – the view stretched for miles. I looked everywhere for the occupants, but couldn't see them. I don't know if they hid when they saw me coming. They would have had to drive up past the farmer's barn, but maybe he hadn't noticed them? Anyway I took a few photos of it. Was it Radio Free Cocking or Radio Free Midhurst? Or even Channel 5 trying to bring some reception to the inhabitants of Sussex?

After this, I plodded along the wide chalk path, which was very muddy, to Buriton Farm. When I last did this walk, on 22 May 1996, it basically poured with rain the entire day – horizontal rain in a driving wind – and we walked up this track and we couldn't see a bloody thing. And we did the whole day's walking without seeing one other person. There's no cover up here at all, and I remember we were so hungry, so desperate to have our lunch, that we eventually found a little yew tree with some sheep under it, kicked them out and squatted under a bush and ate our sandwiches. And when we got to Buriton and phoned for a cab, we didn't dare tell them how wet we were, in case they wouldn't take us. We got on the train back to London from Petersfield and completely stripped off, drying all our clothes in the carriage. It was like a Turkish bath – all the windows steamed up. We sat there, more or less in our underwear, and drank loads of cups of lukewarm tea from the trolley. I hoped it wasn't going to be like that today. It was extremely cloudy, with a stiff breeze, and I could see about 10 miles. I walked through a field of sheep which had been sheared in the last few days; they looked very white, naked and skinny.

The day gradually cleared up and I could see as far as the Isle of Wight and the Solent. As I entered woodland, the track was fenced on my left. In a clearing on the right, by woods on Treyford Hill, I saw a row of burial mounds, known as the Devil's Jumps. Crossing a stile by a wood, I took a closer look. The highest rose about 16 feet, an extremely impressive sight. The track continued through woodland. Leaving it, I could see Telegraph House (from which the first semaphore message was sent) away to the south as I crossed Beacon Hill.

Overleaf: Looking east from Harting Downs.

The track dropped down and I turned to the left at Buriton Farm. After a while I dropped down Pen Hill into a most beautiful hollow before climbing Beacon Hill. I followed the track down, skirting past Harting Downs where the path was somewhat confusing, before picking it up again at a gate just before the car park. Apparently the Harting Downs car park is a notorious lovers' rendezvous and all sorts of activity goes on there, but on this particular morning I was extremely pleased to see nothing more than a few parked cars with sedentary lunchers sitting in them, and our Land Rover waiting to take me to Petersfield Station.

DAY 9
South Harting to Buriton to Warnford

I got up at 6.45 in London, and got the 8 o'clock train down to Petersfield. Then I got a taxi to South Harting where I met the crew and Russell, the South Downs Way Path Warden, who was going to walk with me for a few hours. He was a freindly fellow with an aggressive Welsh terrier, which soon got on everyone's nerves as it mistook the soundman's microphone for another animal. It bit the cameraman's leg and tore his trousers, but we tried to be adaptable. Anyway, we set off, amid lots of gloomy talk about the weather. (Rain predicted.)

My rucksack had broken the day before, so I brought down a fresh rucksack, as I'd been walking with one held together with safety pins, which was too sad for words. I planned to get the original one mended, because I feel very attached to my rucksack, as all walkers do. It's like having a pet really – we don't want to get rid of them, even though we all know rucksacks are completely useless and leak. Just like waterproof trousers, as I'm finding out walking through wet fields of rape and broad beans. All waterproof trousers do is make your legs feel twice as heavy; they certainly don't keep the rain or the water out.

Russell was a chatty companion and we left the car park above South Harting and skirted Tower Hill through a wood, by the road. Uppark, owned by the National Trust, lay to the south. It's an impressive seventeenth-century mansion, which was extensively restored, then suffered major fire damage in 1989 and has been restored all over again at vast expense. The ruined folly on top of Tower Hill, according to Russell, was used as a brothel by the locals in the eighteenth century, and the perfectly rounded little hill it sits on was known as 'the bosom'. We had another half a mile to go in Sussex and then we crossed into Hampshire. Russell was employed by the Sussex Downs Conservation Board, working on the South Downs Way between Eastbourne and the boundary with Hampshire. In Hampshire he works with the County Council on the route to Winchester.

Opposite: One of the temporary route signs which caused me more confusion, and path warden Russell and I take a break during the walk.

Russell told me it was quite common for day-trippers to break down footpath signs and use them as firewood for their barbecues. I was appalled. He had his work cut out trying to placate all the rival users of the paths. He explained:

'The path we are walking on here is 6 feet wide; it's a farm track. The farmer can take his tractor along here. Horse riders can come along here, a mountain biker can come down the hill behind us now… If we get conflict between ramblers and mountain bikers, we try and get all the groups together to sort out the problem and look at opportunities for improvement.'

After this conversation I could see you'd need all the powers of a diplomat in Russell's job. My criticism

of designating long-distance paths is that they draw masses of people to a particular route, all clutching their guide books, and following it religiously, while miles of equally attractive footpaths nearby tend to go unwalked. Long-distance walks take up a lot of resources, need maintenance, and are not always that solitary.

Now I got going on my pet hate, miserable mountain bikers. They never say hello, they've got all this expensive equipment and those high-tech helmets. They come whooshing along and you never know when they're approaching because they don't have any bells on their bikes because they think bells are a bit namby-pamby.

Russell thought this was hilarious: 'I'm in the process of working with other groups to encourage mountain bikers to be more user-friendly. As you say, they wear bright coloured clothes which people don't really like in the countryside. They often wear sunglasses which make them look impersonal, like an android sometimes!'

As far as I could see, they *wanted* to look like androids, or Martians. They couldn't have any sex life, after all that bumping up and down in the saddle.

Russell and I walked for about 45 minutes along a muddy farm track, full of puddles from last night's downpours. After Sunwood Farm we followed a tarmac road for a short distance, turning off on a track to another hidden Downland farm at Coulters Dean. We climbed up a hill, passed Buriton below on our right, and turned left along a wide track into the Queen Elizabeth Country Park, with its organized landscape. Lots of signs for riding and cycling sprouted everywhere.

As we walked through the dreary forested expanses of the Country Park I had a sudden feeling that I'd met my affable walking companion (Russell, not Dillon the excitable dog!) before. He certainly was not my (admittedly prejudiced) idea of what a South Downs officer would look like. No cagoule, no beard, no bike clips. He was a bit of a laugh, even if he *had* removed his gold earring for the cameras.

The story unfolded: Russell was originally from Bromley, but had abandoned his South London home as soon as he could. Born with a passion for the countryside, nature, and all things outdoors, his first job (as a council gardener) was to weed the dinosaurs at Crystal Palace. He took a degree in environmental sciences and became a South Downs Way officer three years ago. I still had a feeling I'd met Russell before. He cracked up laughing: 'It was at a Sigue Sigue Sputnik gig in a village hall in Burgess Hill about 1988!' I'd been dating Tony James, the bass guitarist, and dutifully turned up at this weird event – part of their 'village hall' comeback tour which was, of course, a flop!

Russell had booked Sigue Sigue Sputnik for Burgess Hill village hall. According to Russell, it was seen as a positive move by the council to encourage a wider range of youth activities. They must have been mad! I couldn't remember that night. But it was bound to have been drunken and disorderly, and they were bound to have been out of tune… 'And very short, I recall,' said Russell.

At this point I began to glaze over, realizing that I was dying to go to the loo and the Visitors' Centre was some way away. There were no handy bushes in this environment – too many visitors and mountain bikers, for a start.

Then, thank God, we turned a corner and by the main road and the parking lot was the Visitors' Centre in a wooden purpose-built building. I dashed gratefully into the ladies toilets, past the display of postcards and key-rings.

We left the park, passed through a tunnel under the A3, and climbed up a steep hill to meet the crew at the top. A few years before there had been a thatched hut here, and ancient breeds of sheep and cattle showing what an Iron Age farm might have been like. Sadly, it had been moved to Charlton and the site was now occupied by a tasteful thatched brick building which served as a covered picnic spot. Butser Hill is the highest point on the South Downs and the car park was pretty full. People were strolling around, enjoying the views of the Isle of Wight and Chichester, although the breeze was too cool for the building to attract any lunch parties.

By now it was 1.30 and the crew were panicking about their pub lunch. No one had thought to bring any food for me so we arranged to meet at 2.45 when they would get me some sandwiches. Grey clouds were massing as I said goodbye to the likeable Russell and he gave me a new edition of *The Guide to the South Downs Way*. I gave him my puff-balls I had picked as we walked, in return.

I walked along a minor road, going south and then west over Tegdown Hill. The path was high, the views fantastic. So there was little cover when it began to pour with rain. But this time I was prepared. I tied my hair up, put on my waterproof (allegedly!) trousers and jacket, which thankfully had the hood attached this time, stowed Russell's book and the contents of my rucksack in a series of plastic bags, searched fruitlessly for something to eat (no chocolate or biscuits) and plodded on, trying not to think about my director and the crew, now probably stuffing themselves with pub grub which might be vile but would at least be hot.

I crossed another bare expanse, with an ugly telecommunications mast on my right, and walked along a straight track, with Hyden Wood on my left, till I joined a road. This, I remembered from last year, was one of the more unrewarding sections of the South Downs Way. In my rain-soaked guide book I had simply written the words 'very ugly' next to what I was now passing: an old naval establishment behind barbed wire ('HMS Mercury' proclaimed a sign) which was being ripped down and turned into a housing estate. Why are the Armed Forces allowed to vandalize our environmental gems (Lydd firing range – and now one of the most spectacular sections of the South Downs)? As JCB diggers churned up the earth on my left, another still-occupied naval housing estate of breath-taking ugliness appeared on my right, patrolled by armed sentries and ringed by chain-link fencing and barbed wire. I should have thought the possibility of armed terrorist attack

highly unlikely here. An angry demonstration by aggrieved environmentalists would hopefully be more likely.

This was the rendezvous spot with the crew, but they weren't here and their mobile phone was switched off. It was pouring with rain and I didn't fancy waiting under a hawthorn bush watched by guards, so I turned right along a track by a sports field just after the camp, said hello to two men cutting back the bushes and undergrowth from my path with strimmers (keep up the good work!) and pressed on.

Enclosed by hedges, the path emerged onto the open of Wether Down, by some radio masts, and then dropped down to a road at Coombe Cross. It had stopped raining but there was little prospect of any sun. I stood by a pretty house and tried to raise the crew on my phone. I was starving and cross. My path took a confusing left turn by a field, which I skirted to join a farm road, into the prosperous and well-preserved half-timbered selection of buildings that made up Whitewood Farm.

On the far side of a field, at the end of a really muddy track, I had to painfully climb up to the road. I gritted my teeth and gave a stupendous performance of a happy walker for the benefit of the camera, then collapsed into the Land Rover, devoured two sandwiches as if they were from the River Café, and snarled at the crew. I was so cold I could hardly hold a cup of coffee (and it was June!). By this time it was 4 p.m. and I still had to walk over Winchester Hill, otherwise we'd fall behind schedule.

The director had decided to film me on top of Winchester Hill Fort from a vantage position by the road. 'It would look great on a long lens,' he said. What a surprise! God forbid he'd be tramping over it with me! Old Winchester Hill is a nature reserve and I turned along a well-laid path designed for wheelchair access. Even in this gloomy light, the outline of the fort (Iron Age, with Bronze Age barrows), with its clearly defined raised earthwork, formed a clear and menacing silhouette against the advancing storm. I stood at the very pulse of its curving shape and the rain stopped momentarily. The ground dropped away below me dramatically. I hoped I looked like a 1990s proud Boadicea against the sky for the cameraman half a mile away, but I probably resembled a Titian-haired lunatic. How I longed to sit down, spend time resting my legs which felt like lead weights, and examine the cowslips, clover and profusion of tiny wild flowers at my feet, whilst sipping a mug of hot tea and enjoying a bar of chocolate. But it was not to be – I didn't have any provisions and the heavens opened.

I dropped down the hill, crossed a stile, turned left and wandered along to Peake Farm, where I should warn you there is an extremely confusing set of signs (footpath diversions and so on – just what I didn't need at the end of a long day). I slogged along a minor road with high hedges on either side. At the junction with the A32 in Warnford lay a pub, and thank God it was 6 p.m. and opening time. The publican looked astounded as the crew and I entered the lounge bar, stripped off our wet clothes, draped them over his chairs, and

Stripping off to dry in the pub at Warnford at the end of the day, note I'm drinking cups of tea.

unloaded tripods and cameras and sound equipment all over his carpet. For the second time in weeks I begged a man behind a bar to make me a large pot of tea and find some chocolate biscuits. But he rose to the occasion, totally bemused.

After four cups of tea, three biscuits and a double gin and tonic I could see the funny side of the day (just about!), and at 7 we drove to our hotel in Langrish, where I lay shattered on the bed. Sadly the bath water was lukewarm so I put on all my dry clothes and got under the duvet for 20 minutes. The restaurant was in a cellar-cum-cave, which I found rather oppressive, given that the house itself was so attractive. The menu seemed to be Balkan meets South African, featuring ostrich and wild boar. I had an over-cooked salmon trout and slept like a log.

DAY 10
Warnford to Sutton Scotney

I turned up a road behind the pub I had a cup of tea in, and couldn't find my path. I asked two farm workers where the footpath was and they directed me down the side of a field. Having walked up and down the field twice, and skirted a rubbish tip, I then went down a road marked 'To Riversdown House' on the map. The best-known footpath in this area is the Wayfarer's Walk and, of course, every other path was badly signposted. Around here (close to Winchester) was commuting country; big houses and rich farms, and obviously people just don't want footpaths other than the bloody Wayfarer's Walk..

I had to cross a golf course, which wasn't signposted at all. After that, I made my way down a field, where the path literally ended in 5-foot-high broad beans. So I struggled around the edge, and found two really big mushrooms and saw a deer. Continuing along a muddy track, I met the crew at a village called Kilmeston, where we asked someone where the footpath was, and we were directed to – surprise, surprise – the Wayfarer's Walk. I crossed a very beautiful valley and looked up to the elegant Hinton Ampner across the parkland, a National Trust property.

In the village a Victorian villa had an impressive arch made of copper beech framing the front door. I then followed a series of enclosed drovers' paths north, turning right through tall trees and down across the inevitable golf course into New Alresford. This is the neighbourhood favoured by big money: Sainsbury's, Baring's and Cadbury's.

I crossed over the A31 and walked up a road to the east of town, past dreary new housing estates on my left and fields on my right. Then I suddenly entered a world of pristine Georgian and early Victorian terraced houses, immaculate hanging baskets and a town centre with definite upper-middle-class pretensions. The brightly coloured houses were set around the wide main street – Broad Street. Blue-rinsed ladies strode purposefully in and out of butchers and delicatessens, clutching well-loved tasteful straw shopping baskets.

New Alresford is in fact an old town, founded and laid out in 1200 by the Bishop de

Lucy of Winchester, but not as elaborate as Winchelsea. The bishops built new towns to get cash from rent; elsewhere people would have paid tithes. The Bishop of Winchester also made a reservoir by canalizing the Itchen above the town – which was 200 acres, now just 30.

In the Bell Hotel on West Street I had a drink with Mike Irving and Michael French, who had set up a pub newspaper (naturally entitled *The Bell Times*). It's a kind of local *Private Eye* which prints all kinds of scadalous details about the locals who are thinly disguised by a series of cryptic nicknames. One of the Mikes was an ex-journalist; the other a civil engineer, semi-retired. They made me roar with laughter, telling me about all the intrigues in the secret world of Alresford. They'd even produced a special edition of the paper with me as the cover story: I couldn't imagine they'd sell many copies.

I left the two Mikes and crossed the road to investigate the station, now known as the Watercress Line. Alresford is the centre of the watercress industry – the gently flowing water (with complicated irrigation systems) over the chalk beds apparently produces perfect results. The local preserved steam railway is used to get the watercress to market between Southampton and Guildford, before it wilts. The steam train was painted watercress green and the car park was full of children and railway enthusiasts.

I walked down Broad Street out of Alresford, a very pretty town but a bit like stepping back into another world. Rather like Rye, it was somewhere that Mapp and Lucia, E.F. Benson characters, would live in. There was definitely a competition going on for the most lavish hanging basket. Every shop and house had these extraordinarily luxuriant displays. A little man apparently goes around with a motorized watering can at night, tending to all these hanging baskets.

North out of Alresford, I passed the lake which is home to dozens of birds. The annoying thing was that I had to walk about a mile along a main road, as I couldn't work out the footpaths. But then I turned left and headed north-west along the Wayfarer's Walk and then the Oxdrove Way. These are a series of old drovers' paths that surround Winchester and they've been linked up to make some long-distance walks. This is an area of very rich farming land, and, as you walk down these hidden tracks, you can imagine what it must have been like hundreds of years ago, to travel miles along them driving your flock.

Nowadays, the only flock you'll see going along them is 'New Age' people. I passed two encampments of them: at the first one a large and very ugly lorry was stuck in the mud, obviously caused by the last few weeks of rain, and a man with tattoos all down his arms was forlornly trying to dig it out. His dog was howling inside a hot caravan, and I could hear voices from inside another truck.

After another mile I passed another group of travellers; they had tucked their caravans under hedges in the hope of avoiding detection. There were bicycles lying on the ground, a big pile of twigs for a bonfire, and rubbish strewn everywhere. They didn't seem very eco-conscious to me, I must say.

Eventually the path joined a road just before Itchen Wood to the east of the M3. About 100 yards down the road I passed a lot of colour snapshots torn up in large pieces in a lay-by. They were of the 'Readers Wives' variety, featuring a couple of women in black and red undies with no knickers on. Fascinating…

The Lunways Inn, at the junction of the A34 dual carriageway, was a forlorn sight. This is where drovers used to spend the night, sheltering with their livestock, en route to Farnham. I had visions of it being like something out of *Tom Jones*. Anyway, forget it. The Lunways Inn is now an Italian restaurant which is only open at the weekends. It's closed the rest of the week, completely run down and surrounded by rubbish, and the back garden has a broken greenhouse and a broken fountain with a sad little Roman statue made of plaster.

We crossed over the A34 and just carried on up a dead straight road. Now it was getting really hot, blistering hot, and to my astonishment three runners hurtled past.

After half an hour or so of walking on these broad tracks, heading north-east, we arrived in Sutton Scotney, a village of no architectural merit whatsoever, with an ugly church hall/village hall that had been pebble-dashed. A lot of the villages in this area have a ghostly air to them, as everyone leaves in the morning, dashes to the station, and gets the first train up to London to work.

DAY 11
Sutton Scotney to Andover

I walked out of Sutton Scotney, down a lane past some horses, crossed the A30 and followed an old drovers' road, an attractive lane, to Barton Stacey. This used to be a village with a large Army presence. Now most of the property has been sold off, but the Ministry of Defence still reminded me of their existence by bombarding me with helicopters every 10 minutes or so. My stroll began to resemble something out of *Apocalypse Now*.

As I entered Barton Stacey I noticed that the Army barracks had been replaced by an essential oils factory. If I lived here I'd be constantly applying 'soothing' or 'stress-relieving' oils to my temples with all this racket going on. A local lady told me all the helicopters were practising for their annual flying display at nearby Middle Wallop, which houses the Museum of Army Flying.

I couldn't find the footpath which was meant to start by the playing field, so I strode out into the field behind it and followed a narrow path down one side. Then I realized that my route took me over the northern edge of the firing range (which seemed to extend almost up to the children's playground, a worrying prospect), and I could see that red flags were indeed flying. Sod it, I thought. I just can't be bothered to retrace my steps and go the long way round on the road.

The crew were extremely reluctant to follow me! Eventually they did, and we nervously progressed along a narrow path through the cornfields, coming to no harm whatsoever.

A series of small roads brought me to the backwater of Chilbolton, and I found a footpath between the houses that took me down through the water meadows to the beautiful River Test. I sat on a little concrete bridge over one of its tributaries, ate my sandwiches and picked some wild marjoram. As I tossed the crusts into the clear waters, greedy trout surfaced to snap them up. The Test, once one of the finest trout rivers in the country, is suffering from pollution and has to be stocked with fish.

I crossed the river on a wooden bridge by Wherwell, where dozens of ducks vied with the trout for snacks. Pretty, thatched cottages lined the road through the village and I took a lane on my left which climbed a hill over a disused railway line, and eventually led me to the maze-like network of paths through Harewood Forest. After 20 minutes I was completely lost. A deer crossed the gloom ahead of me. To my astonishment, I managed to find the right path out of the oak trees and climbed up the farm road over the chalk expanses of Cow Down, passing under the A303 graffiti-embellished tunnel (slogans too rude to reproduce here!). I then crossed another field, heading north by some pylons, to emerge onto the Old London Road (now a dead end) into Andover.

The sunny weather of the morning had given way to threatening grey clouds and I was somewhat anxious because all the meandering about in Harewood Forest meant that I was over an hour and a half late to meet Andover's most famous inhabitant! Would he still keep our date?

I speed-walked down this road, passing under an elegant Victorian iron bridge, and ran towards a Rover with its engine ticking over. Reg Presley, lead singer for the Troggs and brilliant performer of my favourite song 'Wild Thing', was smoking a cigarette and chilling out. Reg was a builder in Andover when pop stardom beckoned. These days he lives on the outskirts of town and spends his time on the two passions of his life: playing pop music; and studying crop circles, the strange geometric formations that appear overnight in this part of the world throughout the summer months. Reg has now become one of Britain's experts (if that is the correct word) on the subject, and had recently appeared in a television programme about UFOs.

Reg was wearing an expensive-looking suede jacket and his hair looked (like mine) expensively dyed – his a suitable pop star shade of black. So, when the rain started to pour down, I was pleased that he agreed to drive home and fetch a couple of umbrellas for our stroll into Andover.

According to government statistics, Andover is one of the most prosperous towns in Britain, with an extremely low unemployment rate – under 2 per cent. But it is an ugly town, in my opinion, blighted by the rapid development it underwent in the early sixties. Before it was targeted for expansion by London County Council, Andover was pretty run

Overleaf: The River Test and grasslands at Chilbolton.

down, with a shrinking population. The first families moved into the new houses (built by Reg and his merrie band of local builders) in 1964. Businesses like Twinings followed and now they sponsor floral displays in the shape of company brand names on the round-abouts on the edge of town. Many of the homes built were sub-standard and cost the council £56 million to put right. So there used to be two Andovers, the locals and the Londoners. But now, 30 years later, everyone has intertwined and settled down.

Reg told me that the Troggs had started by playing in local village halls. With his strong Hampshire accent, he explained how his kids grew up with London accents because the children at their school were Cockneys! He pointed out the house he was working on when he heard, on a workmate's transistor radio, that his record had gone up from number 44 to number 11 in the charts. He said, 'Share out my tools, I'm off!' and left Andover to be a pop star.

By now the rain was teeming down and Reg remarked that he hadn't walked into town for 35 years – I was beginning to feel guilty. We'd left the council estates and entered the older central part of Andover, blighted by a confusing one-way system. We passed a plaque to the Troggs in the foyer of the Woolwich Building Society on the High Street (once the Copper Kettle tea rooms where the band had rehearsed). The placing of the plaque had coincided with their comeback album, recorded with REM – *Athens Andover*. Reg has now earned pots of money from his song 'Love is All Around', sung by Wet Wet Wet and used in *Four Weddings and a Funeral*.

Discussing UFOs with Reg Presley in Andover.

Wet Wet Wet was what we were as we made our way down the High Street to the shopping centre for a cup of tea. Reg was moaning about the town centre – ruined by big out-of-town supermarkets. He felt it totally lacked character, and that cars should be banned. His favourite café, the Copper Kettle, was now a building society; the cinema had been turned into a nightclub and the Mikado Café, where he had listened to Buddy Holly on the juke box, had long since closed. Now a modern shopping precinct loomed up like a featureless monolith right by the Guild Hall.

It was 5.15 and the café in the central shopping precinct had to be cajoled into serving us tea – no scones in sight. Reg now warmed to his pet theme, UFOs, claiming he'd seen seven. He described the first one to me:

'It was just an orange orb, but I don't know anything that we have on this planet that can cross a valley going up and down in brightness, then stop, expand about five times bigger and stay there for three and a half minutes, not making any sound whatsoever, and then a crop formation turned up underneath it the following day.'

I kept a straight face as Reg continued in this vein for 15 minutes or so, pressing a gift of a book about corn circles onto me and promising that my walk after Pewsey would be taking me into prime crop circle territory. The Vale of Pewsey seemed to be the Piccadilly Circus for UFO stop-overs during the summer months.

Around us the waitresses had stacked up all the other chairs. It was time to go. I shook hands with Reg, who confessed that most women, including his wife of 36 years, were deep cynics. I told him I'd phone him if I saw anything glowing in the dark as I crossed Wiltshire. Anything inexplicable, that is.

I returned to Andover on a Sunday afternoon. My goal was a straight Roman road heading in the direction of a village called Tangley. Sounds so easy, doesn't it? But when you are taking your route from an Ordnance Survey map, and Andover is a town that is still growing, adding huge housing estates, it's not so simple. Anyway, there's a beautiful nature reserve,

DAY 12
Andover to Chute Causeway

surprisingly, just to the north-west of town. I skirted around that and then headed north around the edge of a council estate. I didn't feel too happy walking by myself with a load of teenage boys staring at me, but I reminded myself that this was England. It was all okay; nothing was going to happen.

I crossed a couple of roundabouts, turned half left and started walking along a track which was absolutely straight and totally peaceful. I didn't see another soul. And then a man came walking towards me in the shadows. I felt a bit spooked, but carried on to Tangley, which turned out to be a hamlet of a few houses with a very pretty flint church. Now I left the Roman road and walked through a series of small hamlets called the Chutes. The cottages were tiny, the thatches exquisite, the gardens well-tended. I passed a bungalow built in the 1920s, with green paint, and with the most perfect English garden. So much so that I spoke to the man working on it, and told him how much I admired it.

I then crossed in front of a large house, Standen House, and started to climb a bridle-way, up the hill. Up here there are lots of 'Keep Out' signs and you have to stick to the foot-path; whoever owns the land doesn't want you to stray one foot onto it. Anyway, I headed up through an enclosed path of trees rising gently up to Chute Causeway. I was skirting the Forest of Chute, which extends over large areas of both Hampshire and Wiltshire and links up with the Savernake Forest. The border country is wild, hilly and secretive. North-west of Andover, the land gradually climbs to elevations of over 800 feet near Chute and Conholt,

Foxgloves near Chute Causeway.

before beginning the descent through downland valleys to the River Kennet and its canal. The hills of the divide are steep and spectacular.

When I got to the top, I admired the magnificent avenue of oak trees in Conholt Park. I could see for miles: to the south, right across Hampshire towards the South Downs; and to the north across Wiltshire to the Salisbury Plain.

I didn't get back to the hotel until quarter to seven, and then I had to leave to go out to dinner with my friends in Alresford. This was the second major coincidence of this walk: I told you before about meeting Hilary Lane in Lewes who I hadn't seen for 25 years. Well, another coincidence happened on the day that I walked into Alresford. I was standing in the High Street and a voice said; 'Janet, it's Rhoda,' and it was my friend who I hadn't seen for over 30 years. When I was 17 I used to see Rhoda and her husband Royce because they were best friends with the person I was engaged to (Rex Lambert, then an architectural student at Kingston, now apparently a successful architect somewhere in Central London). Well, it's a very sad story, as I dumped Rex and called off the wedding, but I stayed friends with Royce and Rhoda for two or three years, and spent a lot of time walking with

them in the countryside around Farnham, Alton and Alresford, where they live now.

They live overlooking the lake; an idyllic spot. We had a wonderful dinner; there was so much to catch up on. I only bothered to tell them about husbands one and three. You can't really fill them in on numbers two and four when you've only got a few hours.

T his countryside on the border between Hampshire and Wiltshire is secretive and magical. Tiny narrow lanes, few signposts, giant holly-hocks and canopies of trees shading the road. Few cars, no other walkers. I was to spend the morning walking through a series of earthworks between the Chute Causeway and Wilton, near the Kennet and Avon

DAY 13
*Chute Causeway
to Pewsey*

Canal in Wiltshire. These grassy protuberances, of varying heights, added to the unreal feel of the landscape.

From Chute Causeway I dropped down a very shady, cool, wooded bridleway. There wasn't a cloud in the sky; it was absolutely airless. At the bottom lay the secluded Hippenscombe Farm. All around me the landscape had just changed. Chute Causeway is a high-level Roman road, and when I stood on it I could look backwards into Hampshire and forwards into Wiltshire. Hampshire was full of big, rolling chalk fields; ahead was Wiltshire, flatter at first, with a lot of Iron Age forts and earthworks. It has a very mystical atmosphere, this particular part of Wiltshire.

I skirted Haydown Hill, on which sits Fosbury, an Iron Age fort. The whole valley, with its steep hills, felt untouched. At 10 o'clock in the morning I saw a deer, and then a couple of partridges flew out of the corn, just in front of me. There were so many flowers – corn-flowers, poppies and daisies. Back on the top, I could see right ahead across the plains of Wiltshire, with the windmill outside Wilton standing up clearly to the north-east.

Skirting around a long-barrow and earthworks at Tidcombe Down (part of the Wansdyke which cuts across Wiltshire), I began to see that the path through the farmland was going to be very overgrown. Tidcombe itself is an immaculate hamlet of two or three big farms, and a flint-covered church. I decided to follow the footpath across the fields to Marten. In a farmyard two labourers wearing camouflage gear directed me to quite a promising track, bearing north-east, but it ended after a few hundred yards. The farmer had planted corn over it. I pressed on, getting more and more lost. I could see Manor Farm, where I was supposed to end up, but the path simply didn't go there.

Eventually I just blatantly walked across some fields of clover and into the outbuildings of the farm where some carpenters, who were working outside, looked at me as if a Martian had arrived. Anyway, they were friendly and wished me well. When I asked them if they'd ever walked on the footpath, they just looked at me as if I was mad. Anyway, I pressed on, heading for the pub.

At one point Wiltshire County Council had placed little yellow arrows at the edge of the field, but the farmer had planted barley right across. When I had walked halfway across, I noticed that, 10 yards to my right, the farmer had cut another completely arbitrary path, so I emerged onto it. Whatever pesticides or chemicals the barley had been sprayed with had scratched my legs, and they felt as if they were on fire.

I finally reached the pub in Marten at quarter to twelve. I was brain dead in the blazing heat. In the pub I was accosted by a couple of dreary bores. And I watched the sight of an entire film crew drinking water and orange juice (not one beer!), we were all so dehydrated.

I decided to press on to Wilton along the road, as I was sick of badly marked paths. But then I thought, if I don't walk these paths no one will keep them open; so I decided to return to a footpath and cross the field to Wilton. And guess what – it had been moved. The farmer had ploughed over it and I had to walk around the edge of a field and got completely and utterly stung by nettles.

As I entered Wilton, two old people were sitting on folding chairs, in the shade under a tree, watching the ducks, who were also sitting in the shade under another tree, opposite a little stream and a pond. A sign said 'Slow – Wildlife'. I turned left and left again onto the chalk footpath that wound alongside Wilton Water, north-east of the village. Although my legs were smarting from the nettles, the view across the water was so beautiful, with the Crofton Pumping Station in the distance, that my good humour returned. The heat was blistering. I skirted the edge of the lake, turned left and climbed over the lock, over the Kennet and Avon Canal.

I could see Reg Paynter waiting for me outside the Victorian pumping station, with its impressive brick chimney. I went under a railway, through a short, dank little tunnel made of brickwork; then up some steps, also made of brick, to emerge by the pumping station itself. After a couple of cold drinks in the café/shop, I watched a black and white video of John Betjeman waxing lyrical about the steam engine at Crofton, in an ancient BBC documentary, and my good humour returned.

Reg now runs the pumping station, having been made redundant from his job as an engineer. He's a steam fanatic, no doubt about that, and within a couple of minutes he'd blinded me with facts and figures, but his mad enthusiasm was highly infectious. As we spoke, steam buffs arrived by motorbike and car, to be given detailed tours by Reg and his band of volunteers.

Crofton Pumping Station houses two Cornish beam engines, the 1812 Boulton and Watt, and the 1845 Harvey of Hayle, restored and now run by volunteers from the Kennet and Avon Trust without any grants or public money, although they've recently been awarded

Opposite: The South Downs near Marten.

some Lottery money. Both engines are steamed from a hand-stoked, coal-fired Lancashire boiler. The 82-foot brick chimney has just been restored thanks to local benefactor, Sir John Smith. They are amazing examples of once-revolutionary technology, left derelict in the 1950s after the canal fell into disrepair and the railway stopped needing water pumped up the hill for steam. The 1812 steam engine is the oldest beam engine in the world, still in its original building and still able to do its original job – pumping water to the summit level of the Kennet and Avon Canal, but only on special 'steaming' weekends. The rest of the time, a modern electric pump takes over.

Given that the water from the lake at Wilton was pumped up to the top of the canal, I asked Reg how the drought had affected things.

He said: 'It's down, nearly a metre down on what it should be. And when you think the lake is 8 acres, that's an awful lot of water that's missing for this time of year.'

Apparently the water table was the lowest it had been in the area since 1767, limiting the movement of barges up and down the canal. Crofton Lock is the highest lock in the eastern section of the canal, and a whole series of locks were needed to make the descent to Bradford-on-Avon.

The Kennet and Avon Canal isn't like the Grand Union – it's shorter and feels more sanitized – but it does pass through some of the loveliest scenery in Wiltshire, and I was now going to walk along it for a couple of days, passing through the Vale of Pewsey. It stretches from Devizes to Reading, linking the River Avon in the west and the River Kennet in the east, with 57 miles of canal. The canal was designed by John Rennie and, according to Reg, had 30 or 40 good years before it succumbed to the Great Western Railway and became derelict. At this moment a train roared past, the track parallel with the little canal, and Reg's point was forcefully made.

Lying in the shade on the grass by the pumping station, I ate a couple of sandwiches, admired their restored ladies loo, then reluctantly bade farewell to Reg and started to walk east along the canal towpath. It was 4.30, baking hot, and the path was bordered by a luxuriant bed of weeds.

I was entering the Vale of Pewsey which felt like the land tourists forgot. The valley is about 12 miles long and is nowhere more than 5 miles across, from north to south. It has some of the richest farming country in the South of England.

Owing to the drought, canal traffic was at a standstill today, though I passed a few truculent fishermen tossing maggots and sweetcorn on the still water in the hope of attracting bream.

After a few miles I reached the Bruce Tunnel. This attractive anachronism was built to bribe Thomas Bruce, Earl of Aylesbury, to allow the canal to run through his land, because he didn't want the ride back to his posh house ruined by a cutting.

At Burbage Wharf I passed a large wooden crane, a replica of the original which stood

on the site until the 1970s. Now I started to pass a series of locks, starting the long drop down as we headed west. I hoped to get to Pewsey before dire fatigue set in. My legs weren't tired, but I was suffering from heat exhaustion.

In the suffocating stillness I saw two herons rise up from the water. The rather taciturn anglers now were out in force, all taking it very seriously. I couldn't see any fish in any of their nets. But one man I talked to claimed he'd caught 15 fish in seven hours, and then thrown the lot back because nothing would make him eat the fish he caught in the canal. I plodded on towards Pewsey Wharf, passing the neat locks of Wootton Rivers. Holiday-makers were moored up on their barges, sitting under umbrellas and sipping glasses of beer.

I lay down on the towpath to rest in the shade and was immediately covered with flies. Later on, someone told me it was the hottest day of the year so far, and I could believe it. At the tiny Mayfield Lock, chippings had been laid on the path which made it even hotter than walking on grass. I began to get a blister on the bottom of my right heel, simply from the heat. Eventually we reached Pewsey Wharf about 6.15. Everybody was extremely tired. The cameraman wanted one final shot of me walking under the bridge, with sunlight dappling the water. Of course, the sun immediately went in and I lay on a bench for 15 min-utes waiting for it to come out from behind the cloud. I was surrounded by tame geese and ducks, and a very fat lady came out of the old lock-keeper's cottage and fed them all a loaf of white sliced bread. The geese seemed incredibly aggressive, but she told me not to worry. We finally did the shot and walked about 50 yards up the road to the pub, called the French Horn, after the horn that was sounded to muster the French prisoners of war who dug the canal.

Pewsey struck me as pretty lifeless, even though it has a direct train to London (unlike the larger and far livelier town of Devizes, just down the road). It has council estates on its western edge, and what the locals call 'Legoland' – the commuter estates – on the east. At Alfred's Pub you can take a sauna for £6 per person during licensing hours; at least that's what the sign said. There were some Georgian buildings and a statue of King Alfred in the main street, but the town seemed to have no vibrancy at all. We drove on to spend a night in Marlborough, to the north of the valley.

The main street of Marlborough is beautiful. It's very wide and architecturally they have managed to preserve a lot of the old town. But the strange thing is, there's no heart to it. It's a bit ruined by Woolworths and Waitrose, but, apart from that, there are no really good restaurants, no good-quality greengrocers or small food shops. There was a grotty-looking pizzeria, a Chinese, an Indian and a wine bar. The public school seemed to dominate the town, to the exclusion of any local night-life.

In the wine bar we asked them to open the windows while we ate because it was incredibly hot, and they said no, they were locked. The food was strange. 'Garnish' is the new buzz word in pub and wine bar catering: next to the dishes were huge piles of

garnish, featuring, spookily, kiwi fruit, apple, raw onion rings and the dreaded shredded iceberg lettuce.

Back in the hotel my room had a strange smell, so I sprayed the carpet around my bed with GIO by Giorgio Armani, popped my blister, and slept like a log. I'd walked about 14 miles but it felt like 40.

DAY 14
Pewsey to Devizes

I left the hotel about 8.40 a.m. It was already blazing hot, hardly a cloud in the sky, absolutely still. Around me the Downs were bleached white with the corn and there were splashes of red poppies around the edges. The landscape was almost lunar. An extremely loquacious taxi driver drove me to the start of today's walk in Pewsey. I asked him about people coming from all over the world to look at the crop circles. He said they regularly got Japanese tourists who turned up in Devizes and asked to be driven to Stonehenge; and Korean and Japanese film crews turned up all the time and hung out for weeks on end. It was very good for business!

I had decided to wear a Calvin Klein nightie to walk in – hopefully it would look more like a chic house dress than slumberwear. Made of orange towelling, it was loose, and I hoped it would soak up the sweat. My legs were still itching all over, and covered in ugly red rashes from my forays through sprayed crops and nettles. Walking along by the canal, through a wide valley of rolling hills set far back on either side, I passed under the Stowell Park Suspension Bridge at Wilcot, which is supposed to be the oldest remaining bridge of its kind in the country. A very elegant, not very deep construction of wrought iron, it gracefully spanned the narrow expanse of water between thick trees on either bank. I thought it looked somewhat fragile and in need of repair.

To the north, I could see the White Horse on the Downs outside Honeystreet. There was much more traffic on the canal today, with plenty of jolly holidaymakers, who shouted hello to me every now and then.

At Wilcot Wide Water, just before Honeystreet, I walked under Lady's Bridge, an elaborate confection of carved Bath stone with elegant feminine fans and draperies lovingly embellishing this folly in the middle of nowhere. Apparently Lady Wilcot would only allow the canal to pass through her land if it was landscaped to resemble posh parkland – hence the bridge, far grander than any other on the canal!

I got to Honeystreet at 12 o'clock. The Barge Inn attracts 'croppies' from far and wide. Outside it, I met Polly Carson from Lancashire, who married a local, and now farms 2000 acres around here, including the hill with the White Horse that I'd seen earlier. A crop circle appeared on their land in 1990. Since then there have been at least 30. Polly, an animated woman with short blonde hair, told me how, when the first crop circle appeared,

The Stowell Park Suspension Bridge at Wilcot, one of the oldest in the country.

television crews and press people arrived on their land from all over the world within 24 hours.

Didn't it cross her mind for one minute that perhaps someone had just gone on to her farm in the middle of the night and made the circle? Polly laughed:

'Well it didn't, because half a mile away, on the same night, a crop circle of very similar proportions and size had occurred, and basically the size of it was enormous, and it would have taken people a long time to do it. And there just aren't that many hours of darkness at that time of year.'

Inside the Barge Inn there was a frenzy of activity. Dutch, Japanese and American accents mixed with the soft local burr. In a room at the back was an information board plastered with photos and photocopies of crop circles — and an ad for the latest fashion,

a crop circle hair cut! I had a beer with Peter Soronson, a jovial, bearded American in a suit. A stonemason and artist who had grown up on a farm outside New York, he had always been interested in crop circles, but had come here simply because there are more of them in this little part of Britain than anywhere else in the world. He spends six months here every summer, paid for by a wealthy American sponsor. Peter records all the corn circles on digital video cameras from a plane. He makes videos which his sponsor watches, and he sells the unedited footage of the corn circles to the BBC, NBC and news channels all over the world. He also sells cassettes of an annual round-up of information about corn circles.

In the Spielberg film, *Close Encounters,* our only way to talk to people from another planet, or another dimension, was through harmonics. Perhaps the symmetry of the corn circles represented a similar set of harmonics and there was a force trying to communicate with us? Well, I was trying to keep an open mind. I'm not an avid *X-Files* watcher and I am a total sceptic, but it did seem extraordinary. Both Polly and Peter could spot hoax circles, and there was no way that the ones they'd seen could have been made by anyone on the land, and the patterns could only be read from the air. So there you are – Reg Presley started something off when he gave me that book back in Andover.

I left the crew in the Barge Inn (Reg's favourite haunt), absolutely packed to the doors with 'croppies'. They were camping out in a field at the back; they were in caravans; they'd come from Korea, Holland, Czechoslovakia to see these phenomena. They were making videos, interviewing each other, as they hung out, waiting for aliens or angels to make their mark on the landscape. Someone called Vince was even painting a mural, a kind of New Wave Sistine Chapel ceiling, featuring corn circles. I left the crew eavesdropping on all the crop circle gossip.

As I left, Peter was holding forth to a captive audience:

'There are more crop circles here than anywhere else in the world and…I think the reason they are here is Avebury. Avebury, some people say, is the belly button of the Earth. The dowsers with their rods say that the energy from the whole planet goes to the sun and comes back from the sun, and therefore the rest of the universe, through Avebury.'

I slipped away, as I thought my cynical presence might be off-putting to the devotees.

I took my two rolls and walked a mile or so down the canal towards Devizes and ate them under the shade of a tree, with no sightseers, no traffic – just perfect really. As pub grub is generally completely unspeakable, I'm only eating prawn mayonnaise sandwiches right across Britain. It's my little experiment. Generally, the prawn sandwich, as prepared by an English pub, is a prawn cocktail shoved in two bits of bread, or a baguette, and then they ask you if you want this mysterious thing called Marie Rose Sauce, which I kept calling Rosemary Sauce. It means some pink goo, which is mayonnaise with tomato ketchup in it. Anyway, today's lunch was a completely synthetic blend of prawns, with the tomato ketchup in it.

I walked on now, along a breathtakingly beautiful canal-side path between All Cannings to the south and Devizes to my west. Spooky hillocks with exposed areas of chalk encompassed the valley, looking completely mystical. I could see why people came here from all over the world. The endless earthworks, the land itself, looking eerily as if someone had arranged all the little mounds. The scale is monumental – it's the nearest you'll get to a prairie in England. Because of the recent rain, the towpath was luxuriant, with loads of different kinds of wild grass, bulrushes, clover, pinks, harebells, poppies, a profusion of wild flowers and birds. It was probably the most beautiful section of the walk so far.

The only people I met, as I approached Devizes, were occasional solitary monosyllabic fishermen. Then two women, carrying a full set of coarse fishing gear, arrived to set up – a most unusual sight. They said that this was their first time on this particular stretch of water, and that most of the men were totally dismissive of female anglers. They had fished in competitions ranging from the Ladies Southern to the Ladies National and were a friendly middle-class pair, well dressed, with gold jewellery and nice clothes. I wished them luck and proceeded on my solitary way.

I came across a tractor which had half-fallen into the water. Its front wheel was in the canal and it made a surreal sight. No driver – very *Twin Peaks*. Maybe he was underwater? There was no one to ask.

As I got just outside Devizes, the cameraman asked me to walk along a bank a bit lower down for a better shot. I knew the grass would be really slippery as it had been raining so much the week before. He assured me there were no nettles, and, of course, the inevitable happened: I fell really heavily down the bank, bruising my backside, and covering my right arm with nettle stings. So it was a sad and weary crew that trudged into Devizes, an hour later than planned.

We met up with John Girvan, the blacksmith, at his forge by the canal, and my temper wasn't improved when I discovered that he'd arranged for the local newspaper and a photographer to be there. I must have looked at my worst – dripping wet with sweat, bitten to bits, and very tired indeed.

After I'd posed for a snap, I talked to John in his workshop, where he made a living making gates and ironwork for the locals, including a signpost in the middle of the town. John soon restored my spirits with his camp manner and fund of entertaining stories about Devizes. He's written six books of local history and does celebrated ghost tours (farmer Polly had taken her kids on one and confirmed his local celebrity status). John's secret passion was women's bras. A happily married man, he was the toast of the local Women's Institute circuit with his famous 'History of the Bra' lectures, complete with props ranging from a wartime bra made with dusters to a 'Millennium' special he'd fashioned with flashing lights in the nipples. He gave me a run-through of his talk in a school-room down the road, delivered in an accent that crossed Kenneth Williams with the local Devizes drawl. I was in fits.

Blacksmith John Girvan outside his workshop.

He pulled more and more extraordinary items out of a suitcase and, although we were in a stiflingly hot school-room, it really was hilarious. We finally finished about quarter to eight, and I went to a pub in the centre of Devizes where they were astounded to find I only needed a room for half an hour – to have a bath and change my clothes. Then I set off back to London.

It only took an hour and a half to drive back. I met up with my friend Paul and we went to see a modern dance piece at 10 p.m. performed outside my old architectural college in Bloomsbury, and then went out to supper – the complete opposite to everything I'd been doing all day. The air in London was very still and muggy, and smelt really dirty compared to that of the Bradford and Avon Canal.

DAY 15
Devizes to Bradford-on-Avon

Devizes, a large and characterful town that dates from Norman times, has a castle (now flats), a large brewery, and a bijou redeveloped wharf area containing a theatre and a museum, but it doesn't qualify for a railway station. That honour has been bestowed on dreary, much smaller Pewsey to the east or bustling Chippenham north across the Downs. So, to continue my journey, I took the train from Paddington to Chippenham, and a taxi back to the canal bridge on the northern outskirts of the town.

I planned to follow the Kennet and Avon Canal west, through the flat, marshy Avon Valley, to Bradford-on-Avon. Dozens of brooks crossed the meadows en route, and every possible drop was being extracted to feed the canal. I was to pass through a marvel of aquatic engineering (if that's the right expression) of the canal world! Twenty-nine locks, in three groups, take west-bound travellers on the canal down 237 feet, over 2¼ miles. They were restored before the canal was reopened in 1990, using donations from all over the world.

Something occurred to me: over 25 years of interviewing people on radio and television – from prime ministers to prostitutes, rent boys to pop stars – I can generally, with my breezy manner, get more than a monosyllable out of anyone, but I had finally met my match: the canal coarse fishermen. Try as I might, I could not get more than three words out of them. All I managed to discover was that the fish on this canal must be the most

over-fed, snacked-out bunch in the United Kingdom. These fishermen spent all day chucking ground bait in the canal in the hope of attracting a tench or whatever, but all they could tell me was that sweetcorn was a bit of a taste sensation for tench. When I asked a couple of men why, they couldn't say. They couldn't even tell me where the idea came from in the first place. That's how uncommunicative they were.

I came to the Caen Hill locks a mile out of Devizes, surely one of the most spectacular sights on all Britain's waterways. A series of 16 locks descended Caen Hill, each with a side pond, like a series of water platforms, full of lilies, ducks and swans, and of course lots of sweaty bargepeople, who had to undo each lock in turn to get up the hill. It took between three to four hours to go through the whole sequence of locks, which was one good reason why I was walking and not barging.

Each lock was named after its sponsors, some of whom came from the USA. The locks were a hive of activity, some barge-renters being more proficient at getting through them than others. A lot of overweight men in unattractive vests looked to be issuing orders to their wives. It seemed like a recipe for divorce!

A little further along, on the opposite bank, I saw two of the strangest animals you could imagine: a pair of llamas in a makeshift wooden pen by the canal. There was a great big brown one which looked like a furry triffid, and a small black companion that had been shaved and consequently looked like a demented Bambi. It seemed to me that their owners had possibly seen *The Good Life* on TV and decided to live out their fantasy of self-sufficiency. The minute we tried to film these creatures, they turned their backs on us and made strange moaning noises.

Then I saw a very welcome sight just before Semington: a little sign that said 'Welcome. By Agreement With The Owner You Are Welcome To Walk Here. A New Woodland Is Being Created For Your Enjoyment And That Of Future Generations With The Help Of the Forestry Authority, Giles Wood, 5000 British Trees Were Planted In 1993'. Of course, at the moment they stood in weedy serried ranks, but I was sure it would look fantastic in about ten years' time.

I was now passing through luxuriant flat water meadows. When I came down the hill from the Caen Hill locks, I saw Wiltshire stretching ahead and thought how boring and flat it looked. But, as I walked through it, a certain quiet charm emerged. The banks of the canal were thick with reeds, grasses and flowers and lots of bird and plant life.

At Semington I crossed a hump-back bridge and was nearly mown down by thundering lorries. I then ate what won my vote as the most disgusting pub lunch so far – at the Sutherland Arms – where I made the fatal mistake of departing from a prawn mayonnaise sandwich and ordering a jumbo cod and salad. I learnt my lesson and planned to go straight back to prawn sandwiches the next day.

In the afternoon heat I decided to take a five-minute break. My feet! When you're

walking along a canal you hardly see any seats at all. Anyway, I came across a very nice bench with a plaque announcing: 'This seat was erected by Semington Parish Council to commemorate their centenary, 1995', and I gratefully took advantage of it.

Now the canal passed over two aqueducts, Ladydown and Bliss, the latter being a tributary of the River Avon. The housing visible from the canal seemed to be either ugly pebble-dashed council estates or upmarket Georgian mansions.

I finished the rest of the walk to Bradford-on-Avon at a steady pace. It was quite uneventful, and very hot, and I saw a lot of dragonflies, and my first heron in this whole stretch of canal. Bradford-on-Avon was tucked away to the north as the canal curved around to the south. Before I approached the town, I passed through Hilperton which had a new marina and a new housing estate of luxury detached four- and five-bedroomed houses – all a bit Toytown. A sense of excitement seemed to stir in the air as I got closer to Bradford-on-Avon. I could tell I was approaching civilization because people were walking along the towpath with House of Fraser carrier bags.

At the lock outside Bradford-on-Avon there were lots of elderly people in charge of barges getting all confused going through locks. You could they had only just started their holiday afloat. There were a lot of Alan Bennett-type conversations and plenty of elderly ladies sitting around watching the proceedings.

There was a café by the bridge, so I stopped there and had a toasted teacake and a cup of tea while I read Stan Hey's thriller, *Filling Spaces*. The central character, Frank Brennan, left prison and came to Bradford-on-Avon for the first time. He'd only ever seen it once, from a prison van window, and thought it looked a nice place. I read two passages from the book and then walked up the road into Bradford-on-Avon. It was exactly as Stan had described it – incredibly beautiful, with Bath stone buildings on either side of the road. The town shot up on either side of the valley, layer upon layer of weavers' cottages, some big mill buildings with interesting pointed windows, grand mill-owners' houses, a jumble of stone, the most perfect example of a mixture of Georgian and industrial architecture. The only thing that ruined it was the fact that it was 4.30, which is rush hour in Bradford-on-Avon. This is when the shops close and everyone dashes home for their tea. Crossing the steep road from the Swan Hotel to the Dandy Lion Pub, as the character does in the book, was a death-defying experience. The Dandy Lion was cosy, with a nice owner – not the one Stan described in the book as having a fat face (she has since left). He offended her at the time by calling her chubby.

Stan explained that, as one of the few crossing points over the Avon, Bradford and its thirteenth-century bridge were swamped with traffic. A wealthy wool town, with 32 mills in the early nineteenth century, it was surrounded by disused quarries on the nearby hills. The posh mill-owners' houses had been converted into offices, restaurants and hotels, and now the mill buildings were being converted into flats for the middle-class overspill from Bath.

Stan Hey and I had met years before. He'd once been a writer on *Time Out* and then he'd done some work on a football series *(Standing Room Only)* I'd done for BBC2. Stan is a highly successful TV drama and comedy writer with a passion for football (he wrote *The Manageress* for Channel 4). He'd moved to Bradford-on-Avon from Chiswick a few years ago and written two thrillers based on the town. He told me he regularly popped into the Dandy Lion for a cappuccino in the morning, as did several other writers, artists and producers from the area – it sounded a very sophisticated place compared to most of the hostelries I'd visited on my walk so far. As Stan has written a lot of newspaper columns about food, I asked his advice about appalling pub grub.

'Make your own sandwiches in the morning,' he replied. 'Take a picnic wherever you're staying.'

This wasn't what I wanted to hear.

Stan has an extremely dry wit and I hoped it would come across on film. He was particularly entertaining on the subject of life in a small town after London.

'On Tuesday during the morning the UK waste dustbin lorry parks outside and blocks out the sun for about an hour, you know.' He laughed. 'We all look forward to that, it's the highlight of our week. A lot of things happen under the surface of a small town but it's not staid by any means. I remember the first week I moved here in 1990 and the crime-stoppers item on the local news was about a guy who hadn't returned a hedge trimmer.' At this point he laughed ironically. 'They had the security camera footage of him, as though he was about to go and do some serious damage with this hedge trimmer, you know. All he'd done was not return it for four days.'

Bath is only about 8 miles down the road, but it's light-years away in terms of culture. As you go into Bath they have credit card police checkpoints, frisking you just to make sure you've got the money to spend.'

Somehow I realized he was joking, but only just!

I left Stan as the Dandy Lion was beginning to fill up with locals and the bistro upstairs started to serve supper. In the dusk I walked up the hill to my bed-and-breakfast, which was in a converted series of weavers' cottages high above, in New Town. My bedroom looked out over the whole valley, which fell away below in terraces – more like Assisi in Italy than Wiltshire. I lay in the bath and looked at the tops of the trees and houses on the other side of the valley, golden in the setting sun.

This was a perfect end to a perfect day, ruined only by going to the hotel everybody else was staying at, and having a thoroughly disgusting dinner. I was back at my hotel at 11 o'clock and Bradford-on-Avon was as dead as a doornail. Every light was out in town – the only movement on the street was four teenagers sloping into the chip shop. I crept into my room, threw my clothes on a chair and was asleep in minutes.

I slept like a log and woke up to discover a completely grey and thundery sky, it seemed that rain was on the agenda. Today's walk was going to take me cross-country to Great Elm.

I still had to overcome the greatest obstacle of the day – the horror of the communal breakfast. I went downstairs, and sitting at the table were two American tourists, one German lady and her English daughter, and a couple of German tourists and they were wittering on about their trips to Bath, Salisbury, Silbury Hill, etc, etc. I have no conversation first thing in the morning, and felt somewhat conspicuous. It was all I could do to tell the Germans that I was walking across England for a film. That was a bit of a conversation-stopper, so I collected my notes and a cup of coffee and bolted back upstairs.

Later on I walked down through the very busy town to the café by the lock to talk to Vicky Crystal, a local councillor who is campaigning against the appalling stench from a nearby food processing plant. She's formed a protest group called NOSE (No Offensive Smells in the Environment). I listened to her complaints sympathetically enough, as I wouldn't like to be woken up each morning in summer to a disgusting pong which made me close all doors and windows. But I pondered the rise of the NIMBIES (Not In My Back Yarders), as I crossed the canal and started to walk up a steep hill, leaving Bradford behind me.

I'd noticed on my walk across rural England that it had become a battleground between farmers (who now have to be basically businessmen), and people who live in the country-side, and people who use the countryside. These three groups do not necessarily see eye to eye. Farmers say they farm in the way government encourages by subsidy; and they have to run farms as businesses. Consequently, when I moan that they plough across footpaths, they say they have to farm fields economically; and when I moan that they put pesticide on the crops, they say, well, they have to achieve a certain level of production. Then you have all the people who live in the countryside who don't want new roads going past their houses or smells of the kind Vicky had been talking about. Finally, there are people like me, who come to the countryside for leisure and have certain expectations regarding access, footpaths, and so on. We want the countryside to be unspoilt for us to enjoy. As far as I could see, bigger and bigger battles would be fought over rural England as people's leisure expectations increased.

Musing on all this, I reached the top of the hill, met the film crew and was about to climb a stile and enter my first field of the day when I was confronted by an angry farmer! He demanded to know what we were doing, and wasn't very happy at all about us filming on the footpath in the field, because he had a lot of cows and calves, as well as a bull, in there. But once he recognized me, his manner suddenly changed. He was all sweetness and light, and we engaged in a very useful conversation about footpaths and how hard it is to keep them up. According to him, footpaths were created for milkmaids and farm workers, or country people who needed to get to town, not for groups of 30 ramblers at a time who

would frighten his cattle and might leave gates open. Anyway, he wished me well with my walk, and we shook hands, temporarily friends, tantrum over.

I then walked high on a hill by a radio mast, and in a little copse I saw the biggest puff-ball mushroom I'd ever seen in my life – it must have been almost 2 feet across! It had spored and had lots of brown holes in it. I thought it looked like something out of the *X-Files*. After this I walked down the hill, enjoying the views of the Mendips ahead, and crossed some fields. I was looking forward to visiting Westwood Manor, a fifteenth-century house owned by the National Trust with a topiary garden and Jacobean and Gothic additions. But guess what? It was closed. (Apparently it's only open on three afternoons a week for three hours at a time, which isn't very good news for members really.) And the guide-book opened with the disparaging sentence: 'Westwood Manor is not one of the great stately homes of England.' Talk about putting people off.

Anyway, as I crossed more ploughed fields, and got very hot, I saw a sight I'd not seen in 10 years. In the middle of a pasture was a circle of white blobs, each one as big as a saucepan. It was a huge crop of puffballs. Much more exciting than a crop circle! I called over the crew and they filmed me worshipping at this mushroom shrine. Each one was easily the size of Reg Presley's brain. I picked three of the biggest and turned my orange zip-up jacket into a makeshift rucksack, using a couple of knots and some pieces of string. Then we set off across the fields towards Rode, carrying these monsters of the mushroom world, which weighed at least 6 pounds.

At this point I discovered the next problem with this part of rural England – bulls. My maiden name might have been Bull, but I am still intimidated by them. Walking through a field containing a very large and menacing specimen, I made a detour through a wood. I passed some mill buildings at Tellisford by the River Frome, and a picturesque bridge over the river, and reached Somerset. (Wiltshire was now behind me.) Approaching Rode about 1 o'clock, I was pretty tired, having lugged those bloody puffballs about 4 miles up and down hills and over stiles. But I was determined to get them back to the crew car, so we could have a delicious dinner.

As I got closer to the village, I saw that Rode church was very interesting. It had twin spires which were really pointed. It looked early Victorian Gothic and completely eccentric. I walked up the road, past some dreary council houses, to explore. Outside was a lot of builders' rubbish and loud banging and sawing noises were coming from inside the porch. A slim man, in his thirties, with a neat and precise manner, introduced himself as Andy Hooker, a violin-dealer, who'd always wanted to live in a church. He'd bought this fine specimen in order to turn it into his dream home. The church had been built in 1824, designed by Henry Edmund Goodridge (1797–1863) who built other extraordinary buildings in the area. To me it was inspirational, as good as Gaudi's La Sagrada Familia Cathedral in Barcelona, and sitting in the tiny village of Rode.

I crossed some fields down into the village of Rode, past some very pretty houses. I walked down to the river and followed it to the A36, passing a field with three bulls in it. They approached me but I stood my ground and they backed off. Crossing the A36 was frightening with lorries thundering past inches away from me. I then turned into the driveway of a cottage; it had been sold and the owners had removed the footpath sign and the stile. Following the track around, I could hear the sound of a weir on the River Frome in the background. There was a large bull in the field in front, but I headed off to the right, contouring off to a lane where I met the crew.

Vena and friends in Lullington.

Now I was in real Somerset countryside – rolling hills, lush small green fields, high hedges. I walked down a little lane into the village of Lullington. At the junction, just outside the village, was a spectacular folly built in the high Victorian Gothic style, castellated with turrets, designed by Thomas Wyatt. It was the lodge at the back entrance to Orchardleigh House. The village consisted of a tiny group of thatched cottages around a green and on it I talked to three old people. One of them, Vena, went and got her autograph book for me to sign. She'd lived there for 30 years, and her husband had been the gamekeeper at Orchardleigh. The autograph book was exquisite with only one other entry in it, and that had been written in 1919; I felt honoured. We all took each other's photograph, and then it was down into the grounds of the big house, where we crossed the golf course. Vena had shown me the Savills catalogue which revealed that the house and grounds were for sale. Apparently it was in the hands of the receivers. It was a Grade One listed building, but planning permission had been secured to turn it into a 200-bedroom luxury resort – how we dread those words…

Suddenly it poured with rain and, as I crossed one of the greens, I met Julian Baker, an osteopath, who immediately told me that one of my shoulders was higher than the other, my hip was out and I was having back trouble, all of which was true. The crew just laughed at me. The truth was my back had been a bit sore. I told Julian I had been walking with magnetic insoles in my shoes that day but they just kept making the soles of my feet tingle, they didn't seem to extend their magic upwards to my lower back. I arranged for him to come to the Woolpack Inn in Beckington, where I was staying that evening, to give me 'a good going over' (if that's the right phrase) and he said he'd do it for the price of a pint.

Having left the golf course, I entered the woods, and saw rows of cages containing baby pheasants which would be released at six weeks old. An irritating footpath diversion meant

I had to skirt around a field of barley and get scratched as well. Then it was up into the village of Buckland Dinham on a busy main road. The church there had a really beautiful border of antirrhinums. But rural peace and quiet must only be attainable if the villagers install double glazing to blot out the sound of the lorries constantly going to and from the nearby Eden Vale milk factory.

The crew went back to the hotel and I walked on alone, down completely deserted lanes between high hedges. The sky was clearing now, the sun came out, and it was a nice warm, slightly steamy evening, with the insects out in full force. Great Elm was a very pretty village, partly destroyed by the lorries coming from the nearby quarry that thundered through it. I crossed the road and went down a steep pathway where there was the most beautiful duck pond.

After crossing a stream, I climbed up through a wood, and suddenly a train appeared from nowhere. I was at the top of a gorge, on a steep cutting, and as the train trundled through below, I walked through the wood, emerging onto a main road at a place called, slightly worryingly, Murder Combe. I waited about 15 minutes and eventually the crew turned up. We went back to Beckington, to the Woolpack Inn, which was very comfortable, and had a good dinner for once. The chef, Michael, cooked my puffballs and they tasted delicious.

My session with the golf course osteopath certainly did the trick. I overslept and woke up at 7.55, feeling completely groggy. I threw everything back in the suitcase, went downstairs and had breakfast. We then set off back to Great Elm, where I interviewed Maureen Lehane Wishart, a mezzo-soprano, who holds a music festival there and residential music courses throughout the summer. A lively woman who's sung the world over, she was entertaining and enthusiastic company. She had applied for money from the National Lottery to expand her music courses, and I wished her well.

DAY 17
Great Elm to
Shepton Mallet

Maureen and I drank coffee in her cluttered kitchen which was full of dressers with pottery on every surface. She told me she regularly turned it into a concert hall and managed to cram up to 80 people in, to enjoy string quartets, singers and pianists, as well as chamber music. She served food from a trolley as well! The festival (which also has performances in other local venues, like beautiful Mells Church) was dedicated to her late husband.

Maureen explained: 'Apart from being a musician, he loved his food and wine, so every concert has food and wine attached. We have cream teas for afternoon concerts and we have morning coffee for morning concerts.'

With her no-nonsense approach to music and food, Maureen should quite clearly be running somewhere like the Royal Festival Hall or Covent Garden, where trying to get anything to eat or drink involves endless queuing and battles to get the attention of a few

over-worked servers. When I met her, she was in the process of refurbishing Jackdaws, the house at the end of her drive, to make it into a centre for her residential weekend courses, where professionals could work on everything from folk fiddle to flute workshops.

I crossed some pastureland where cows grazed peacefully. Then I came to the village of Whatley, about half a mile from the quarry that dominated the area. Apparently, 300 lorries a day pass down these narrow lanes, making life intolerable for the residents. I only had to walk a short distance along the road, but I immediately felt threatened and harassed by the heavy traffic thundering past. Then I walked down a road, through woodland, towards Chantry. An ominous sign outside a house declared 'Guard Dogs Loose'. The three huge barking monstrosities that hurled themselves at a fence made me feel even more paranoid.

I was looking for a path on my left, through a wood, which was very badly marked. Though, once I was on it, it was pretty obvious. Walking through the sun-dappled beech and chestnut trees, I started to relax. But suddenly the dreaded 5-foot nettles re-emerged, and I wished I'd worn my trousers instead of stupid short black shorts.

By 11.40 a.m., I walked from the stream to the village of Chantry, where a funeral was taking place in the wonderful Gothic church designed by Gilbert Scott. The narrow road was lined with cars and the coffin was just being taken in, with about 20 mourners dressed in black. It all added to my general feeling of gloom and doom. Why does this part of Somerset feel like this? The farms are really smelly and the farmers are surly. I walked through one farm in Chantry which stank to high heaven.

At the end of the village I turned onto a little road to Bulls Green, where I came across an amazing sight – an entire garden filled with garden gnomes, painted animals, plastic flowers and little windmills, with a sign announcing 'Pixie Land'. This exotic melange of appalling taste really cheered me up. I then strolled through the northern edge of Asham Wood.

After this, I passed through the village of Downhead (nothing much happening there) and climbed a huge hill, up through pasture, to a disused radio tower. Looking eastwards, I could see for at least 20 miles – a fantastic view.

In Cranmore Wood I ate some wild raspberries while walking up a broad track. At the end of a high field was the spectacular Cranmore Tower, a 150-foot folly, 953 feet above sea level. It was built in 1862 for the Paget family, and has been restored and turned into a house.

Descending towards Shepton, I got completely lost. There were five different footpaths marked on the map, criss-crossing each other like lattice; the only trouble was, I couldn't work out which one I was supposed to be on. I walked down through fields, climbing over gates. It was a very pretty route, downhill, through empty country lanes. After Waterlip, I went through somewhere called Chelynch, then cut along the road to a tiny hamlet called Bodden, and down the hill into town.

Outside Shepton Mallet, on the A361, the traffic was already gridlocked and the summer hadn't even begun. Naturally, the traffic lights were out of action and roadworks

My day was brightened considerably by this joyous display outside the village of Chantry.

were in progress. I walked into town as the children were coming out of school. It was 3.45 p.m., I still hadn't had lunch and I was in an extremely bad mood. The town centre, with a pedestrian precinct, had little to offer in the way of gourmet eating. In the end I settled for egg and chips at a café. The egg was greasy, the chips were soggy, and the baked beans – well – they were just baked beans.

Shepton Mallet once had a flourishing cloth industry, and weavers led riots against the introduction of machines. I couldn't imagine anything like that happening today. The pedestrianized centre around the fifteenth-century market cross was lined with cheap shops, many of which were boarded up. Posters for heavy metal bands and truck derbies reinforced the impression of a dearth of cultural opportunities. I finished my tea, and walked over to the prison to wait for the crew. This was by far the most interesting building. It is the oldest inhabited prison in Britain, dating back to the reign of James I, and is surrounded by a high wall which makes it look like a French medieval fortified town. I walked all the way around it with the crew and we were stopped by a prison officer, who had obviously been watching us on a security camera. I found it hilarious – what sinister motives could we have for filming the bottom 10 feet of their wall? Anyway, we called it a day at 5 o'clock.

DAY 18

Shepton Mallet to Wells to Draycott

I walked out of Shepton Mallet through an ugly council estate along Draycott Road. It seemed almost cold, the mist was well down over the hills, and I was worried that when I walked along the top I wouldn't get the view down into Wells I'd been hoping for. After a steep climb up the hillside to the west of Shepton Mallet, past the cemetery, I crossed a field heavy with dew and saw a man out walking his dog.

The sun was beginning to burn off the haze – it looked as if it might be a really hot day. As I reached the brow of Windsor Hill I saw another man, who'd been out for an early morning walk with his dog. He was sitting on the back of his car, taking off his boots, and we exchanged a cheery hello. Unfortunately that was the last bit of good news for the next hour.

I turned left and into a farmyard. According to my map and the *Channel to Channel* book, there should have been a route to a quarry, but all I met was a large sign saying 'Private Land, Keep Out, Guard Dogs Loose, Access to the House Only', the usual stuff. Anyway, I decided to press on.

I went through the gate and suddenly two enormous dogs started barking and leaping up at me. I wasn't sure how friendly they were, so I decided to beat a hasty retreat. I then looked for the footpath marked on the map, but there was no way I could find it. On my Ordnance Survey map, three paths met at a dismantled railway embankment at the bottom, to the north of Ham Woods. All I can tell you, readers, is that those three paths are not marked in any way, shape or form. I was getting crosser and crosser and spent 20 minutes going through a stream that wasn't on the map. Having found the dismantled railway cutting, I climbed over an electric fence and then, as I was leaving the woods, turned back and saw a yellow footpath sign – God knows where that path started!

I continued west, crossed a road which led down to Croscombe, then headed north-west along a very overgrown path. Having gone over the stile to the road that went up to Crapnell Farm, I passed through a field with four bulls in it and prayed that the crew would not telephone me on my mobile to find out where the hell I was. The countryside was a lush green and there were little dewy spider-webs in the grass. I tried to put myself in a good mood, but I was really hot and it was only 10.30. All the mist had been burnt away by now, and around me were rolling hills and woods. I met up with the film crew and we followed a bridle track west, north of Dinder Wood. Now we were on the top of the hill above Wells, but we couldn't get a clear view of the Cathedral which was somewhat disappointing.

Skirting round through the King's Castle Nature Reserve, I met Jim Docherty, sitting in his camper van. He turned out to be the Footpath Inspector for Mendip District Council, so I gave him a right ear-bashing about what I'd just been through, and he came up with some flim-flam about 'Well if you'd stuck to the East Mendip Way you wouldn't have had a problem, etc, etc.' When will all these footpath inspectors realize that ramblers want to walk on *footpaths*, not just long-distance paths?

The imposing west front of Wells Cathedral.

Jim was an impressive figure – bare-chested, with a flowing mane of white hair and a matching beard. He wore a small pair of blue shorts and was as brown as an old leather handbag.

Anyway, the good thing about meeting Jim was that he gave me an even larger-scale map of how to get into Wells and explained how to follow the footpath to a place where I would get a view of the top of Wells Cathedral. At this point I had the King's Castle Nature Reserve to the north of me and a golf course to the south – doesn't that just sum up the dilemma of the British countryside today? Going over Tor Hill, I did just about see the top of the cathedral framed through the trees. Then it was a steep drop down onto the road. I followed the fourteenth-century moat of the Bishop's Palace into the market-place of Wells, and stopped at the west front of the cathedral. It's an astonishing sight, the cathedral, which never fails to take my breath away.

I first came here as a schoolgirl. I wanted to get into architectural college, so I came to Wells to draw and photograph it for my portfolio. Wells was choked with traffic then and I

was disgusted. Now it's just choked with tourists. There's a new bypass, cars are banned and the streets are cobbled. Not all the traders like it, but it does improve the cathedral and all the approaches to it. The building sits like a serene masterpiece. Few things make me crosser than reading in Pevsner's *Buildings of England* that, although he considers it one of the finest examples of architecture of its time in the world, he doesn't think the west front is really that great. Isn't that just typical of him, to find fault where everybody else simply finds perfection? The construction of the cathedral took place in two stages, from 1180 to 1240, and from 1290 to 1340. Its interior is dominated by the fourteenth-century scissor arches, but, for my money, the offending west front, flanked by solid towers and holding tier upon tier of statuary (about 400 figures in all) provides a visual feast like no other church in Britain. Pevsner calls it an 'image-screen' – and he's right. There are apostles, angels, saints and martyrs, all piled one on top of the other. Only the lower level is missing, prised off by the Duke of Monmouth's followers in 1685, during their rebellion against James II.

I spent an hour in front of the cathedral, admiring the front and watching the people come and go. Even the ghastly accordion-playing by a busker stationed in the archway through to Market Street couldn't dampen my joy. The day had been entirely saved by the gloriousness of architecture. It really can raise your spirits like no other art form.

Feeling spiritually refreshed, I walked through the town and bought a wooden jigsaw at the extraordinary Falkland Islands Agency shop I came across, and then went back to my hotel to lie down for half an hour to escape the blistering heat and hordes of tourists in Wells city centre before making my ascent of Ebbor Gorge.

At 2.30 I felt slightly less exhausted, packed my rucksack and set off westwards. It was still boiling hot. Coachloads of elderly tourists passed me as I crossed Cathedral Green and said goodbye to the cathedral. I headed up New Street and entered a narrow cobbled passageway by a sign that announced 'The West Mendip Way'. I was on a footpath that ran beside some immaculate tennis courts – so perfect I decided they had to belong to the Cathedral School. On closer inspection, they turned out to be immaculate because they were made of plastic grass!

I crossed over the bypass on a brand-new bridge. To the east the radio tower dominated the horizon. That must have caused a stink when they put it up. Ahead of me on a playing field, a boy was flying a kite. Standing on the bridge over the bypass, I looked to the south-west and saw Glastonbury Tor very clearly, and behind me the very pretty, fifteenth-century church of St Cuthbert's, often mistaken by tourists for Wells Cathedral. Wells seemed incredibly genteel, a world away from Shepton Mallet (where, on the night I arrived, three teenage drunks and a woman with track-marks up her arms were drinking on a bench in the High Street and some children were feeding chips to a group of desiccated-looking pigeons). No, Wells and Shepton Mallet couldn't be more different, I mused, as the footpath passed through the grounds of the Blue School. As the children were on holiday, it was eerily

quiet. After heading up through fields and the last bit of suburban Wells, I walked along the top edge of Underwood Quarry on cliffs hundreds of feet high. Below me, in the huge crater, was a giant crane, silent. To the south were the rolling hills of Devon, basking in a blue haze.

As I approached the Wookey Hole caves, I met an old gentleman who told me he was 80 but went out walking three days a week. He was on a 7-mile circuit encompassing Ebbor Gorge and the radio tower. The heat didn't seem to bother him as much as it was bothering me. Wookey Hole – which is supposed to be a major tourist attraction – seemed strangely quiet in the afternoon.

It would all have been very different 90 years ago, when the Wookey Hole Paper Mill was the largest of its kind in Europe. Around it was a thriving community of mill buildings, a church, workers' cottages and a school for the children of the 200 or so mill workers. The mill was sold in the 1950s following the decline of the handmade paper industry, but it has been reopened and now exports its specialist papers (made on Victorian machinery) all over the world. I found it relatively easy not to be diverted from my path through Wookey, and passed a whole series of signs to the caves with no pain whatsoever. Mind you, about 300,000 visitors annually are not of my persuasion!

The village was pretty, if somewhat over-manicured, and there was a Cluttons 'For Sale' sign in front of a particularly ugly bungalow. In front of the restored mill, music was playing loudly (tasteful, electronic music, I should point out), and a neatly tended bowling green had a sign that read 'The Wookey Hole Bowling Club' with a picture of a witch on it.

Having climbed out of the village on a narrow road past a wonderfully old-fashioned sign which announced, 'Unsuitable for Charabancs', I toiled uphill through a wooded valley in the cool shade, thank goodness. Then I was off on a footpath over very red earth towards Ebbor Gorge. Apart from the old gentleman, I hadn't seen anyone else walking this afternoon. Strange how near you can be to a city centre and yet, when you walk, how isolated you are too.

I was now in the heart of the Mendips, the hills that stretch for about 20 miles, from the headland of Brean Down, in the Bristol Channel, to the market town of Frome. In Saxon and early medieval times, Mendip land was a royal forest where kings hunted red deer; there is a story that in 941 King Edmund narrowly escaped death when his hounds chased a stag over the cliffs at Cheddar in thick fog.

Above: An ancient sign near Wookey Hole en route to the Ebbor Gorge.
Overleaf: The Somerset Levels below Cheddar with the Mendips in the background.

The hills are limestone, with deep craggy gorges, underground caverns and streams. The hard-wearing, weather-resistant white stone is used everywhere, from drystone walls to Wells Cathedral itself. The area is an uneasy combination of dairy farming, tourist honey-pots (like Cheddar and Wells), and quarries which provide employment but scar the landscape and clog the roads with heavy lorries and the air with fine dust.

As I entered the leafy splendour of Ebbor Gorge, I took a sharp right turn and climbed upwards on thousands of newly made, wooden steps. The crew, however, had gone up the bottom of the gorge, which got narrower and narrower, and then they climbed up and we met at the top by two completely different routes. It was annoying really because I missed the view that they had of the gorge from the bottom, but at the top there's a stone platform – natural stone that's all eroded – and you look south for at least 20 miles. It was a sensational view and I enjoyed the breeze.

Then we climbed out of the gorge the wrong way. We had to retrace our steps, and go down and up again, to emerge to the north where we could see the Bristol Channel over in the east, and a series of undulating fields bounded by stone walls and filled with sheep. We turned right, along an old drovers' lane, and met two wardens with a dog, repairing stiles. They fell about laughing when I recounted how we'd all got lost in Ebbor Gorge. It turned out that it was because I'd entered the gorge on a public footpath! English Nature have erected signs that tell you where to go, but they start from the car park. Silly me! Obviously, long-distance walkers aren't catered for in this part of the country, which is totally geared to day-trippers.

Ahead lay the isolated hill-top village of Priddy – its vast village green lay silent and empty. In medieval times this was a busy place where wool was collected for the mills down in the valleys. Each August an ancient sheep fair commemorates its past, around the thatched stack on the green. Today, as Priddy was shopless and café-free, I settled for a luke-warm bottle of water and a piece of chocolate; I felt somewhat hard-done-by as I walked out of the village at 6.15 in a westerly direction in unreasonably hot sun, along a little road with cornflowers growing in the verges. After about half a mile, I headed off to the west, across some slightly undulating fields.

To the south lay a series of Neolithic burial mounds. The Priddy Nine Barrows were constructed about 1500 BC by the Beaker People, so-called because they arrived in Britain with the first knowledge of metal and drank out of cups. The landscape seemed to be imbued with a sense of isolation and bleakness, in spite of the lush grass. Maybe it was the spirits of the Beaker People speaking to me from the spooky humps that housed their remains, or perhaps just hunger and fatigue brought on by my long walk – I don't know!

I began to see the horizon in the distance. The sun was setting but it wasn't going to be a perfect sunset – there were too many grey, fluffy clouds. To the south, though, it was clear, and there was an electric blue sky over the southern hills. To the west lay the Bristol

Channel; the islands off Weston-super-Mare (Flat Holm and Steep Holm), Cheddar and the flat plains lay beneath us. The Cheddar Reservoir reflected the dying sunlight like a big round mirror. As we came over the brow of the hill, heading west, the view was breathtaking. Slightly to the north was a gliding club. Gliders took off every 15 minutes or so and circled above us, in the evening light.

I sat on a hillside looking out towards the end of the English part of my journey, which meant I was halfway. It was exciting to see the sea for the first time for weeks and weeks.

As I dropped down in to the village of Draycott, the holiday traffic was clogging the roads as people went home after their days out. I got back to the hotel in Wells at about 8.30, and had exactly 10 minutes to have a shower and clean up before dinner.

The narrow roads were already crawling with holiday-makers in their cars anticipating a cracking day out. I left the village of Draycott and walked up a little lane, a back route into Cheddar, that was quiet and provided a suitable opportunity for contemplation before I entered the tourist nightmare ahead. The fertile fields below me in the valley were full of

> **DAY 19**
> *Draycott via Cheddar Gorge to the M5*

produce that enterprising locals were flogging on roadside stalls – strawberries were the top seller this week.

I was meeting comedian Bill Bailey who was to accompany me on my inaugural trip to Cheddar Gorge. He was a local lad, with the soft warm accent of one born in Devizes. He grew up in a village outside Bristol and went to school in Bath. He'd lived in London since he was 19, to pursue his music and comedy ambitions. Having seen his act, I think he would have found it hard to progress much in suburban Keynsham. He looks like a rock roadie, with long hair and dark T-shirts, but mixes rock, classics and surreal humour like no one else on the comedy circuit.

I walked up the main street of Cheddar amongst a steady stream of fellow pilgrims all gazing into the shop windows which lined our route. They were stuffed with tourist trash and I wondered if Lourdes was like this. Cheddar seemed to have Holy Cheese Witches and Grottoes, where Lourdes had Virgins, Holy Water, Grottoes and Miracles. Having left their cars and coaches, my fellow walkers had a purposeful air about them. They were going to shell out quite considerable sums of money to see natural wonders, like rocks and so on, turned into twentieth-century areas of wonderment with names like 'Heritage Centre', 'Crystal Quest' and 'Jacob's Ladder'.

I met Bill and his two Lakeland terriers, Rocky and Ruby, outside the Cheddar Gorge Cheese Company, which the manager wouldn't call a museum but said was 'living history'.

Overleaf: With Bill, Rocky and Ruby in the Cheddar Gorge.

By the rubbish bins were boxes, which had once contained traditional Cornish pasties, labelled: 'unbaked, frozen made for Country Choice by Butcher and Baker Foods of Dudley', which I believe is in Birmingham. One box was labelled 'Cheddar', and another labelled oddly – 'Leg Bender'. Behind us, a stuffed sheepdog and model of a farmer boomed out recorded greetings to attract visitors. In a cheesy Somerset accent, the farmer entreated:

'Hello my dears, welcome to Cheddar. Step inside my model village and see genuine farmhouse Cheddar cheese being made. Ooh ahh, 'tis right tasty is that by far. Oh! Oh! There's scrumpy cider, country wines to sample… lots of sweets and treats for the kiddies too. That right Bob?'

Sadly, whoever had dreamt up this idea had been a *Carry On* films fan, for the dog regularly injected 'Ohs' and 'Ahs' and 'My Dears' in a Kenneth Williams accent, reducing us to hysterics. According to Bill, a man with a pipe and dog guarding churns was a potent symbol of West Country tradition. He promised me that the gorge would be hewn not from rock, but made cunningly from solid tea rooms! We wanted to walk up Jacob's Ladder, a series of steps to the top of the gorge, but were told we'd have to pay £2.50 because it belonged to the Cheddar Gorge Showcaves Empire. We coughed up even though there is a public footpath at the top of the 274 steps. Bill was very good company and I bought him a model wizard joss-stick holder in the shop because he made me laugh so much.

I found Jacob's Ladder a complete disappointment. I'd lain in bed that morning envisaging a sort of stairway to heaven, formed from rock by tremendous forces aeons of time ago; what I got was a dank, dismal set of concrete slabs with a nasty iron rail and hundreds of overweight German and Dutch school kids blocking my path as they toiled up.

At the top, we were reading some totally over-the-top sign about the prehistoric evolution of Cheddar Gorge, when a very officious man bounded up. When I cheerily asked him if he had really come all the way up without stopping, he drew himself up ramrod straight and asked me if I had permission to be filming in the Cheddar Gorge Showcaves Park. Well, this guy was like Colonel Blimp or something. Bill was behind me in a mass of suppressed hysteria. Of course we hadn't got permission but, after moving his head up and down on his shoulders like a neurotic budgie for two minutes, the man realized he wasn't getting anywhere. I then said we were on a public footpath and he departed as rapidly as he'd arrived. From then on, Bill was in his element, saying wasn't it bizarre to have such a thing as a show cave, a bit like a show house, as if you'd suddenly ring up and say, 'I was thinking of buying a show cave. Have you got any I can look at and do they have electricity?' Anyway, we went on in this vein, imagining conversations with show cave salesmen for about half an hour as we climbed ever upwards.

The path was completely eroded and the earth showed through everywhere because of the pounding from tourists. The path to the West Mendip Way has been moved back from the edge of Cheddar Gorge to prevent further erosion, but of course if you walk on

the West Mendip Way you don't get to see down into the gorge itself, so it's really hard to know what to do. At various points along the route there were spectacular views from rocky platforms. I was astounded at the size of some of the people who were struggling up the gorge – not just one stone overweight but several. Anyway, everyone seemed in very good humour and, astonishingly, the person with the worst breathing wasn't a human but a large Great Dane. By the time we got halfway up I thought it was going to pass out with asthma.

We finally reached the top of the gorge after about half an hour. So far we hadn't seen the famous killer sheep. Apparently, a wild breed of Soay sheep (originally from Scotland) have been multiplying like wildfire, dislodging rocks, causing injury and even death. Now a local battle was raging between those who wanted cows culled rather than sheep. After all, as one letter-writer pointed out, the limestone gorge was a wildlife area, and the sheep had been there for centuries. Rainfall is a greater cause of rocks falling, and tourists dislodge more earth than Mother Nature or four-legged animals!

After a stop to get our breath back, we dropped down a steep muddy path. Some time later there was a sign where the routes parted; one said 'Steep, slippery slope to the road', and the other one said 'Longer route'. The longer route turned out to be just as slippery as the shorter route because it had been raining the previous night, which I thought was very entertaining. At the road Bill and I parted company. He flatly refused to walk right back up the other side of the

Pastureland on the north side of the Cheddar Gorge, I'm striding out for a picnic lunch.

gorge, and I couldn't blame him. He got a lift in a car and said he'd meet me for a picnic lunch at the top in an hour. I crossed the road and went up a track into the National Trust nature reserve at Black Rock. At first the path was stony. I was in a continuation of Cheddar Gorge, on a wide track with steep sides. Then the path became the most beautiful wide carpet of velvety green grass and sheer black rock on our left. This part of the gorge seemed tourist-free and peaceful. The path curved round to the north. At this point I saw a whole line of parked film trucks and just laughed out loud. After another 100 yards there was a table laid out with urns serving tea and coffee, and three women standing alongside it holding paper cups. They told me they hired out and handled animals, and the production being filmed was *Animal Ark*, a drama for television. The film crew were slightly over the brow of the hill; we could see them in the distance. Another officious young lady came up with a walkie-talkie. When I asked her where the lunch van was, she wouldn't tell me. She had no sense of humour whatsoever.

After another hundred yards, we went through a gate and I realized I would have to climb back up through a forest to get up to the higher level of the gorge. This time the path was gentler, not like the concrete horror of Jacob's Ladder. Anyway, at this point, through the mature forest of Long Wood, the path was completely empty, dappled with sunlight and sheltered from the wind. It was a steep climb, but after the gorge it didn't seem that bad. At the top we were on a plateau again. On my left were fields of oats and corn, the deep azure blue sky and the wind blowing in my face very, very strongly. I walked a couple of miles west on the West Mendip Way, through pastureland, and stopped for a picnic lunch at Ashridge Farm.

After lunch, I walked down the road to Tyning's Farm and then headed north-west from behind the farmhouse, along the West Mendip Way, through a beautiful forest of very tall pine trees, hundreds of feet high, Rowberrow Warren. My path was crossed by forestry tracks, but it wasn't too hard to find the way using a large-scale map. I dipped down briefly, crossed a stream, followed it, and emerged at the top of Lippiatt Lane, which dropped slightly down into the outskirts of Shipham. I skirted around to the south of the village, with fantastic views out to the coast, and dropped down through the back gardens of some bungalows (the Somerset retirement version of Beverly Hills).

Shipham, once a thriving mining village, now had the look of a place stuck in the 1950s: an old-fashioned garage with ancient pumps and a matching village shop. I crossed the main road back into Cheddar, dropped down a steep slope to a stream with a brand-new bridge across it, and started the climb up Winterhead Hill, heading for Sheep Shelve Farm which is about 3 miles away.

It was exhilarating walking over these rounded hills in the direction of the sea, seeing it get closer and closer with the wind beating in my face. Along Winscombe Drove, a high-level old drovers' road heading directly west, with high hedges on either side and sandy

ground underfoot, 6-foot bracken on either side perfumed the air. The fields were a luxuriant green (even though the hay had been already cut), bordered with dark green shrubs and hawthorns. Every now and then there were pine trees amidst rolling hollows, a very sensuous landscape. It was late afternoon, I'd walked the West Mendip Way most of the day and I hadn't seen another person walking in my direction. True enough, in Cheddar Gorge I had seen lots of holiday-makers, but, once I'd left, they had vanished. Everyone was sucked, lemming-like, into that one small area.

I crossed the A38 which was pounding with holiday traffic. Directly off the A38 lay King's Wood. A sign told me it was an ancient semi-natural woodland probably dating back to before the eleventh century; my path followed the old Anglo-Saxon boundary crossing Wavering Down and Compton Hill. The landscape had suddenly increased in scale, from small rounded hills to magnificent downs with broad backs and heathland.

I stopped at the bottom of Wavering Down and waited for the crew. Our celebratory cream tea arrived in a plastic crate: lots of tea, scones and clotted cream. We laid it all out on a plastic ground sheet – the only cream tea we'd had on the film so far. We all ate between two and three scones each and felt really bloated. Then I climbed to the top of Wavering Down. I'd eaten so many delicious scones I couldn't climb up on top of the trig point, but someone lifted me up. Even though it was blowing a gale I could see for miles, down to the coast and the Somerset Levels to the south. I just breathed in the air and enjoyed the view.

Then I set off walking across Wavering Down. The heather was already out – a deep pink, almost fuchsia colour – and there were tiny little yellow flowers. It was like a carpet of small bright colours. The sun went behind the cloud… and I could already hear the roar of the M5. It's so depressing to be in a place of such utter beauty and hear the noise of a motorway in the background. To the east I could see Compton Hill and Crook Peak. I was going to turn down to the motorway before then and meet my taxi on the motorway bridge. It would be a fitting end to a day that had started in Cheddar Gorge. I climbed up the slope to Crook Peak and met a man who was rebuilding the drystone wall in the evening sun.

One last hill as I skirted Crook Peak – the noise from the M5 was really strong now and, depending on which way the wind was blowing, very intrusive. The sun came out and I walked across a wide grassy path – totally idyllic. By a wrought-iron gate a sign proclaimed 'The Bungalow'. And yes, it was a bungalow that faced the M5! After battling with nettles I emerged onto a narrow, deserted B road running parallel with the M5. I walked it as quickly as I could because the bridge over it was further away than I'd anticipated, and my taxi would have been waiting for ages.

At my hotel I had the honeymoon suite, complete with primrose-yellow sunken bath and a lace-cloth-covered dining table in an alcove. From the window I could see right across the valley to the west. It was a light, airy room – I was sorry I was only in it for one night.

Woke up at 6.15 feeling a bit anxious, don't know why. I went straight back to sleep, and was in a deep dream when I was woken by banging on the door. Time to get on the road again.

I looked out of the window. The sky was covered in grey clouds and it was extremely windy. Not a good sign for a day in Weston-super-Mare!

I started on the bridge over the M5 that I'd reached the previous night, and I walked past Forgotten World, which is an attempt at a homespun theme park celebrating gypsies. It looked extremely sad, nestling right by the motorway. In its back garden were the rotting frames of half a dozen caravans, and I could see some exotic-looking chickens wandering around in front of the house. Ted Atkinson, who runs Forgotten World, builds gypsy caravans to order using traditional plans. His theme park offers woodwork and gypsy folklore, Romany music and dancing; it just seems to be in a most unromantic setting.

Even at 9.30 in the morning the noise from the M5 was deafening. I turned right down a lane, crossed a field covered in clover and daisies and progressed through the village of Loxton and onto the West Mendip Way, on a drovers' path climbing steadily up Bleadon Hill. Loxton had some fine buildings for such a tiny village, including a thirteenth-century church with a beautiful carved cross just outside the porch.

At the top of Bleadon Hill I turned west at a confusing group of tracks, and headed along a very muddy bridleway with views over to Weston-super-Mare. The path joined a road and travelled west along the ridge for about a mile. To the west I could see Weston-super-Mare; to the south the Levels, with the odd hill rising here and there. The Levels, with no hedges but lines of willow trees, criss-crossed by waterways, drains and ditches, sit between the Quantocks, the Mendips and the coast.

This was obviously a prime residential area, with outstanding views, and I passed a series of lavish bungalows and upper-middle-class homes. Suddenly I came to one that surpassed them all! It had high wrought-iron gates embellished with huge eagles, their wings outstretched, which hung from imposing stone gate posts. Emblazoned on the gates was the immortal word 'Graceland'. They were firmly shut and there was high-tech video equipment to deter unwelcome callers. The house, a pink confection that would have been more at home in Memphis or Louisiana than the outskirts of Weston-super-Mare, lay at the end of a long driveway. The owner must have been curious to see a giant red-haired rambler peering through his gates. He came out to meet me, looking as if he'd just got out of bed, with his slippers on, jeans and a Juventus football shirt. He had thick dark hair, an Italian-looking face, a gold tooth and gold earring, and, apart from revealing that he owned a fish and chip shop by the pier in town, he was smiling but unforthcoming. George (as he introduced himself) picked up his daughter Demi, who was dressed in an extremely expensive check

Opposite: The trig point at the top of Wavering Down.

cotton frock with a white collar. George must be doing well: it would take a lot of cod and chips to build that place. He smirked enigmatically as we said goodbye – a mystery man.

Opposite Graceland I took the footpath down the hill, past some ponies and donkeys in a field. Having gone down through a meadow with many different kinds of wild flowers, I emerged into the village of Bleadon opposite some council houses and holiday bungalows, all very much in the south-west England Riviera style.

I got a bit lost in Bleadon, finally finding my route out down the back of some gardens, through well-tended allotments each with its own little hut. I passed through a very large farm at Purn, and miraculously found the right path again. The buildings, farms, workshops and barns, were of fine local stone and quite imposing.

Just as I thought I'd done all my hill-climbing for this part of the journey, I had to climb another one, and then turn back on myself south. The West Mendip Way certainly twisted and turned to get into Weston-super-Mare. Ancient stones formed natural steps to descend the hill. Then there was a horrible stretch of about a quarter of a mile along the A370, which I found almost impossible to cross. After a railway line I was on a sandy flat path over Bleadon Levels to the sea following the banks of the river. I turned into a marina by a sign saying 'Keep Out: no footpath through the boatyard'.

At the road I turned left and emerged on the beach by a caravan site at Uphill, at the south end of Weston-super-Mare beach. The tide was as far out as it could go, exposing miles of mud flats. As I walked north along the sand, it was blowing a gale. I started to walk on the mud because the loose sand was whipping against my skin like sandpaper. There was nobody on the beach, except for a lone runner and one small child bravely making a sand-castle in what seemed like a tornado. I headed towards the Grand Pier and fish and chips.

Despite the awful weather, I was elated to have completed half my journey. I walked over a carpet of tiny shells in the sand, with no one bothering to pick them up. Closer to the town, pockets of holiday-makers with their overcoats on were having a short stroll and putting on a brave face.

Weston-super-Mare, like so many British seaside towns, has had changing fortunes since its heyday as a Victorian resort. With the second highest tidal range in the world (up to 45 feet) it means a long walk over dreary mud flats for a paddle. In this age of armchair channel-hopping and Disneyland, the public want their good weather guaranteed and physical effort cut to a minimum. How can Weston compete with Majorca?

But the real phenomenon in Weston is the huge number of charity shops – over 42! I popped into the Tourist Information Centre near the Grand Pier and picked up a map. After fish and chips and about six cups of tea, I felt strong enough to brave the gale. Armed with my map, I set out to distribute some donations (from designer T-shirts to books) that I'd bought to Weston in my rucksack. My own T-shirts were a bit grotty so I'd persuaded a pop star friend to recycle some Dolce and Gabbana and Calvin Klein numbers my way.

In all the shops, from the RSPCA to Oxfam to the Red Cross to the Sea Cadets, it was the same story. They ruthlessly undercut each other's prices, indulged in lavish themed window displays and kept a strict look-out for crumbly shop-lifters. One window featured a full-length, size 22, white satin wedding dress, complete with veil. Such is the fame of Weston thrift shops, coach trips are now organized from the Midlands, Wales and the West Country. These day-trippers don't bother with the beach: they just get their maps and fill up their suitcases on wheels with bargains, clothing whole families, buying records, finding shoes and even dinner services. The notes provided by Weston's tourist office told me that the Beatles had played at the Odeon in Weston for a week in June 1963. Jeffrey Archer had lived there and chosen Lord Archer of Weston-super-Mare as his title. But Weston's most stylish export is surely John Cleese, born there in 1935. How entertained he would have been by the thrift wars: over 40 shops fighting a cutthroat battle for the hard-earned pounds of Weston's bargain-hunters, all staffed by genteel ladies in twin sets and pearls wearing 'Doreen' name badges.

In the RSPCA shop I purchased a small silver-plated trophy for £3.50 and awarded it to David, the director of all the films so far. I would have another director, John, for Wales. David had put up with my tiredness, tantrums and sandwich rages with good humour. How would I manage in Wales, where wind, weather and mountains loomed high on the agenda? I'd walked over 245 miles, but the real physical challenge lay ahead.

Above: Fun on the pier at Weston.
Overleaf: Weston-super-Mare, the end of the East to West walk.

South to North

Cardiff to Conwy

The second part of my coast-to-coast odyssey would take me from south to north across Wales, starting at the water's edge in Cardiff Harbour and ending 274 miles later at the magnificent Conwy Castle. I'd decided to use Tony Drake's little book *The Cambrian Way* as the basis for my route, undeterred by the fact that it involved climbing the Black Mountains, the Brecon Beacons, the Rhinogs and Snowdon – about 61,000 feet of ascent, or a couple of times up Mount Everest!

I knew that the middle part of Wales was under-populated and relatively under-walked, and I was resigned to the crowds I would encounter in Snowdonia. This journey would also be a chance to revisit my roots: after all, my mother is Welsh and still lives in Llandudno. I grew up in a house in Fulham, West London, where Welsh was spoken on a daily basis, as my mother's sister lived next door and my Welsh granny would come and stay for pro-longed periods as she got older. My father (born in Fulham), my sister and I were the outsiders, excluded by language and culture. As a small child, being Welsh seemed to mean a lot of cleaning (done by my Welsh granny or *nain*) and a lot of sitting around in the Welsh dairies we had discovered locally, while the three Welsh-speakers spent what seemed like hours talking in their native tongue to the shopkeepers.

My route would take me through Mid-Wales, near Tregaron, where I'd spent a lot of time in the late sixties, when my first husband's family owned a farmhouse high up on the hills. I'd spend the last day of my journey through Wales walking near Llanfairfechan, where I'd spent all my holidays as a child, staying in my grandmother's white-washed stone cottage, with its wash-house and toilet across the back yard and the iron mangle occupying pride of place en route to the loo. I still have relatives living in Llanfairfechan, and it hasn't changed much. *Nain* is buried in the Welsh cemetery there.

My day began down in Cardiff's docks, now in the throes of redevelopment. I started by the small, white Norwegian Church, now an arts centre, on the waterfront. I walked out of the docks, with their new roads and office blocks (somehow lacking a heart in my opinion), and took a dead straight road from the docks to arrive in the one-way system that signals the start of downtown Cardiff. I was to meet the Welsh singer/songwriter Donna Lewis in Bute Park, and we planned to walk together up part of the Taff Trail through the city.

I passed a lot of expensive men's clothing shops in St Mary's Street and stopped for a coffee in a Victorian shopping arcade. The town centre was mostly Victorian and Edwardian, and it was bustling with life – in complete contrast to the docks. Cardiff has only been the capital of Wales since 1955, and, because only 6 per cent of the population speak Welsh, it is viewed as not very Welsh by people (like my relatives!) from the North. In fact, Wales

Previous page: Cardiff Bay in the throes of redevelopment.

suffers from a north–south divide, with plenty of development in the valleys around Cardiff (valley boys come into town each Friday night to spend all their money – hence the clothes shops) and a strong sense of identity in the north, with Snowdonia and the coastal holiday towns and retirement resorts. Neither the people of Cardiff nor those of Conwy care too much about the problems of those in Mid-Wales, as I was to discover during my walk.

Cardiff Castle was remodelled by the fabulously wealthy Third Marquis of Bute; he met the architect William Burges when he was 18 and together they constructed their fantasy version of the Middle Ages. As I planned to explore Castell Coch, their other tour de force, I decided to press on with my walk and meet Donna. She was waiting by a fake stone circle in Bute Park, small, thin, attractive and blonde, wearing no-nonsense hiking boots, a T-shirt and black fleece hiking trousers.

Donna's story was a fascinating one. She was born in Cardiff but now lives in Woodstock, New York – where she has to explain where Wales is. Her dad was a jazz pianist. Donna played the piano from the age of six, and by 14 she was writing songs and recording them on cassette. She was a big fan of Elton John and Rickie Lee Jones and attended the Welsh College of Music and Drama, studying classical composition, piano and flute. She trained as a teacher but, after working in bands in Cardiff, moved to Birmingham and toured European piano bars: five hours a night, six nights a week.

Then she put together a basic four-track studio at home and set about recording her own material, which was ignored by record companies in Britain until she went to America four years ago, and did the rounds of the record companies with her demo tape. Despite getting a bit of interest, she came home without a deal and went back to the piano bar circuit. She was saved when her tape was passed on to Atlantic Records. Atlantic found her, flew her back and signed her up.

To me, Donna was interesting because she never gave up. This woman just kept plugging away, determined to continue writing and making music. She was clearly extremely strong-willed under the soft exterior.

Donna and I walked along through the grassy expanse of Bute Park, with its manicured flower beds and broad, well-maintained paths. Then we turned off, along a narrow path which follows the River Taff. At first it was easy going, but then the path rapidly degenerated into a mass of brambles and 5-foot nettles. I was glad we were both wearing trousers.

We struggled along the narrow path, passing a couple of magnificent weirs, one of which had a brand-new suspension bridge over it for pedestrians and cyclists. The path improved somewhat as we entered a series of parks. The only trouble was that we were on a route favoured by cyclists who seemed to think it a bit sissy to have a bell.

Anyway, we walked on, chatting away, totally engrossed in each other's company. After Donna's lucky break her first single was voted the most-played record of the year in America. Of course she was still almost completely unknown in Britain; she released her

record here but we pooh-poohed her because we hadn't discovered her first. Donna was flying to Los Angeles on Sunday to record the title track for a new Fox film, *Anastasia,* with Richard Marx. In the meantime, she and her husband were staying at her parents' house in Cardiff, sleeping in her old bedroom!

Above: Walking the Taff Trail with Donna.
Opposite: Beyond the traffic, Castell Coch on the hillside north of Cardiff.

After walking for a couple of hours, Donna and I said goodbye – she was going home to work on her part in the duet she was going to record on Sunday. I walked on by the river, entering another public park where I had a picnic on the grass by the river. Then I left the crew and followed the Taff Trail up towards Castell Coch, skirting the edge of a road past some modern housing estates and a very interesting pumping station for the Glamorganshire Canal. The gadget was called Mellingriffith Pump and had recently been restored. It was surrounded by 6-foot steel railings so you couldn't get anywhere near it, but my notes told me it was one of the most important industrial monuments in Europe, a water beam engine built in 1807 to lift water up to the canal.

Then I crossed a road and walked through woodland onto a stretch of the canal, north towards the castle. It was a nature reserve – totally idyllic. The canal was overgrown with rushes and reeds, and carpets of waterlilies. School children were having picnics on the banks: a very pleasant way to spend an afternoon, although the twittering of the birds was somewhat undermined by the hearty roar of traffic in the background, and it wasn't even rush hour.

When the canal ended abruptly I took a little stone bridge to my right, and climbed up a series of steep steps through woodland. At the top I emerged onto a horrific spaghetti junction. I went over and under one major road and one feeder road after another: the sound of the traffic was deafening. Ahead of me I could see the hills and Castell Coch; behind lay Cardiff. I couldn't help thinking what terrible damage we do to the environment with the car, and how beautiful and peaceful it had been walking along the canal for the last half-hour. Still, I was looking forward to Castell Coch: it was, after all, one man's fantasy; a dream castle, completely useless and redundant, housing a fantastic bed, complete with crystal balls on the corners!

I walked along a road and came to the main street of Tongwynlais, which must once have been a little village but was now just another suburb of Cardiff. I turned right, in front of a pub, up Hill Road, and started to climb up to Castell Coch. After about half an hour I turned left up the castle driveway, having passed the inevitable golf course on my left.

The castle looked deserted. Inside, from the windows of the top floor in Lady Bute's

Merthyr
Tydfil
A 470

M 4 (E)   M 4 (E)
M 4 (Dn)   M 4 (Dn)

↑   ↑

100 yds
100 llath

bedroom, you could see all the way down to the sea: my route due south, past the castle, to the docks beyond. Castell Coch had just been a pile of stones when the Marquis of Bute commissioned William Burges to create a fantasy castle for his summer residence in 1872. It was eventually finished 20 years later, but Burges never saw it – he died in 1881. With its three circular towers of different heights rising from the hillside, this castle is a folly built in stone, complete with drawbridge. Timber balconies surround the central courtyard and the lavish interior consists of just four main rooms: two bedrooms (one for Lord, and one for Lady Bute); a dining room; and an octagonal double-height drawing room, decorated with scenes from *Aesop's Fables*. The guide told me the castle had been used for many films and TV commercials, including one for a Lebanese mattress company. In this one, a handsome young prince searches the castle for Sleeping Beauty, finds her in the bedroom and kisses her, but she doesn't wake up because she's sleeping too soundly on her comfy mattress!

When no one was watching, I stepped over the silken ropes and lay down on the magic bed with its crystal balls at the corners. The horsehair mattress was surprisingly lumpy! No gorgeous prince materialized so, after a couple of minutes fantasizing about my life as Lady Bute, Queen of the Walkers of Britain, I opened my eyes, went down to the café and ate a large scone.

It was the end of my first day in Wales. It was a shame I couldn't spend the night in the castle – the decor was exactly my taste and I was sure that prolonged exposure to such whimsical madness would inspire me and speed me on my way. But, sadly, it was not to be. I made my way back to spaghetti junction and the real world – so much drabber by comparison.

DAY 22
Castell Coch to Machen

I left Castell Coch by the car park, took a broad track up through the woods to the top of the hill, followed it and came to a road junction. There were brief tantalizing glimpses southwards to the Bristol Channel. At a road I turned right, and then slightly miscalculated where to turn back again and took the wrong path, adding about half a mile to the journey.

Having skirted the hillside, I climbed steeply up Thornhill which had a radio transmitter on top. I turned left at a main road by a pub, and then right along another track that took me through woods, following the Ridgeway Footpath.

The views had opened up now and I could see down into the valleys on either side. Caerphilly lay beneath me to the north. To the south lay Cardiff. The disappointing thing about this otherwise exhilarating high-level footpath was the fact that the M4 ran roughly parallel with it and slightly further south, maybe a couple of miles, so the sound of the traffic was carried by the wind right up to where I walked.

I skirted around a disused quarry, heading east. It was strange to arrive in Wales and find so early on that I had to adopt such a circuitous path. The path through England had seemed so direct, but my route through Wales was to follow mountain ranges and would therefore twist and turn enormously. The path came out by a small pub that was being renovated, and I took a little country lane behind it. All along this section of the route farmers had posted signs saying: 'Please walk slowly. Do not frighten the sheep. The lambs will die.' It made me wonder what on earth people did when walking here.

After this, I joined a forestry track, which was more or less flat for half a mile, and then started my descent in the direction of Machen. It was pleasant walking weather but extremely boring to be walking through a forest when I couldn't see anything. I was longing for more views of the valleys, but it was not to be. As I approached Machen I joined a narrow road that crossed over a bridge, and then went on to the main road and the High Street itself. I turned right, found a road called Church Road, turned left, and there was the Land Rover waiting to meet me.

I'd expected this part of the route to be about 7 miles, but it turned out to be nearer 8½, with about 850 feet of climbing. So, instead of taking the couple of hours I'd anticipated, it took closer to three and a quarter. I hoped it wasn't an omen for the route ahead.

I woke up and looked out of the window to see big black clouds. There were brief sunny intervals en route to Machen, and then as I got out of the car, which was returning me to Machen, there was a torrential downpour. I turned up the road by the old post office (now the village store), and after 100 yards turned right up a path by a chain-link fence. Ahead of me

DAY 23
Machen to Pontypool

lay the first hill of the day, with a BBC television mast on the top. It was covered in fir trees and a big cloud obscured the summit.

I was wearing a new kind of waterproof that I'd borrowed from my friend Janet: an extremely lightweight nylon poncho. It covered me like a shroud, with a couple of horrible flappy bits hanging down between my legs like tails, but I didn't care. It was much lighter than a Gore-Tex jacket, and, as I had to climb two hills today, I wanted as little as possible weighing me down.

Crossing a bridge made of old railway sleepers, I started the ascent through the forest. Looking south to the coast, it was sunny, but there were big black clouds ahead, and I could hear the roar of the rush-hour traffic heading into Cardiff below. As I climbed up I could see the huge developments in the valleys: Caerphilly to the west and Newport to my east.

I climbed steadily through trees that were at least 100 feet high. The lower branches were all dead – only the tops were green. This made for a rather sombre start to the day, but at least I was protected from the showers, with only the occasional drip filtering

through. Then the sun came out and shafts of light dissected my path, lighting up the rain-drops and falling on a thick carpet of sodden pine needles. I emerged from the forest and skirted the northern edge of the pasture which dropped steeply away to my right.

I was already boiling hot. It was time for the first costume change of the day: off came the nylon waterproof. I re-entered the forest for a short stretch and then emerged onto common land covered with bracken. Below, to the south-east, was a working quarry. I turned left immediately, up a track through the bracken, and made the steep ascent to the television mast. It was time for the second change of clothing: off came the fleece shirt. I tied it round my waist, shoved my sunglasses on, tied my hair up and prepared for the climb.

The path was extremely slippery. Below me in the quarry the lorries clattered away. The only other sound was me, gasping for breath. Ahead lay the white pole of the mast against a clear blue sky, with white fluffy clouds behind it. The final ascent to the radio mast was a bit easier. I could see Risca, my next destination, so I headed north-east, downhill, towards it. Ahead of me was a slag heap which looked like a giant Iron Age barrow – magnificent.

Risca, with its neat rows of terraced houses, nestles at the bottom of Ebbw Vale, with the road running through it. The town was a centre for brick-making before coal was mined there in the nineteenth century; 142 men and boys were killed in an explosion at the Blackvein colliery in 1860.

There's something about the colour of the grass in Wales – it really seems greener than anywhere else. It's the colour I remember best as a child when we drove up the A5 to Wales every summer for the holidays. Somehow it all changed colour when we crossed the border, and became this lush, emerald, mystical green; the green that meant lots of rain.

The road dropped down to Risca through the forest. Below me, the traffic was getting noisier. I crossed under the busy A467; the short channel was full of graffiti and smelt dis-gusting. Thankfully, it was only a few yards to a stone bridge over the Ebbw River. I crossed the valley floor, past a recreation ground with elegant arched iron railings, and through a council estate where people were out walking their dogs. Life in the valley was just starting up on a weekday morning. On the corner of the green, three women stood and chatted, each holding a dog on a lead.

I turned left to go under the railway line, and the path then went through thick bracken. My legs got stung by nettles but, as it was going to be so hot climbing the next hill, I couldn't face putting trousers on. There was a very pretty stone bridge over the narrow Brecon Canal and, as I walked along the towpath, the light was dappling the grassy verges of the canal. I doubted any boats came along it – it looked quite silted up. At the next stone bridge I took a narrow tarmac road which climbed steadily northwards, up out of the valley, then became a footpath just below some fir trees, still climbing up the valley. From the head of the valley, by a small car park at Pegwn-y-bwlch, I made the final ascent up a broad grassy track to the top of Twmbarlwm: at 1874 feet, just a warm-up for the mountains that lay ahead.

The fort at the top of Twmbarlwm.

On the top was an Iron Age settlement, built circa 500 BC. What a great location! There were steps up and down each side of the fort, and it was surrounded by a low wooden fence with a ditch around it. I left the settlement and turned north, on a broad, well-used track. It was muddy underfoot from all the rain, well cropped by sheep, nice and soft under my feet. The sheep had been recently shorn. They looked very white, and somewhat startled as they emerged from the bracken and caught sight of me.

It seemed strange to be walking alone along a long ridge when, below, I could see dozens of big factories humming away. I was in another world. I quickly ate some lunch, as I could see the rain approaching from the south. Then it absolutely poured. I put on my nylon poncho – my legs got wet but I didn't care.

After a long, slow climb to the brow of the hill, I then skirted round above a reservoir, eventually dropping down onto a tarmac road leading to the Lamb Inn. The road passed through pastureland; sheep grazed amongst the gorse which still had a few yellow flowers. I looked back: the hills seemed black and gloomy. In the front bar of the Lamb Inn a band of afternoon drinkers, plus sheepdogs and a couple of kids, were silently staring at Sky TV. It poured with rain outside – there was no sense in rushing anywhere. I went into the back bar, started to strip off my wet clothes and apologized to my Japanese guests, who had been waiting for half an hour.

Mr Tanaka was wearing a suit, and spoke extremely formally and politely. He was the General Manager of the Sony plant at nearby Bridgend. Mrs Tomoka Toda's husband was a senior manager at the Panasonic plant in Cardiff. She'd come to Wales four years ago, was a keen walker and a big fan of all things Welsh. Mrs Toda had brought us a delicious home-made lunch: rice balls wrapped in seaweed, vegetables, green tea, hot saki and fried pork with spicy sauce. It was a million times better than any pub lunch! And the saki heated up my soggy limbs like a dream. She also brought me a yellow silk good luck charm, with a Japanese motto on it, from her local shrine back in Tokyo. I was to carry it with me for the rest of my journey. Mrs Toda was very giggly and soon had me in fits with her stories about the Japanese back home who miss Wales so much they've formed a club.

Mr Tanaka estimated that around 25 different Japanese companies have opened up in Wales, making them the largest single employer after British Steel and local government. Mrs Toda extolled the virtues of the Welsh: gentle friendly people with close family ties. She'd even learnt to make laver bread. When her friends visited from Japan, apparently they all stopped their cars and rushed into the fields to photograph the sheep! Feeling somewhat full up, I noticed there was a break in the rain, so I said goodbye to my new friends and headed down the road towards Pontypool.

The road soon became a muddy track. Little harebells bobbed in the rain at the side of the road. Pontypool vanished under a cloud and it was like a river underfoot. As I reached the bottom of the hill, I realized I was in the middle of major road works. The rain was sheet-ing down. I picked my way through a series of roundabouts and traffic queues (the rush hour had already started). Heading north across the valley, I went into a petrol station to ask the way, and use the loo. It took hours to get all my clothes off and on again. And then, when I came out, it had stopped raining! The sun had come out, and 25 yards up the Usk Road were the wonderfully ornate gates of Pontypool Park, a triumph of wrought-iron-work, decorated with bunches of grapes and green leaves and brown stems all the way up the fine columns.

Richard Hanbury from Worcestershire moved his family here in the eighteenth century and they pioneered the tinplating and iron industries, leaving a network of tunnels running right under the town. The town hall was built to celebrate the birth of Hanbury's son, and another family member built the Italian Garden in the town after a honeymoon in Italy. The park I was passing had housed the family home (now a school) and these swanky gates had been a present from the Duchess of Marlborough.

I walked on up the road about 10 yards and took a footpath by a green iron fence. The path climbed steeply up. It was narrow, with brambles and nettles on either side and hawthorn trees overhead. Then I emerged onto the edge of a field and the path became a wide track, still with the stone wall of the park on the left. As it levelled out, there was another fine view to the east of the valley and the factories. A rainbow was poking up over Newport.

I was now on a series of farm tracks and drovers' roads, undulating up and down, heading due north out of Pontypool. I wondered why I'd chosen to carry on and walk tonight, at the end of such a long day. Charming though the Japanese had been, it was a somewhat formal conversation, and I felt enclosed by the pub. I wanted to get out in the fresh air and spend the last couple of hours of the day by myself, just walking alone. There was a freshness in the air, and I was looking forward to a night out. I climbed up one more hill with a castellated octagonal tower on the top of it. Its windows were firmly shuttered, there was a little flagpole on the roof, and a sign on the side said: 'This 230-year-old tower, rebuilt after wartime destruction, was opened 22 July 1994, by His Royal Highness, The Prince of Wales.' Around the tower were six stone benches, each one gazing out at a different view. This was the famous Pontypool Folly, built by the Hanburys in 1765, and apparently destroyed in 1940 in case the Luftwaffe used it to locate a munitions factory nearby. It seemed an appropriate place to end the day's walk.

I was driven back to my hotel through Pontypool. The centre of the town was completely dead: half the shops were boarded up, including the Economic Development Agency office. When the flyover is finished none of the traffic will ever stop in the centre of town. My hotel was in Usk and after supper, which wasn't very good, I drove to Pontypool for my night out.

At Pontypool United RFC, there was a training session going on on the pitch, and inside the club-house there were about 50 women, very seriously line dancing to country and western music. A woman on the stage was issuing instructions: she had a fringed Stars and Stripes shirt on, and a cowboy hat. Several of the women were identically dressed and all were in jeans. It seemed a very complicated thing to take up. Out of the 50 or so dancers, there were only two men. The lounge bar was full of rugby players who'd finished training.

My next stop was the Pontypool Working Men's Club. It was in an amazing new building that had cost over a million pounds, and Malcolm, one of the people who ran it, took me into the bar, which was packed with men, and fewer women, with children playing pool and darts at the other end. I talked to some of the oldest members and they said Pontypool isn't the place it was. Apart from Tesco's, there's nowhere decent to shop in the centre of town, and unemployment, although it's only running at 8 per cent, has taken the life out of the place.

Everybody I'd spoken to in Cardiff had been really rude about Pontypool and said what a dump it was. I admit that the centre of Pontypool is ugly, and the road works have taken the heart out of the town, but what's really good about it is the people. They were a million times more entertaining than loads of other people I'd met on this journey.

After I'd been plied with three huge gin and tonics I felt there was a serious possibility I might start singing, so I was reluctantly dragged back to our car by my director, fearful he'd never get me out of bed in the morning to start walking again…

DAY 24
Pontypool to Forest Coal Pit

I started my journey by the Pontypool Folly. My route lay northwards, along the spine of the ridge separating the two valleys, with Blaenavon on my left and Abergavenny to the north-east. Soon I'd left Pontypool, and the Saturday morning golfers, behind. I climbed up a grassy hill, Garn-wen, and was on to open moorland, with a confusing set of tracks. Irritatingly, I took a path that just petered out in a bog, so, using my compass, I tried to aim for some pylons ahead without dropping down. What had seemed like a simple moorland tramp was proving to be a wet, slow trek. I walked for an hour completely alone. Although I could see a lot of activity in the valleys below, all the locals were obviously busy driving to Tesco's or Sainsbury's instead of walking up here and helping me find my route!

I passed a radio mast on the left, dodging huge puddles as my path had become a stream. White strips of terraced houses lined the valley below. Eventually I picked up a better track and emerged onto a little road that crossed from one valley to the next, by a sign announcing Blaenavon's local forest, with a picnic table and a couple of seats. The chilly wind meant it was free of snackers. I turned right up the road, and after 100 yards or so I picked up my next path (thankfully signposted) and spent a pleasant 45 minutes speed-walking on a recently cut route through the heather. I passed over the rocky outcrop of Carn y Defaid and headed for a radio mast, around which the rocks lay exposed.

Here I crossed onto a road and found a sign saying that Sir Harry Llewelyn's famous horse Foxhunter was buried under some stones by the car park nearby. I looked for a head-stone, but couldn't find any sign of one. Having walked over to the peak of Blorenge and the trig point, I dropped down to a cairn and looked down to Abergavenny below, and Sugar Loaf to the north-west, which I'd be climbing later on. It was a fine day – the clouds were scattered but it was extremely windy. I put on a cheap, green, nylon hooded jacket, as an experiment. At least it would keep the wind out of my ears.

The direct path down was almost vertical and very slippery. Far below, I could see a party of ramblers coming up with their maps flapping in plastic folders round their necks. Having stumbled down through brown, scratchy bracken, I soon found a narrow, muddy sheep track, which eventually joined the main path. At the bottom of the hill was the Monmouthshire and Brecon Canal. The way to Abergavenny lay under it, through a tiny tunnel, dripping with water, that ran under a house. A large sign directed me to it.

The canal had been built in 1794 to carry iron ore, limestone and coal from Newport to Pontnewydd. Now, apart from rowing boats carrying holiday-makers, nothing was trans-ported along it. I dropped down a wide path on the other side of the canal, with a stream merrily gurgling on my right. It was an ancient road, with grass poking through the tarmac and moss covering the stone wall on my left. I passed a cemetery and a Victorian church and crossed over a road by a sign with a map of the area – so rusty and eroded it was barely legible. Now my path was covered with fat plums which had just fallen off a tree in the

hedge. I passed a garden centre, went under the A465 and skirted some very intensively farmed allotments. Eventually I turned right by the River Usk, following it to a fine stone bridge, past a Victorian cemetery full of sombre yews and cedars.

I followed the main road towards Abergavenny for a couple of hundred yards, but I didn't have time to visit the town centre; I was meeting Welsh playwright and theatre director Ed Thomas in a vineyard just outside town, and we planned to climb Sugar Loaf mountain together. At a roundabout I turned left and headed through an industrial estate, past a factory selling 'Green Farm Frozen Potatoes'. Not for me the heady charms of Abergavenny's tea shops or Museum of Childhood. Not that I cared! I'd already booked myself into one of the best restaurants in Britain for dinner – the Walnut Tree – which just happened to be a few miles away!

I passed the ugly modern hospital and turned up a narrow lane with stone walls on either side, following signs to the winery. Ed was an attractive man in his early thirties, with short grey hair. He didn't look the slightest bit Welsh to me (more Spanish or Italian) but maybe that was my prejudices coming out. He was sitting outside in 'the tasting area'. We shared a couple of glasses of the Welsh wine, which I have to say for my palate tasted a bit thin. The bottle labels had a picture of Sugar Loaf which looked just like Mount Fuji to me!

To get to Sugar Loaf, we went through a series of fields with very confusing footpath signs heading upwards in a north-westerly direction. We walked up a narrow tarmac lane and into a wood, went over a stile and had a pleasant walk up through the woods.

Ed, 34, was born and bred in Cwmgiedd in the Upper Swansea Valley in the Brecon Beacons. He writes in both English and Welsh, usually on the theme of modern Wales and its identity crisis. If this sounds gloomy, it isn't – I found Ed very witty! His play, *House of America,* is about a young man in a dead-end Welsh valley who dreams of being reunited with his long-lost father in America; meanwhile the opencast mine eats its way towards his home. Ed's one-line synopsis: 'The American dream in the South Wales valleys, but it's the wrong dream in the wrong town.' He told me the play had been turned into a feature film, just shown in Edinburgh and at the Sundance Festival in America, and it was about to open in Britain. He said he didn't feel the slightest bit British and he wanted Wales to be part of a federal Europe; he thought it was time for Wales to re-invent itself and get more confidence.

The extraordinary thing about Sugar Loaf is that it isn't very much higher than Blorenge, probably only 100 feet or so, and yet it's much more spectacular, both in its shape and in the views you get from the top. It's simply a more majestic mountain. An extinct volcano, the top is bare, covered in very closely cropped grass, with a rocky outcrop. On the way up, I was delighted to discover lots of bilberries. Ed claimed not to have eaten them before, and said they looked like rabbit droppings, but I forced a few upon him. The final ascent, at 45 degrees, was extremely steep, with some stone steps cut in the rock. Ed surged ahead,

the macho male coming out in him, while I plodded along at my usual steady pace, as taught by my Sherpa in the Himalayas a few years ago.

On the top, we could clearly see the Black Mountains, my next port of call, rising up impressively. Looking back towards England, there were the Malvern Hills, and the green fields beyond, south of Pontypool and the valleys. Sadly, the distant hospital was a bit of an architectural eyesore, and it was blowing a gale. We headed down – an easy and enjoyable stroll along a grassy path that soon brought us out by the edge of a wood where we turned left. I saw a large cep mushroom that someone had picked and then just tossed away – how depressing! If I'd been going home I would have picked it up and taken it with me.

Above: At the top of Sugar Loaf with Ed Thomas.
Opposite: A view of the mountain in autumn.

Ed had been talking about the identity crisis Wales and the Welsh suffered from:

'How would you feel if every time you travelled nobody knew where you came from, so your country doesn't exist, so your nationality doesn't exist, yet you have a passport from somewhere called Britain which you don't feel any part of. The British passport means nothing to me. But it's the only passport I have. What I want to write is universal stuff from a little place called Wales and that's it. If it's not universal it's crap. Fair enough?'

This new Wales sounded light years away from the Wales of my childhood and holidays in Llanfairfechan with my Welsh granny: a birch rod over the back door and a lot of soulful old people; Welsh chapel and hours spent waiting while my mother gossiped in Welsh and bought bacon in the Co-op.

As the afternoon drew to a close, we reached a little cottage that had a sign saying 'Forest Coal Pit Post Office'. The door looked firmly shut and there was no phone box, although the sign in the window said it was open.

Ed was desperate for a cigarette but Forest Coal Pit didn't even have a village shop; it was a few houses at a crossroads. So we walked back up the road, passing a lady who was staying in a holiday cottage, busily filling a carrier bag full of delicious-looking small plums from a tree by the side of the road.

After walking for 20 minutes, we found a phone box and eventually Iwan, our driver, appeared in the Land Rover. We dropped Ed back at the vineyard by his car and I got ready

for my gourmet dinner, putting on the baggiest clothes I could find in anticipation of a huge meal! Then I got a taxi to the Walnut Tree Restaurant – and what a terrific place it was! Franco Taruschio and his wife, Anne, who own it and run it, were welcoming, hilarious people. There was a big display of Franco's cookery books on the counter (apparently there are about four out at the moment) and he told me that he'd come to England from Italy in the sixties. His wife was English, but her parents had moved to Brecon. He went to visit and fell in love with the area; they bought the Walnut Tree 30 years ago, and have been making a success of it ever since. He'd just filmed a six-part series for BBC television.

The restaurant and bar inside the plain white building serve exactly the same food, and this evening the restaurant was packed. I had a taster of spinach tart, then Franco brought me a little slice of cold suckling pig with pickles, because he wanted me to taste it, and that was all that was left. I had a couple of glasses of wine to put me in a good mood after waiting so long for my lift, and then I had my real meal. I can't believe I was still hungry – that just shows how far I'd walked! I started with carpaccio of monkfish and for my main course I had guinea fowl with wild mushrooms and spinach, and a plate of delicious runner beans and new potatoes. And a bottle of Chianti Classico!

Finally I had a glass of dessert wine and ice-cream, which tasted of thick cream and whinberries (a cross between raspberries and loganberries). Franco told me he loved going out to collect wild mushrooms and that there were absolutely masses of them in the forestry land. He was planning to go out on a mushroom expedition that Sunday. I asked him if I could expect any more good food as I made my trip northwards through Wales, and he just laughed. Then Franco pressed some lemon grappa upon me, after which the minicab trip back to Abergavenny seemed to pass in a dream. I got back to the hotel and passed out, jeans straining at the waistband.

When I woke I found a copy of his cookery book resting on top of my case, autographed by him and his wife. They had certainly cooked the best meal I'd eaten on the trip so far.

DAY 25
Forest Coal Pit to Capel-y-ffin

I had a fitful sleep, probably because my digestive system was coping with an overload situation. At 7.45 there was banging on my door – time to get up. I looked out of the window – it was a pretty normal Welsh sky, grey with bits of blue.

The hotel owner was so anxious to please me that, when I asked for fresh fruit, he brought me a large dinner plate. On it was: half a grapefruit with a maraschino cherry; a pear with its skin on; an apple with its skin on; a banana ditto; a kiwi fruit ditto; and a bunch of green grapes. Sadly, I'm not up to preparing my own fruit salad first thing in the morning. He then provided me with a cornucopia of slices of lemon and orange arranged around two poached eggs on a slice of brown bread.

After breakfast, we drove over to Forest Coal Pit, and I walked down the road to the junction known as Fiveways. This area was once full of charcoal burners who made charcoal in pits in the forests to fuel the iron works nearby. I crossed a field, pursued by a hysterical barking dog and a flock of flapping geese.

I'm sure worried homeowners round here are concerned about their property, but in this particular valley they seem to have bred an extremely noisy type of sheepdog, who, on seeing a woman with a rucksack, long legs and a lot of red hair, feels compelled to bark about five times louder than any other bloody dog I've encountered on this route. It was like a knife right through my brain, and pre-10 a.m. I didn't need it.

My little road came to a beautifully restored Baptist chapel with a new roof and brown paintwork. A sign on it said, 'S.T. and J.T. Builders, 1837'. All the gravestones had been cleaned up, and two children's gravestones were placed on the wall. There was a lot of very fine stone carving in the churchyard, and it was a very special place. Looking around, it seemed that all the locals had either died young, or lived to a ripe old age. There were plenty of 87-year-olds and 21-year-olds with not much between. I really like reading the quotations: 'We are confident I say, and willing rather to be absent from the body, and to be present with the Lord'. Another one proclaimed: 'Be ye therefore ready also, for the Son of Man cometh at an hour when we think not'.

Next to the chapel was a sweet little cottage, with nettles growing in the front garden and boarded-up windows. It had a new slate roof, but no one appeared to be living there. In the field behind were two ponies and their foal. I followed the tarmac road up and curved round to Upper House Farm, where I was going to have coffee with fellow long-distance walker, Shirley Rippon.

As I walked through the fields on my way to her house, I found some field mushrooms, which I picked for her. Shirley was thin and super-fit-looking, with short grey hair, a vivacious face and striking eyes. A rabbit sat under a portable cage on her lawn – a four-legged mower, drinking from a dish that said 'Dog'. A year ago, at 53, Shirley realized her lifelong ambition when she spent three months walking from Land's End to John O'Groats – 1200 miles. Shirley took photos, wrote a diary, visited stately homes and museums, and climbed Ben Nevis, carrying a backpack and staying with friends and relations.

Her daughter joined her for a fortnight and her husband acted as road manager. She had to be highly organized, carrying six maps at a time and using the post to send old maps back and get the next set. The longest walk she did in a day was 28 miles, to get to the nearest campsite past Bristol. (That was one of only two or three miserable days.) Shirley said walking had become like a drug – she hadn't been able to settle down since. She loved the solitude and sense of freedom but also the camaraderie of walkers who seem to form part of a separate society: when she was on the Pennine Way 50 or so walkers started the same day as her and she got to know them well over the two or three weeks' walk.

We walked up to the top of the hill above her house – and passed Dial Carreg (the 'Revenge Stone') which is supposed to mark the spot where the Norman Richard de Clare was murdered by Welsh locals in 1135, in revenge for his killing of a Welsh lord.

Shirley pointed out the Black Mountains that lay ahead, with the Hatterall Ridge running parallel and to the east of the one we were on. Offa's Dyke crossed it, and the Vale of Ewyas lay between us. Our route was an old drovers' road from Abergavenny to Builth Wells, and in the twelfth century about 130 people lived on this bleak, windswept ridge. Shirley confirmed that the chapel I'd so admired earlier was still very well used. We said goodbye and I struck out along the drovers' path, heading due north for Capel-y-ffin and climbing over Garn-wen – which means 'White Tower' – although it was a cairn of not-very-white stones.

I walked on the ridge and then on to the little summits of Bal-bach and then Bal-Mawr. Although the Black Mountains look very green and heathery, they are in fact red sandstone, forming a long dark wall dividing England and Wales. The hard life of the sheep farmers here was commemorated in Bruce Chatwin's unforgettable novel, *On the Black Hill.* My path even went near Vision Farm, whose name Bruce Chatwin borrowed for his story of twin brothers eking out an existence in this isolated area. The mountains are really flat-topped hills and broad ridges, distinguished by their extremely steep slopes. The beautiful Vale of Ewyas below me has drawn all sorts of exotic travellers to live in it over the years, but few have had the gumption to stick it out like the local farmers Chatwin wrote about.

I could see the ruins of Llanthony Priory below. Set up around 1118, the locals weren't friendly, and after a Welsh uprising in 1135, the monks fled, and only used Llanthony as a summer residence. The poet Walter Savage Landor bought the estate in 1808 and set about improving it, but it all came to nothing and the ruins of his house stand above the priory.

The wind was absolutely howling and I could barely stand up along the ridge. After another quarter of a mile, I dropped down and, by a cairn, I took a path dropping down to Capel-y-ffin on a steep, eroded, stony track. At the bottom I crossed verdant green pastureland where I could still make out old wall patterns in fields that are now covered with grass.

I walked down a small road to the Grange Trekking Centre. Sitting on a wooden seat, I had a cup of tea. Behind me in the field were two donkeys and a horse, to whom I fed the remains of my lunchtime sandwiches. They repaid me by farting in my face.

Later, I walked up the track to look at the monastery: a large white building with two wings and pointed windows. A small child came out and said hello – her mother whisked her back in. Outside the house was a statue of the Virgin Mary, and a wooden bench. I walked over to the remains of the church that Father Ignatius had never finished building. His tomb was in the middle, with a cross on it and tiles. The Father was originally Joseph Lyne from Barking, who renamed himself and came here to start his own monastery – building it in 1870 and starting the church in 1872. A yearly pilgrimage of his devotees still draws 200 or so!

The ruins had a 'Keep Out: Dangerous' sign on them, and on the noticeboard was the latest newsletter, telling us about the progress of the appeal fund to get the ruins restored. There was also an old picture of Father Ignatius, with some of the local youths. I hate to sound disrespectful, but it did kind of cross my mind that there was more to Father Ignatius than met the eye, and that he might have been slightly too fond of young boys.

The artist Eric Gill bought the monastery in 1924 and tried to set up a commune there, but locals were suspicious of his sexual reputation. Matters weren't helped by his taste in clothes: he favoured tunics instead of trousers and the odd pair of red silk underpants!

Capel-y-ffin means 'chapel of the boundary' – between Brecon and Monmouthshire. It consists of a church, two chapels, a handful of houses and a phone box.

I walked back down the lane to the crossroads. The phone box was painted grey. On the other side of the road was the very beautiful St Mary's Church: a simple white structure built in 1762, with a slightly crooked wooden spire. In the churchyard were several carved stone gravestones, including one by Eric Gill, which had a tribute to the village carpenter on it.

I then walked about a mile up the road to the youth hostel. Walking through leafy woodland, the river far below, I climbed up gradually and turned left up the driveway where I met Diana, who was very jolly and wore black Reebok trainers, green jeans and a youth hostel T-shirt with a badge that said 'Di – Manager' on it. She took me on a tour of the building, a 200-year-old farmhouse, with a four-oven Aga running on solid fuel. Di had a little counter with a cash till; she sold food and made meals; and there was a kitchen if you wanted to cook your own, with rows of gas cookers. Upstairs there were bunk rooms for men and women.

Di's hostel was only 7 miles over the hill from Hay-on-Wye, with its middle-class weekenders, its bookshops and its posh literary festival, but it might as well have been 700! She said the weather was totally different, too. It was now 6.30 and I was tired. I said goodbye to Di and secretly looked forward to the blissful day I was going to have, walking through the Black Mountains completely alone, to Crickhowell.

Everybody was pretty muted, still thinking about the death of Princess Diana. The papers were full of nothing else. I caught the train from London to Newport at 9.40 a.m. and was driven up to Capel-y-ffin.

DAY 26
Capel-y-ffin to Crickhowell

I walked between two restored cottages, then over a stile and up the hillside, on a pretty steep and stony path which was covered with bubbling water splashing its way downhill. The earth was an astonishing red ochre. My goal at the end of this valley was a mountain called Lord Hereford's Knob, about a 2-mile climb ahead. If the weather held, I hoped to walk the entire 16 miles to Crickhowell. It's rather like three sides of a rectangle, heading north, then west, and then south.

Most of the walk would be on pretty well-defined tracks without too much climbing, and, although there were some peaks, by and large it would be over a series of ridges. One Saturday in May 96 I walked about 16 miles, from just above Pandy, up the Offa's Dyke path, and down into Hay-on-Wye, in aid of Macmillan Nurses. I did the walk then with my friend Janet, and Rosanna Bulmer, who'd organized it, lived nearby. It was pretty cold and windy but we had a terrific time.

I did it because my friend Lucy was seriously ill with bone cancer, and she found the services of her Macmillan nurse so important and special. Well, Lucy died last August, just over a year ago, so I said a prayer for her and dedicated this bit of my walk to her, because on that occasion I walked absolutely parallel to where I stood now. Then I looked across from Offa's Dyke onto today's route and thought how spectacular it looked. I never would have walked it with Lucy, because she hated walking! But she was a very special friend of mine, so I was going to think about her when I got to my first peak today, and remember all the good times we'd had.

I headed north-west, up a V-shaped lonely valley, on a sheep track. I aimed for the brow of the hill, which I hoped would bring me to a faintly marked track I'd seen on the map. Unlike the horrible boggy quagmire I'd struggled through above Pontypool, this was easy ground to walk over – close-cropped bilberry bushes and soft, sleek, green grass underfoot. There were occasional patches of reeds and black peaty puddles, but nothing to compare with last week's bog. Below me lay the Gospel Pass; and the twin flat tops of Lord Hereford's Knob (or Twmpa) and Hay Bluff formed an exhilarating symmetry.

Although there had been recent rain, there were large sections of bog where the ground was quite firm underneath, so it was obvious that the hills were suffering from the drought of the past few years. Skylarks popped out of the heather around me. And after 20 minutes more plodding, I stood on the edge of Twmpa. Ahead lay a patchwork quilt of English fields. And to my left, westwards, stretched out a series of ridges that I would be climbing. To me, the Black Mountains are a special, enigmatic landscape. Their ridges stretch out, bony and undulating, like a sheep's back when it's been sheared. I felt a real sense of achievement climbing this by myself. This morning, with blue sky and the best weather I'd had so far in Wales, was magnificent.

By the trig point five white ponies were grazing. A large crow suddenly flew out of the heather – what ugly birds they are. And another walker was striding up the hill on the right. I'd only just noticed him, so lost was I in the dynamics of the landscape. We exchanged greetings. He looked like one of those well-bred public school men you find living round here, with a battered cotton-brimmed hat, jeans with splits at the knees, and a healthy-looking suntan. Two women with rucksacks were toiling up, about 100 yards behind him. He was carrying a tripod with a small camera bag. When I asked him where he was going, he said he hadn't decided yet – it was such a beautiful day he'd come up to take photographs.

Climbing out of Capel-y-ffin and heading for Twmpa.

I could see for at least 25 miles – hard to photograph though. Behind me, to the south-west, I could see Sugar Loaf, its silhouette very distinctive amongst all these rolling hills.

Dropping down from the cairn, I skirted across the flat ridge at the head of the valley. The path was pretty eroded on the way down (lots of mountain bike tracks), then it became a soft, green carpet. After a short while there was a cairn marking the crossing track from Grwyne Fawr Reservoir in the valley to the south (one that I'd left a few miles back in order to walk higher up on the ridge). Now I was heading south-west, with exciting steep drops to my right.

At a trig point I could clearly see the ridge I would be climbing, stretching away to the south-west. It was a broad eroded way, with lots of boggy patches. At this point, I couldn't believe it but I was plagued by a wasp, for about 200 yards! Big, black clouds, which had temporarily covered the sun, disappeared and the day returned to tip-top weather. Rising up on the path from the reservoir were two people on horseback, the only figures to be seen for miles in this direction. Sheep, splotched with bright blue dye to identify their owners, stared at me with astonishment and then just resumed munching. Now my path turned south towards Waun Fach, over rolling hills.

Up ahead of me, 50 yards away, a hawk hovered. A man climbed up to my path from the valley floor. Earlier I had see him a mile away — my only other companion in this vast landscape. He had white hair and a hearing aid in each ear, and told me he was completing an 8-mile circular walk — incredible for someone of his age, which I guessed to be about 70.

I was pleased to get to the trig point on the top of Waun Fach, as the last 100 yards had been a very steep and very eroded climb. It was 2.20 p.m., so I decided to have some lunch. The trig point was a big concrete boulder sitting in a sea of mud, which stretched for 10 yards all around it. Anyway, I picked my way through it, but there was no one to take my picture. This unattractive spot (2660 feet) marked the highest point in the Black Mountains.

Now I have to make a particularly sad confession: here I was, enjoying a spectacular walk in great weather, and what had been my secret anxiety for the past two hours? Whether my specially purchased Marks & Spencers couscous with char-grilled vegetables had anything to eat it with! All the way up, I had forced myself not to look, and I'd mused on how I'd eat crumbly couscous with my fingers. Having delayed having lunch until about half-past two, the moment was upon me, and I sat in a howling gale and extracted the Marks & Spencers container from my rucksack. It had the magic words written on the lid: 'fork included'. It's small things like these that make the walker's day. Later I lovingly washed my tiny plastic fork and stowed it in my rucksack for future forkless emergencies.

The wind was cold, so I quickly got going again, heading west now. I could see my path stretching ahead, following a series of pretty narrow ridges and culminating in a fort.

The path across was extremely eroded: thousands of feet have tramped this way, and hundreds of mountain bikes. Then it was down a rocky slope onto the ridge, wide, flat and grassy, where someone had made a shelter out of the flat slaty stones. About 45 minutes later I stood by the sad little cairn on top of Mynydd Llysiau (2173 feet).

I rounded a little hill top and saw two carved paving stones set into the ground. It was really hard to read their inscriptions, but I thought they might be giving directions. Just before the hill ahead, which had a standing stone on it, I took the right-hand fork, not bothering to climb the hill.

Now Pen Allt-mawr rose up in front of me and I skirted the flat ridge round to its base. I hoped this was the last peak for the day; the final 50 feet was extremely steep and very, very eroded, but as I stood on the summit, exhausted, I saw that I was still facing the final peak — Pen Cerrig-calch (2300 feet). The flat track across the ridge to it was so eroded it was like a white scar. The summit lay ahead, and from then on my route was downhill.

At the trig point, the sun had gone in and I was pretty tired. The top was a glittering pavement of white stones, all eroded. Straight ahead was Sugar Loaf, the mountain I had walked up two days before. I'd walked in a great big loop, and come back to it. Below me lay Table Mountain, a strange little protuberance which isn't a mountain at all but an Iron Age

Ponies on the top of the Black Mountains.

hill fort. I sat out of the wind where a stream crossed the path and put on an extra pair of socks for the final descent. Having eaten a bit of cold pasta and three Jaffa cakes, and drunk half a bottle of water, I got up to wend my weary way down. Above me, I saw two walkers in short-sleeved T-shirts and shorts. What macho men!

I'm afraid I didn't feel it necessary to climb to the top of Table Mountain. My wide, mercifully soft, green path, went to within 100 yards of the rocky summit and then turned to the left. The two young men I'd seen before were sitting staring across the valley. I stopped to talk to them and I have to confess they weren't macho at all, but extremely nice. Their mum lived locally and they were visiting her and doing a circular walk. They wished me well and I skirted the south side of the hill, heading towards Crickhowell, which nestled in the valley below, a cluster of grey and white houses. As I walked along a series of lanes, bridle paths and footpaths I noticed that at every junction there was a 'Private: Keep Out' sign to stop me straying from the path.

The sheep round here looked far more rounded and happy than the poor scraggy ones I had seen up on the moors. These were a different breed, with black faces, ears and legs, and white coats. And this grass was pretty luxuriant compared to the offerings up top.

Now I was out of the wind, it was really hot. I followed a road downhill and ahead I could see terraces of houses, and a welcoming terracotta church spire. Civilization! It had been a good day's walking, and I was glad it was a pleasant evening. I'd cleared my head after the depression of the weekend, with Princess Diana's death, and today's newspapers. I felt I'd made a fresh positive start to the week.

In suburban Crickhowell men were strimming hedges, children were playing on bikes, and people were gathered around their televisions for the 6 o'clock news. You know you're in suburbia when you see a sign by a council estate that says 'No Horse Riding', and when you look in the driveway of the council house immediately behind it, what do you see? A horse box.

The cottages on my right had been gentrified, with hanging baskets and petunia-filled window boxes everywhere. I passed the Swan pub, festooned with flowers. At the end of the road was a fine castellated wall, with a large cedar tree. I turned onto the main road by the petrol station. I'd walked about 16 miles – a hot bath was my next stop.

At the hotel I watched the local television news, and found that there was already a row brewing in Wales about whether a proposed monument to Princess Diana should be in Caernarfon in the north or Cardiff in the south. Endless people came on to have their say, and there were queues up at municipal offices all over the country to sign books of condolence. I turned the TV off and went in for dinner, sitting by the large 'Janet' sign on my table, as requested. I felt a bit like one of those victims in a religious war who had to wear a sign and be paraded through the streets.

The hotel had just installed a music centre, which they switched on while we were eating. Elvis Presley's 'Love Me Tender' blared out eight times – I'm not exaggerating. Then I noticed that the owner actually looked like a fat version of Elvis Presley, but with white hair.

By 10.15 I was back in my room (thankfully a Presley-free zone), poring over my maps and thinking about the Brecon Beacons, my next mountain range.

DAY 27
Crickhowell to the Torpantau Pass

Saturday, 6 September: it was Princess Di's funeral and the whole country was in mourning. I got up at 6 o'clock and put the television on, and already crowds were gathering. Having left London on the 8 o'clock train from Paddington to Newport, I got a lift back to Crickhowell. I was walking with two friends, Janet and Darryl; and Alan Thomas, who runs the Dragon Hotel in the High Street in Crickhowell, was going to be our guide. Alan is so mad keen on the area, that he's become part of the local Mountain Rescue Team. He also takes parties of

people from the hotel out walking. His enthusiasm for the area was apparent before we'd even gone 100 yards down the High Street. He was full of local gossip, pointing out the large, double-fronted, elegant house at the bottom of the High Street bought by the sound engineer for Oasis, and exquisitely restored.

The High Street in Crickhowell is absolutely beautiful. Opposite the Bear Hotel there was a little stone arcade which housed a market, but because of Princess Diana's funeral, there were cloths over all the stalls and nobody was there. The town was silent, with no cars on the road.

As we headed on down the High Street, Alan pointed out the line the river had flooded up to, a few years ago. We crossed the fine stone bridge over the River Usk, which has more arches on one side than the other, and, in spite of the funeral, I was glad to see a woman fly fishing, just below the weir.

We crossed another main road and went up a series of lanes to the Brecon and Usk Canal, where we crossed over a little bridge and walked up a series of footpaths climbing up the hill above Llangattock. We then took a stile to the right to the base of the tram track for the old quarry. This was a limestone quarry that formed a high cliff to the south of Llangattock, and we planned to climb to the top of it.

Basically, we slogged up a series of tram tracks which were very steep (about 1:3) and overgrown. Even so, you could clearly see the large stones that had once held the sleepers; there were bolt holes in them. And in other stones you could see the grooves cut by the cable through sheer use, where the trolleys carrying the stone used to come down.

After the first track, we were all a bit hot and sweaty and I sat on a bench that someone had thoughtfully provided and looked out over the valley. Then we climbed the second tram track, which went off at an angle to our left, and as I reached the top of it, feeling somewhat exhausted, I saw a large, fat man sitting on a stone just to my left, with a white pork-pie hat on, wearing sunglasses, and next to him was a little girl with a soft drink in a can. He said, 'My God, it's you,' and we both burst out laughing. He was a local man who had played rugby for many years (well, that was pretty obvious from his enormous size), and his wife was watching the funeral on the television so he'd decided to bring his daughter out for a walk. He had me in fits: apparently the very next day he was supposed to do a giant cycle ride for charity, but he was off work sick and so the doctor was coming round to the house first thing in the morning to see if he could do it. He also told me he cycled 600 miles a week on his bike but, looking at his girth, I found that somewhat hard to believe.

When we got to the central part of the quarry where there's a dip, we started to make our ascent, keeping to the right of the loose shale and climbing on all fours up a very steep

Overleaf: Crickhowell with a view of Table Mountain beyond the town.

grassy slope. This wasn't that dangerous, but it was pretty exciting. I was OK as long as I didn't look backwards. When I got up to the top, we were on the edge of the moorland, and we had the most beautiful view north across the valley to Crickhowell, and the Black Mountains were ranged in front of us. I could see Table Mountain, that I'd come down the previous day, really clearly.

We walked along the top edge of the quarry, heading west, until we found a little dip where we could get down out of the wind and sit and eat the first of many snacks. Alan was so nice: not only had he agreed to be our guide, he'd also brought us a load of rolls.

We then headed across some very exposed moorland. It was a good job we had Alan with us, as this section of the moor is relatively featureless and stretches for about 4 miles. You literally head due west. Eventually you cross a minor road, the B4560, but you have to watch where you're walking, as there are a lot of sink holes, caused by water collecting underneath the moor. Alan explained that fog and cloud can make this quite a dangerous walk if you don't know what you're doing.

Anyway, to the south we could see Ebbw Vale, and the edge of Merthyr Tydfil. We crossed the road, went on to grassier terrain and climbed to a trig point after a mile or so. After that the path was literally a series of sheep tracks through the heather, aiming slightly south-west, for about another 3 miles.

At about 4 o'clock we got to the Chartist Cave, which was a series of rocky outcrops on the moor. The limestone boulders were piled up as if by a human being, but it was just the product of wind erosion. Next to one of these wind-made cairns was a cave where the Chartists stored their weapons when they organized their rebellion in 1837. Alan very kindly made us cups of tea, and told us that we had another two hours' walking to go, even though we could see our destination, the ridge below Pen y Fan. We were feeling somewhat fatigued, so this was not good news. To cheer us up, Alan rang his daughter on a mobile phone and ordered her to meet us at the other end with some drinks. Janet and I started fantasizing about gin and tonics and cream teas, and Alan just laughed.

From the Chartist Cave we followed a largely westerly route over the brow of a hill, then dropped down on a sheep path to a road. We walked down it (which was a bit of a relief, quite honestly, after three hours of slogging it through the heather), then took a small track off to the right, which took us to another quarry. We skirted the upper edge of a fir plantation, with beautiful, silvery green trees. This quarry was spectacular, with ruined stone arches on our left. We followed a stream right into the heart of the quarry, then turned right along a wire fence, and headed west.

The quarry was abandoned – it was just like a Wild West town. There were some buildings, and we could clearly see where they'd just finished hacking the stone. Apparently it was a very popular site for television commercials for cars, and that very day they had been shooting an advertisement for Mazda.

We followed a narrow path alongside the wire fence, until we came to a horrible sight. The owners had obviously been given permission to start working this part of the quarry again, and it was full of very ugly Portacabins, cranes and earth-moving equipment: a total eyesore.

Then, to my horror, we started climbing up again, over a series of grassy hills, heading north-west to the Torpantau Pass. My legs were really tired at this point, so at 5 o'clock we sat down and I had yet another sandwich (my third of the day). I drank some water, and felt somewhat revived. Then we followed a faint, wide, grassy track, along the brow of the hills. It was a bit like being on a switch-back.

By now the sun had gone behind the clouds and it was quite cold; my face felt whipped by the wind. Finally we reached a trig point and turned down a well-defined path to the road below. We headed thankfully down a grassy slope, to the road and then to the car park. Alan pointed out the track I was going to have to take the following day, up to Pen y Fan. I couldn't really think about that, my legs felt so tired. Suddenly his daughter appeared in his car and, from the back, she extracted two large gin and tonics for me and Janet, and a container of freshly made scones, a big container of jam, and another of clotted cream. What a perfect end to the day.

Alan had been a charming and informative companion; you couldn't wish for someone more entertaining to tell you about the area. I had an early dinner, watched the 'highlights' (if that's the right word) of Princess Diana's funeral on the BBC, and fell into a deep sleep. I'd walked about 13 miles, but it felt like 130!

Although my bed was comfortable at the Nant-ddu Lodge, I was obviously very tired, physically and emotionally, and I spent most of the night waking up. At 5 o'clock in the morning, I wrote out everything in the remaining programmes, in order, so that I could see what was missing, and talk to John, the director, about it. (He was astounded when I handed over this list at breakfast at 8.15). I worked till about 7 a.m., then fell into a deep sleep, as always happens, to be awoken by my alarm call at quarter to eight, feeling very cross.

DAY 28
Torpantau Pass to the Storey Arms (Pen y Fan)

I tried not to take my ill-humour out on the crew, but I would have given anything not to have climbed Pen y Fan that day. My back was stiff; my knees were sore; and worst of all, I just didn't seem to have any energy.

I got in the car and we drove up to the Torpantau Pass where Wayne, a National Park Ranger, was waiting to walk with me. He was an interesting character, who'd joined the Army, served in the Falklands, run an antiques business, and now worked for the National Park. He was bound to be a good walking companion because of his range of experiences: from stripping pine dressers to Port Stanley. My kind of conversationalist!

Wayne explained that the Brecon Beacons National Park had been established in 1957 and contains distinct mountain ranges: the Black Mountains in the east, the Brecon Beacons and Fforest Fawr in the centre, and the Black Mountain in the west. Most of the park is privately owned and covers 522 square miles of high grassy ridges and wooded valleys. The lower slopes provide grazing for thousands of sheep. Apparently there is a lot of tension between landowners and the National Park – particularly over planning matters, as new building is severely restricted and the Park even have the right to tell you what colour to paint your house.

Pen y Fan was the most popular summit, although the route we were taking wasn't the one most favoured by day-trippers. Their preferred route was the gentler slope up from the Storey Arms to our west. But it wasn't just walkers who were eroding Pen y Fan; over-grazing by sheep was causing serious damage to the moors; and Pen y Fan is also used as a training ground by the SAS. Wayne said it was a common sight to see soldiers in combat gear, carrying heavy packs, running up and down the hills. Well, there was no chance of me running anywhere; my legs felt like lead.

From the road opposite the car park we went steeply up by a stream, climbing through tussocks of heather on a steep narrow path that was extremely eroded and had already been restored with steps. We got up to the first ridge, via some fir trees on our right and a river on our left, and headed due north until everything flattened out at about 1800 feet. Now we were on Craig y Fan Ddu, which was extremely boggy.

Then we just walked around tussocks for about a mile, heading north-west, but there was no path to follow. Eventually we came to a path which crosses from north-east to south-west, where the ground drops sharply away below. Here I met the Brecon Beacon Park Erosion Team, led by a very tall, thin guy called Marcus who was doing an exquisite job of re-laying a very over-trodden path along the edge of the ridge by cutting beautiful green pieces of sandstone and re-paving the path, just as the Romans had done. It was a work of art. One of his mates had already opened a large plastic container and was devouring sandwiches for breakfast. Marcus explained that, once their work was complete, they scattered a special hardy seed mix between the stones to get the grass growing back as quickly as possible. This particular path was a military training route, so we ramblers couldn't be blamed for the erosion – I point the finger at big beefy soldiers.

Wayne told me that this part of the National Park receives over 100,000 visitors a year. It's one of the most over-walked paths in the whole of Wales, because of its accessibility from the southern valleys and the fact that everyone wants to say they've climbed the highest point in the Brecon Beacons. Even at Christmas, apparently, it's packed.

We hadn't seen too many people so far but then we'd come up on the less popular

Opposite: A view from the most popular part of the Beacons, the slopes of Pen y Fan.

route, and the thick cloud was obviously a deterrent. But, even as we spoke, walkers were emerging through the cloud.

Now I was faced with my second climb: a steep ascent north-west to the summit of Cribyn. From the summit of Cribyn I could see a death-defying path that ran north down an escarpment which dropped away on both sides. A couple of SAS wannabes jogged past wearing sweat pants with vast packs on their backs.

The views from Cribyn were spectacular: Brecon lay a few miles away to the north-west, and the cloud was clearing all the time. Then we had to climb back down again, round the rocky edge of Craig Cwm Sere, before making the final ascent of Pen y Fan. Cribyn's 2608 feet high and Pen y Fan is 2906, so there's not a lot of difference in it. The final summit was pretty steep, but the top was disappointing. The first thing I saw were two parties of 20 school kids being bossed about by teachers. Then there was a load of walkers who were already on to their lunch.

It was totally crowded – the Piccadilly Circus of walk world! I was so disappointed I can't tell you. Cribyn was much more spectacular (slightly more pointy and a first-division mountain), whereas this was definitely a second-division one. Anyway, we stayed there long enough to feed the ravenous sheep. These are probably the most aggressive sheep you'll ever meet. You've only got to open a sandwich packet and they rush towards you, tongues hanging out, virtually ready to grab the food out of your hand. They're beyond tame, they're really pushy!

I followed a pretty well-worn track to the obelisk commemorating Little Tommy Jones who disappeared from his home in the 1920s in a village far below. His remains were found up here; obviously there was foul play, as no child of five could possibly have walked up this far.

From the obelisk we skirted round in a southerly direction, heading back to the Storey Arms (not a pub but an outdoor education centre). We then dropped down to a river, went over a stile and followed an extremely eroded path all the way back down to the A470. We could see hundreds of walkers coming up the easier route in the opposite direction.

My day on Pen y Fan had provided some fantastic views. I'd enjoyed the way the cloud had swirled around me and then receded, and Wayne was good company. But ultimately I'll never go back there – it's just so over-walked and there are so many arguments for discouraging people from picking off all these peaks in a macho way One of the pleasures of climbing a mountain is to sit on the top of it alone to clear your head and just stare into space, and you can forget that on Pen y Fan.

Opposite: The imposing face of Pen y Fan, the highest point in the Brecon Beacons National Park and, unfortunately, for me, the target for too many walkers.

Today I planned to attack my next peak or two with Robert Croft, the 27-year-old spin bowler for Glamorgan and England, a big star of Welsh cricket, together with Alan Ward, a Brecon Beacon Park Ranger. The Army were on manoeuvres with Dutch soldiers, and a petrol station en route to our start had inexplicably been turned into something out of *Apocalypse Now*. All the pumps were draped with green netting, and in the forecourt, instead of Ford Fiestas, there were tanks and tents.

Alan was a bearded man, I'd guess in his forties. He'd walked all over the world and in his holidays liked to lead expeditions in places like the Himalayas. So, basically, he spent the whole time walking. I asked him if his wife minded: he laughed and said she didn't want him to lead many more than one or two treks a year, because he used up all his holiday walking with other people.

I was looking forward to meeting Robert Croft, who was going to join us for the second part of the walk. On the news, that very morning, I'd heard that he'd been selected to play for the England team in the forthcoming West Indies tour. It must have been a very exciting day for him. He'd already played for England a couple of times before, but this was a real honour. Robert had grown up in the valleys just south of here, played rugby and then cricket.

We climbed up and over the first hill, Fan Fawr (2409 feet), which was pretty easy after the horrors of the day before. It meant rising up to avoid having to walk through rivers, so we skirted slightly north-west of the summit. First thing in the morning, the climb was quite difficult, but then I'd been walking for many days now, never doing less than 10 miles. If you're over 50 like me (I don't want to show off) it does take about an hour to get going, but then I've got stamina!

We took a series of sheep paths, heading for a ridge. There were many different routes to choose from here, and the going was relatively easy. Once over the ridge, we were in a broad, wonderful expanse of common land; the rivers which flow into the Ystradfellte Reservoir all fanned out below. We came down the western side of Fan Fawr, taking care not to drop too low down into the valley, because the ground was extremely boggy where the rivers converged.

We then headed south-west again, up the second ridge of the second fell called Fan Llia (2071 feet). The weather was getting hotter and hotter, and I was soon slapping on the block-out cream. As we dropped down to the Roman road, I saw a couple who must have been in their sixties walking along it. They were having a wonderful day out: the man already looked completely sunburnt.

Before the road there was a large standing stone, Maen Llia, and I had to walk through a pretty boggy area to get to it. It was very impressive: about 12 feet high and very narrow, ovoid in shape, rather like a Barbara Hepworth covered with lichen. It was put up

by the Beaker People 4000 years ago and points north to south. Was it an early road sign or an object of worship? Musing on this, I walked up to the road, which was actually only about 25 yards further, and sat on a wooden stile waiting for Robert Croft, cricketing superstar.

Alan told me that this part of the park was called Fforest Fawr, but there isn't much of the ancient forest left. It was once the medieval hunting ground of the Lords of Brecon, and poaching brought severe penalties, including maiming or execution. After enclosure in 1815 much of the land was sold and cleared for sheep farming. Now most of the trees are Forestry Commission conifers.

Robert turned up after about 20 minutes, completely wrongly dressed for walking! He had a pair of very expensive sunglasses on, which he didn't remove at any point, short hair that looked as if it might have had gel on it, a chubby, happy smiling face which looked as if it needed sun-block on it (but I wasn't going to be so cheeky as to tell him); a brand-new Reebok sweatshirt with its logo emblazoned right across the front (again, I couldn't face telling him that the BBC wouldn't be so happy about that!); a pair of very pale grey, brand-new sweat pants; and, worst of all, brand-new white Reebok trainers. How could I tell this man that we were about to climb one of the Brecon Beacons, that boggy ground could appear at any minute, and that it might put a sudden end to the elegant sartorial image he was so anxious to present?

Alan, the Park Warden, nearly fainted: he tried to persuade Robert to put on a pair of walking boots – but to no avail. Anyway, as the sky was getting bluer and bluer, it seemed pointless to argue about walking boots, anoraks and wet weather gear. Robert was a tall man, about 6 foot 1. It was hard to tell how fit he was from the track suit he was wearing. He was good company – funny, witty, very proud of being Welsh and married to a Welsh girl – he still lived not far from where he'd grown up. His favourite activities were pheasant shooting and fishing – a real country boy.

First we had to climb to the summit of Fan Nedd, which rose very steeply up a 1:3 track above us. This was a simple, straightforward climb, and we set off at a cracking pace. We simply headed south-west from a path which started just over the road from the standing stone, aiming for the cairn which was clearly visible on the northern edge of the summit. We followed a path up, with the river on our left.

We got to the cairn on Fan Nedd and realized that the actual summit, the trig point, was about half a mile to the south-east, so we walked over there. What a magnificent view we had to the south: we could see all the valleys where Robert had grown up. Then I told him that this was only the first summit of the day, and we were going on to Fan Gyhirych (2381 feet). He seemed a bit taken aback, especially when I pointed out that we'd now have to go down a little in order to go back up.

From the summit of Fan Nedd we went down a few hundred feet on a gentle grassy

slope in a north-westerly direction. At the bottom we crossed a stream and then climbed right back up again, and that was a killer: but not too big a climb. At the top was a gate, and on the other side a farmer's track heading north–south. There we met the crew who were sitting in Land Rovers with our lunch. This meal, if you can call it that, was the worst so far – mine was a strange sandwich of brown sliced bread with bits of coleslaw inside it. The other sandwich was cheese slices and that was it. I actually hurled the coleslaw sandwich to the ground and berated my driver. That very night I was going to sit down and write out what constitutes the perfect packed lunch: it would be Xeroxed and issued to all providers of food in the future. When you're doing a long walk, the high point of your day is reaching the peaks and then having a decent sandwich. And if the sandwich is rubbish, that so diminishes your pleasure. I know it sounds obsessive and stupid, but all walkers reading this will know what I'm talking about.

Robert the cricketer was completely shocked. He stared open-mouthed as I stamped on my coleslaw sandwich. He wasn't eating very much. He had a white cheese sandwich and a soft drink. But I was starving, having been walking day on day. Anyway, by filleting and rearranging all the strange sandwiches on offer, I eventually managed to make up one that met some of my requirements. I could see that my raving temper tantrum over the coleslaw sandwich fiasco would be the talk of his local that evening…

Wasn't it galling, I asked him, playing for the English team? Robert was tactful, but divulged that several of his team-mates were learning Welsh so they could be rude about people without getting reported by the umpires. He spoke South Walean Welsh, and claimed it was slangier and easy to pick up than the version spoken in the north. I asked him if he thought the Welsh had been slow to promote their home-grown talent. 'Sometimes, I think the Welsh people are a little bit embarrassed to do well if you know what I mean. I come from an area which keeps people's feet on the ground – and maybe we get a little embarrassed to do well because you might get termed a bighead or something along those lines, so that might have something to do with it.'

After lunch (if you can call it that), we walked along a track heading for the summit of Fan Gyhirych. When Robert saw that reaching the summit wouldn't involve that great a climb, he perked up. (Earlier, he'd kept asking how much longer the walk was going to take.) Fan Nedd (2175 feet) is not that much lower, but Fan Gyhirych is the most beautiful mountain to approach: the ground dropping sheer away, with cliffs hundreds of feet high on our right.

As we made our way up the grassy slope to the summit, we saw two people with microlights. I'd seen a van parked on our track further up, but had not given it any thought. Obviously these fanatics had emerged from it. Ahead of us, one just gathered up his equipment, and jumped off the edge of the mountain. He soared up high and then a second man appeared and did the same. They were like two man-made butterflies hovering above.

At the summit of Fan Gyhirych with England and Glamorgan cricketer Robert Croft.

As we got nearer to them, one dropped back to earth and then the other. I had a very good talk with them. It turned out that one was a builder and decorator from the valleys, and the other said he did a 'bit of this and a bit of that'. The bit-of-this-bit-of-that man was wearing an earring. They were both very jolly, didn't mind being filmed at all, and told me that flying was their passion. They were wearing all-in-one suits a bit like pilots, crash helmets (which seemed a good idea), and gadgets called variometers which showed whether they were rising or falling, by bleeping.

From here, it was a relatively easy climb and the summit was flat and eroded. There was a cairn to the north and spectacular steep slopes on three sides. It was a fine moment: I think Robert Croft was pleased he'd climbed it too. It was really windy around the trig point; you could see Brecon clearly to the north, Llandovery, and my route ahead. The ground dropped away so steeply I felt I understood why those two fellows were so addicted to jumping off mountains and hanging in space. Robert had been in the news recently for getting involved in a shoving match with another player (and receiving a £1000 fine!) so I made a little joke about pushing him over the edge.

The route down was extremely steep. In *The Cambrian Way,* the author suggests an easier route by heading further south and taking the slope gradually. But as I was in the presence of two macho men – Alan the Warden and Robert – we went more or less straight down this 3:1 slope, which was a real knee-killer. We crossed a couple of streams and I was dying to go to the loo, so I stopped. They, of course, dashed on ahead. The final descent was even steeper. The men were waiting for me at the bottom, by the stile. Luckily they hadn't seen me falling over twice.

We came out onto the main road by a pretty little stone tower where the cars were parked. I shook hands with Robert and thanked him for being such good fun on the walk. He seemed very hot and sweaty. That's the funny thing about cricketers: they're like tennis players – not always as fit as you think they are. After all, all they have to do is run about and chuck a ball, but I would say that wouldn't I – a woman who's a cricketing Philistine.

Afterwards I drove to Brecon and bought a new pair of fleece trousers. It might have been 75 degrees today but I was anticipating storms in Snowdonia. Am I just a pessimistic Capricorn?

DAY 30
*Fan Gyhirych to
Llyn y Fan Fach*

Today I was to walk the Black Mountain, not to be confused with the Black Mountains I'd enjoyed a few days before. The Black Mountain (singular) is the name given to the vast mountainous area that forms the western part of the Brecon Beacons, containing the source of the distinguished Rivers Usk and Tawe.

I was to travel through a part of Wales which has the country's highest suicide rate amongst farmers, vets and doctors. The Samaritans have set up offices in Brecon and Radnor to try and help. Eking a living from the land here means relying on subsidies, working all hours, and living in isolation. At the same time, this part of the Beacons National Park is being heavily promoted as part of a tourist drive, marketing the Welsh landscape and its mythology to the Americans. The mystical lake of Llyn y Fan Fach now suffers the indignity of being a reservoir for Llanelli, but I didn't expect that to be featured in the come-to-Wales propaganda! The whole area is a vast common, with huge flocks of sheep wandering for miles.

Waiting for me by the little stone tower was Wayne, the Brecon Beacon Ranger I'd climbed Pen y Fan with. We left the crew and climbed up the hillside, heading north-west over the brow of the hill. I immediately felt cold and wet, and it started to rain so I put my waterproof trousers on. The first hill is always the worst, so I climbed up a couple of hundred feet and felt shattered. Then we followed a wall down the other side to a B road where the crew were waiting for us; and I could see the ridge that runs north–south, Fan Hir. About 20 yards ahead, the River Tawe was in full spate and I had to cross it to start the

ascent towards the ridge. There was much debate about this, but I just couldn't be bothered, so I took my shoes and socks off and actually waded through the stream. I've walked through far worse – it was quite refreshing.

We then climbed up to the right-hand side of the stream, Nant y Llyn. Away to the north I could see some stone circles. The trick was to find the path, for it was quite a steep ascent at first, with a series of waterfalls to reach the first lake of the day, Llyn e Fan-Fawr. The lake itself was very beautiful, with a long, red escarpment running south and rising up like a forbidding wall. I kept the lake on my right and faced the wall of rock which I would have to climb.

Now it was starting to rain intermittently and I posed on the promontory by the lake, trying to look like the Lady of Shallot, but actually just looking like a bedraggled nutter. I started the climb up, which was extra-slippery in the wet weather. The narrow, bright red path wasn't too bad, except at one point where it was very severely eroded. As I approached the top, I headed to the right, and the pass of Bwlch Giedd.

At this point it began to pour down. Luckily this was after I'd gone over the most eroded sections. I balanced on a rock and put all my wet weather gear on. The escarpment I'd been so looking forward to seeing disappeared in thick cloud, and my mood deteriorated.

Anyway, there we were, standing on the top in the pouring rain. All we could see was the edge to our right, where it dropped away. So, standing a safe 3 feet back from it, I followed a somewhat eroded path to the first trig point at 802; magically, the cloud lifted and I could see the narrow escarpment ahead – jutting forward to the north. It was like an *Indiana Jones* movie. The cloud lifted, fell, and swirled about, and the sunlight came though it, making this one of the most atmospheric moments I've had on any walk. I went forward, through a series of cairns, and then on to the cairn on Fan-Foel. It was magical. I was on a fairytale promontory of rock, the kind I had dreamt about and painted so many times as a teenager.

After this high point, I turned and headed south-west on the grassy moorland, dropping down a seductive dip, but sadly realizing I'd have to climb back up again. There was a little stream at the bottom, and then I climbed up the grassy slope of Picws Du. This rose up in front of me like a roller-coaster, with a sheer rocky cliff falling away on my right – so exciting!

From Picws Du, I followed the edge of the escarpment, with Llyn y Fan Fach lake far below me. This exquisite pool, cradled in its perfect setting, is the subject of the following myth from the *Mabinogion,* the classic Welsh epic.

Once upon a time, a poor country lad met a beautiful young lady sitting on a rock at the water's edge at Llyn y Fan Fach. He offered her some bread but she refused because it was hard-baked. The next time he returned with some unbaked bread, but she refused that too. He returned once more with some unleavened bread, which she accepted, along with

his proposal of marriage, subject to her father's agreement. The next time he arrived at the lake he met the father and his five identical daughters: the deal was that he could have the daughter, with as many sheep and cattle as he could count, if he could pick out the right one. Fortunately the girl made a sign with her toe and the lad picked the right daughter. Dad now gave him the dowry of cattle and sheep, but with the proviso that, should the lad touch her three times with iron, she would have to return to the lake with all her dowry. After some years of marriage he broke the taboo and she disappeared back into the lake.

Though I tried very hard, I could not see any maidens beneath the waters hundreds of feet below, but it can only be a matter of time before Mel Gibson and Gwyneth Paltrow are recreating this bizarre tale on celluloid.

A path dropped sharply off to the east, down to the head of the lake and the dam. I chose to take one that headed due north, down the flank of the mountain, an easy climb down, picking up a stream on my left, down to a farm, through a gate and down a track to a little bridge by the road. It had been the most wonderful day. And the weather was really fine again. The next stage of my walk would pass through the rolling hills to the sheep town of Llandovery, taking me through some of the loneliest and least-visited areas of Mid-Wales.

DAY 31
Blaenau to Llandovery

It was Sunday and I was walking with my friends Janet and Darryl again. We got a lift to the place where I'd finished the previous day, a hamlet called Blaenau, and started by the little bridge over the river. We walked about a mile along a very narrow road in a valley to the north of the stream, the hills rising up steeply on either side. A couple of cars passed us, their occupants returning from chapel. We were just below the moorland. Opposite a farm road on our left, we turned right up a verdant green track for a couple of hundred yards, and then turned right again where it crossed a footpath.

We had started walking at 11.20, later than I'd wanted to, but I was pretty tired. As we were walking, a fine, misty rain started – not really wet enough to make us put on water-proof trousers, but wet enough to wear waterproof jackets and to pull them over our heads so our hair didn't get soaked.

Our goal was marked on the map as a Roman camp, just after a hamlet called Blaenllechach. We tried to walk across the tops of the moors by picking up tracks every now and then, and dipping down to streams, which we crossed with varying degrees of difficulty. The earth was red and muddy; the rocks were mossy and slippery. At one point Janet slipped in and her boots got wet through.

Eventually we reached what we thought might be the Roman camp. On the map it

Blaenau to Llandovery **Day 31**   **139**

looks so impressive, but when you're up on the moors there's a succession of softly round-ed hills and you can't actually see a camp at all!

Now we fantasized for a while about what life must have been like for the Roman soldiers sent here. Imagine: one minute you're a centurion commanding a regiment in somewhere exotic like Assisi or Perugia (anyway, somewhere hot and sunny, with loads of olive oil, wine, women, song, lots of designer vegetables). And the next minute you're in this place. There's thick mist and fine rain, every hill looking exactly like the next one. Life must have been pretty grim: lamb, possibly a few local wenches, bilberries and mead – somehow it wouldn't compare with risotto and Chianti!

We reached the road at a point called, on the map, Bylchau Blaenclydach, turned right and, about 100 yards later, picked up a track heading due north, slightly below some hilltops. This was a very pleasant piece of walking, with a patchwork of green fields in the valley below. On our right was the Usk Reservoir, which we saw from the first hill. Darryl wanted to head north from cairn to cairn, but by this time Janet and I were pretty achy and not too keen on his plan, which seemed a pretty macho thing to do when there was a perfectly agreeable path about 100 feet below. Anyway, we fitted in with him – don't ask me why!

We climbed over a stile, turned down the hillside on a track, and then suddenly turned right off it, heading due north. The sun came out and, as we passed between two hills, we thought it looked a very good spot to have lunch. So we sat down, spread out our nylon jackets and ate some delicious ham sandwiches. It was 2 o'clock. We'd been walking for two and a half hours and we seemed to be about halfway to our destination.

I imagine this was one of the ancient routes used for centuries to drive sheep from the high moors to market in Llandovery, gradually descending through a succession of hills, the landscape becoming more inhabited with every mile.

After lunch, the track dropped down extremely steeply. We passed a farm on our left which was completely deserted and derelict and walked along a small road for about a mile to a pretty little village called Myddfai. There wasn't a single person in sight. We passed a pub called the Plough. Through the door you could see the bar full of men drinking their pints, and hear the television, but nobody was on the street. The cottages were painted in attractive colours, and decorated with hanging baskets. Having turned up towards Myrtle Hill, we soon passed a chapel on our left. It was a rather austere building with three cars outside, and some very unattractive polished granite and marble tombstones. I listened to see if I could hear any singing, but there was none. The church in Myddfai looked a hundred times more welcoming and homely than the chapel, that was for sure.

Our weary legs took us up through some woods and then along a little leafy green lane behind another derelict farm, which would have made a very pretty home. The back garden was completely overgrown with weeds. All the signs were obvious – that sheep

farming doesn't pay and no one wants to take over the businesses when the old farmers die. Once you get outside the villages, this is a depressed and depressing environment.

Then we passed through a series of fields and some woodland, and crossed a new wooden footbridge over a stream. Turning left and then right along a series of tracks, we went through fields and then woodland, past an old farm. Someone was doing it up, because the bushes had been cleared and there was a new track. Now we were walking through smallholdings (farms with relatively small fields, a few sheep, very few cows). It all looked pretty poor and run-down.

In the middle of one group of farm buildings was a caravan that someone was living in while they tried to keep the business going. Then we picked up a farm road heading north, entered a forestry plantation, turned right, and picked up another track. Suddenly we were on top of the hill looking down into Llandovery. We passed through another derelict farm.

This time disaster struck. I went to climb over a stile but my legs were so heavy that I caught the plank on the way down, and I fell heavily on the ground with my foot still hooked on the stile. I banged my right thigh extremely badly. Luckily I hadn't pulled any bones out of alignment, but I was going to have really bad bruises on my legs.

Having got my breath back, I walked slowly down the hill into Llandovery. The town nestled in the valley below, with hills stretching far away to the north. It sat between the River Towy and two smaller streams flowing in from the east, joining by the castle. The view to the north across the valley was sensational but, sadly, we were soon very aware that we were back in civilization after our quiet hours on the moors. We could hear the roar of motorbikes and cheap cars being driven at high speed up and down through the town by people with nothing to do on a Sunday afternoon in summer.

The castle was barely visible, in amongst all the houses. Finally we emerged into a new concrete farmyard, all very clean. We walked through it and onto a road, and turned left into the town along the High Street. We soon found ourselves in Market Square, though 'square' is too big a word for it.

Llandovery seemed to be a place that had lovely buildings but was now on its uppers. It somehow lacked the liveliness of Crickhowell. But it could have been because it was a Sunday and all the shops were shut, so I decided to reserve judgement until market day.

I had read the Victorian writer George Borrow's description of Llandovery in his rambling tome *Wild Wales,* in which he mentions it as a 'pleasant little town in which I halted in the course of my wanderings'. Janet, Darryl and I had decided to follow in Borrow's footsteps by staying at the Castle Hotel, a large black and white building proudly standing at right angles to the road by the castle. It was closed; I rang the bell and a young man showed us in. We were the only people staying there. My room had a plaque on the door announcing it as 'The George Borrow Room'. It could have been my Welsh granny's

bedroom in Llanfairfechan, back in the 1950s, with a Victorian mahogany bed, a satin bed-cover and piles of cushions.

The young woman who was the owner said dinner could be a problem – they were shut on Sunday evenings. (I was thinking – but you *are* running a hotel aren't you?) We could have some plates and get a Chinese takeaway, she suggested. The look on my face must have persuaded her this was a non-starter! What about some George Borrow-style hospitality after we'd walked nearly 12 miles? Anyway, she returned with a small baby and said her father would cook us supper. We were pathetically grateful. It turned out that she and her husband had bought the hotel two years before and were slowly restoring it. She bought us a homely supper of steak, lots of fresh vegetables and delicious, luxury rice pudding with roast pears. We ate alone in a large wood-panelled lounge.

After dinner I rang up Elton John and told him how good I thought he was at Diana's funeral, and how much I enjoyed his song. He was packing to go to New York. I stretched out on the cosy George Borrow bed; the mattress was a bit saggy but I didn't care. I had nice crisp, white cotton sheets and hoped for 10 hours' sleep. The bruises on my legs were already forming, as well as a great big lump. Thank God the summer was nearly over and I wouldn't be wearing short dresses for a few months.

I returned to Llandovery a few days later to continue my walk and see the sheep market on Wednesday morning. Having checked back into the Castle Hotel, I asked for a plank of wood to be put under my soft mattress in the George Borrow Room. It was the most perfect evening – not a cloud in the sky. I put my shorts on and felt so good I decided to walk out of town along the high-level road, to relax and enjoy the good weather.

DAY 32
Llandovery to past Rhandirmwyn

Auctions and markets mean drinking. A century ago there were 57 pubs in Landovery – now there are 14, which stilll seems a lot for such a small town. The Romans built a fort here and the Normans a castle, the ruins of which were on a little hill outside the hotel. Llandovery today seems a shadow of its former self: lots of grandiose Victorian buildings, from the Town Hall to the bank, but it's off the tourist trail. Compared to the bustling streets of Brecon, it seems asleep, with a dead town centre, although the little square and back streets couldn't be prettier, or the people friendlier. I felt it needed some visionary to come along and revitalize it. Now the money's gone out of sheep farming it needs a new purpose. The railways destroyed its business as a coaching stop and the posh Victorian public school, Llandovery College, sits on the road leading out, disconnected from the daily life of the town.

I walked east along the A40, then left by some municipal offices, and north, through streets of very pretty, different-coloured cottages. Having skirted around the hospital, I met

up with the A483(T) and headed north-west out of town, turned after the church, crossed over the railway line and climbed steadily up an extremely beautiful narrow lane, heading

Llandovery – grandiose buildings in a sleepy town...

almost due north. It climbed and climbed: in the hedgerows were sloe trees full of fruit. I passed farms with cars parked outside, people inside watching television and having their dinners; at one a pair of wellingtons and a cat were parked on the back porch. I thoroughly enjoyed this little lane: it rose up and curved round, and I saw more and more hills rising around me; then I looked back and saw the sun dropping away to the west. The whole of Llandovery lay below, and the valleys of the Brecon Beacons were gradually exposed as I climbed.

As the road climbed up, I realized that the large-scale Ordnance Survey map and *The Cambrian Way* describe it differently. At one of the highest points in the road it bent round to the right, but I had to take a fork going directly north (a grassy track but still used by cars). After about a mile, a B road crossed it, and in front of me was a farm. On the Ordnance Survey map it looked as if there wasn't a footpath, but I went through the gate and between the buildings. The drovers' road I was on continued along the other side of the farmyard.

I passed through a series of fields, on my perfect drovers' road, and all the gates were tied up; it was obvious that the farmer didn't want walkers. I was on high-level pastureland and could see for miles. It was really pleasurable, and I felt that I was walking on extremely old paths, used by cattle and carts for centuries.

Away to my right, the farmer was cutting hay. He just ignored me. He was probably the man from the farmyard I'd just walked through. Now the path started to drop down. It joined a road which I followed down a steep hill. Below me was the River Tywi, sitting at the bottom of a beautiful wooded valley.

I took a leafy, wooded path, still dropping down towards the river. Once again, I got lost at somewhere labelled 'Gwernpwll Farm' in my book. After about 100 yards, I saw someone coming towards me, and I asked her the way to the river. She was American, but she knew. She directed me back past a barn, and I picked up a little footpath that ran through woodland. I crossed a field and came to the River Tywi.

Having wasted about half an hour looking for footpaths, I wanted to make up some time, so I followed the easterly bank of the river along a well-trodden path. The river was wide and peaceful and the sun was still shining. After a while there was a campsite on the right. At the end of it I turned left and crossed the river over a bridge. Eventually the track went through some bracken and emerged onto the road. I walked past a pub where people were eating outside, and continued along this tiny road; the river valley was absolutely spectacular.

I turned right down a road marked 'Dead End', which wiggled its way back down towards the river. Then I went through a gate and found a broad, grassy track that curved north-west, along through woodland on the right, with a steep hill on my left. A burial chamber was marked on the map, and I could just about make it out.

The path was obviously not much walked, although it was marked on the maps as a bridleway. I passed a couple of caravans that looked as if people had been living in them, in the middle of nowhere. I couldn't imagine how they'd got there. Then, a little further on, there was a caravan site, and my track emerged into a farmyard where a very noisy pair of dogs barked at me. But I carried on walking. I now have nerves of steel so far as barking dogs are concerned. Beyond the gate was a sign informing me that this was a farm with a fierce dog. What a surprise!

I got a lift back to Llandovery. I was so glad I'd done this walk. It had loosened up all my arms and legs, and mentally chilled me out. I went back to the hotel, had a bath, unpacked and went out to eat at a pleasant restaurant in the square.

The next morning I got up very early. It was market day and the town was bustling with trailers, Land Rovers and ancient vehicles passing the hotel and on their way to the auction mart. There are two breeds of sheep native to this area: Welsh, with all white faces; and 'Beulah Speckled-Face', which have black and white faces. Sheep were being loaded from trailers

DAY 33
Llandovery

into pens in the auction building, to be sold 20 or so at a time; £80 or £90 for good-quality yearlings and only £20 for older sheep.

I met farmer Bernard Llewelyn, who lives in Carreg Cennon Castle near Llandeilo, about 11 miles away. Bernard's worked out how to make money from sheep farming: he was the adviser on the BBC drama *Drover's Gold,* and provided all the cattle! He also supplies old and rare breeds of sheep for filming, and gives talks about farming issues on Welsh language TV. Bernard explained how, until the advent of the railway, Welsh farmers used professional drovers to take their cattle, sheep and pigs to market in England, sometimes hundreds of miles away. Cattle were shod, pigs were given little woollen socks with leather soles, and geese might have their feet protected with tar and sand.

Droving was a respected profession, requiring a licence; a man had to be over 30, married and a householder. (This was to prevent anyone from running off with the profits.) Anyone found droving without a licence faced a fine of £5, together with a term of imprisonment for breaking the vagrancy laws.

Llandovery was an important resting place for the drovers and their animals. The cattle were nourished in the fields to the north of the town, while the drovers made use of the numerous pubs. They also carried the 'Ship Money', collected by the agents of Charles I, to London, and the rent paid by Welsh tenant farmers to their landlords, and today the town's rugby team is still nick-named 'The Drovers'.

I put it to Bernard that this area of Wales was having a hard time: to me Llandovery was a town that the heart had gone out of. A lot of shops were for sale and quite a few of the pubs had closed, unlike Brecon with its tourists. An article in the *Daily Telegraph* a couple of days before had spelt out the gloomy story: the Farmers' Union told the government that young people weren't interested in taking over the family farms and begged them not to cut subsidies, saying that hill farming offered a totally unattractive career, with low pay, long hours and a soaring suicide rate.

But, according to Bernard, this isn't a new story:

'My grandfather tells me about putting milk on the train in the 1920s, sending it to London and picking it up again the following day. By the time he got it back, it had gone sour, simply because there was no market for it. The saddest thing of all is the fact that we haven't got young people who are prepared to make the sacrifices that you need to, to become a farmer. They see their contemporaries from school and university, on a high salary or wage, with disposable income that perhaps farmers don't have. What they say about a farmer is that he tends to live very poor but die very rich. A lot of young people don't find that acceptable today.'

As the cattle auction got under way, I said goodbye to Bernard and spent some time in the café in the High Street, drinking the weakest instant coffee I'd had in a long time and studying my maps. I'd walked about 105 miles from Cardiff and acquired a giant bruise on one leg, a lot of gloomy information about sheep farming, a pretty good suntan, a Japanese good luck charm, and a whole collection of waterproof jackets (from cheap to expensive), none of which seemed to work.

The next stage of my walk would take me up a rarely walked river valley, with government minister Chris Smith for company. I read his cuttings, watched by two single mums and a pensioner. Would the Minister for Culture be interested in the problems of sheep farmers? I knew he was a keen walker, but would New Labour live up to all their pledges and ensure that the Access to the Countryside Bill became law? I couldn't see Tony Blair or Peter Mandelson with a rucksack. The Welsh might have their Assembly – but did north or south really care about the forgotten zone of Mid-Wales?

I was to meet Chris Smith at the Royal Oak pub near Rhandirmwyn, now a small hamlet of holiday cottages north of Llandovery, nestling on the western slopes of the River Tywi valley, but once the site of the largest lead mine in South Wales. By the end of the eighteenth century, 400 people worked here (including a large number of women) but by 1900 the mine

was abandoned, leaving 23 miles of levels and shafts. This village is truly out of the way: electricity didn't arrive until 1955, and the village school closed in 1969. Now it's a village divided between Welsh-speakers and incomers seeking solitude.

The publican made me a plate of scrambled eggs and, after a while, Chris Smith arrived: he's a very engaging, personable kind of guy, doesn't stand on any ceremony and it's all, 'Call me Chris'. We filmed him putting his boots on, and then we were driven up in the cars to the exact spot I'd already walked to, a couple of miles down the road at a bridge at Gallt-y-Bere.

This was an extremely beautiful valley, though the sky was totally overcast. The River Tywi was shortly to split in two, and we crossed to the western bank. On either side the limestone hills rose up, rounded and craggy. It looked more like North Wales or Scotland than the cosy landscapes I'd seen around Llandovery. We headed north, and then the river split again, and we followed the River Doethie. Having walked quite a way along a very easy track, we crossed to the eastern bank of the river where the hills rose up extremely steeply above us.

We passed the Dinas Nature Reserve, which is completely covered in trees, with rivers almost totally encircling it. On it is Twm Shon Catti's (Thomas Jones') Cave. (He was a Welsh folk hero who stole from the rich to give to the poor.) To the north lies Llyn Brianne, a large reservoir which produces hydro-electric power.

The River Twyi used to be an excellent river for salmon 20 years ago: now there are none on this stretch. They have all been poisoned by acid rain, caused by coniferous forests drawing in the acidity from the air which is then absorbed by the falling rain.

We went past a farmyard and the valley narrowed – it was an idyllic spot. Sheep grazed on the steep slopes on either side. Above us were ugly forestry plantations, but even they looked attractive in this setting. We were climbing gradually, and I started feeling hot, so I took my jacket off – then it started to rain. When I put my jacket back on it stopped raining. It was that kind of day.

The narrow path was somewhat muddy; it had obviously rained a lot over the last couple of days. In places the path was partly obscured by bracken: we felt we were venturing up into a truly unexplored and lost part of Wales; a place where no one lived any more, hardly anybody walked, and the only inhabitants were red kites and sheep.

After following the river for a couple of miles, having crossed little side streams and occasionally looped back, we went slightly uphill, slightly downhill and slightly curved round

little billowing hills that caressed the edge of the stream. We then took a slightly more north-easterly route, still following the river, climbing higher and higher up the valley, and it became more spectacular as it grew more isolated.

Chris Smith was an extremely good walking companion. We chatted about everything: when the sound man wasn't recording us we talked about the BBC, gossip, Elton John, culture, Damien Hirst. When he was recording us, we talked about walking, the arts, charging for museums, architecture and so on. Time passed extremely quickly: we set a cracking pace, so much so that the camera crew, whom we hadn't worked with before, started moaning.

Chris, of course, is a famous walker, who has bagged all the Munroes in Scotland and appeared in the TV series *Wilderness Walks*. I was sorry I wasn't offering him a mountain, but pleased we were both discovering a wonderfully unspoilt river valley for the first time. As I pored over my soggy maps, Chris admitted that, like me, he was a closet map freak:

'I love those wonderful old Ordnance Survey maps that you used to be able to get which had a sort of cloth backing…and they stood up to rain and storm and God knows what else. They were wonderful. Bring out the modern paper ones in the middle of a blizzard and they either flap all over the place or they get completely sodden. There's nothing quite like the Ordnance Survey.'

Suddenly we met two Germans, coming the other way, carrying posh laminated maps. They were on the Five Rivers Walk; they told us they loved Wales because they saw so few people when walking. They'd found out about the walk through the Internet! Chris was delighted; he's a big fan of new technology and New Labour are not only working with Microsoft and Bill Gates on educational projects, they also want to put a computer terminal in every classroom. I think another teacher in every classroom would be better, or a fund for school trips so all children can enjoy museums and galleries instead of staring at screens, and I told Chris that.

By now we were both struggling with the rain and wiping our spectacles frequently. At one point we took a track slightly too far uphill and had to cut down through some bracken. I fell down on the wet ground three times; my backside was covered in mud and soaking wet – but we just laughed. Chris was that kind of companion.

Finally the track met a T-junction with a much better dirt track coming across us, and suddenly we were at the youth hostel in Ty'n-y-cornel. This was a lonely spot for a youth hostel. No one lived in it and there was an 'honesty box' to put money in for tea and coffee. The walk had taken much longer than I thought. We had our sandwiches outside, but when it started to pelt with rain we went indoors and Chris made a pot of tea. We had a talk in the kitchen and I asked him when his passion for walking had started?

Opposite: A good companion and a very experienced walker, the Minister for Culture, Chris Smith.

'Although I was born in North London, I spent most of my teenage years in Edinburgh, and that's so convenient for getting out into the hills. I really envy my Scottish colleagues the ability to head for the Highlands at the drop of a hat. One of the wonderful things my school did (this was when I was about 13) was to send the whole of my year away for a fortnight, all around Scotland, doing different things. I ended up with a group of about 12 or 15 who went way up in the north-west of Scotland, and we spent some time plotting the regeneration of the old Caledonian pine forest and measuring the new growth of trees and all that sort of thing, but we also climbed mountains. And I came away completely hooked and ever since then I've just loved climbing mountains.'

I really enjoyed our tea-time talk, sitting at the old kitchen table, though our discussion was disrupted by the cameraman backing into the frying pan and making a lot of clonking noises.

Anyway, at 4.30 I said goodbye to Chris; he got in a car back to London, and I continued up the track. By now the rain had stopped. Now I was to walk north-west along 3 miles of rough terrain with no paths and meet them by a telephone box at Nantymaen. John Bush, the director, offered to walk with me because he wanted the exercise.

We decided to follow a series of low ridges, really just rounded hillocks of tufty grass. That way we stayed clear of the bog, only dropping down into it occasionally. I'd look to the east and see hill after hill with nothing on it: not a house in sight. All I could see in the distance was forestry plantations: this truly was the loneliest place I'd encountered so far. The rolling grassland seemed more like the prairies of Montana than Mid-Wales.

At the phone box, my lift was waiting. On the way to Tregaron I saw two red kites – such distinctive birds, with their forked tails and beautiful chestnut colour.

By 6.30 the hills were bathed in a soft light; even the sheep looked quite pink. I entered Tregaron and nothing was happening. I parked in front of the Talbot Inn in the square. There were only two or three other cars there and four or five irritating kids playing.

I'd spent quite a lot of time near Tregaron in the late sixties, when my ex in-laws, the Street-Porters, had a farmhouse high up on the hills outside town. It didn't seem to have changed one bit, apart from the addition of a shop selling crafts and Welsh gold in the main square. At the Memorial Hall, line dancing (what a surprise – the secret passion of the Welsh!) was due to start at 7.30.

I sat in the Land Rover and dozed. Suddenly, at 7.25, when everybody had had their tea, or dinner, or whatever, the town ripped into life. From nowhere, cars appeared and disgorged women and the odd bloke, all heading purposefully for the Memorial Hall.

Within 15 minutes the square in Tregaron had been transformed from half empty to totally packed. I went into the Memorial Hall. In a large room with a wooden floor, there were at least 50 people marching up and down in lines to the sound of Dolly Parton. Unlike Pontypool, there were more men this time. The age range was astounding: there was one

In the bar of the Talbot Inn, with my present – a beautiful carved stick.

girl of about 10, a couple of ladies of well over 80, and everything in between. There were couples in cowboy hats and jeans and boots with silver bits on them: there were women in just their ordinary house gear. There was a very fat girl in trainers, who seemed to be doing it to keep fit and having a whale of a time; there was a couple of old ladies in skirts and slippers. It was the most wonderful cross-section you could possibly imagine – an advert for line dancing being the thing that keeps the community together!

I left the line dancing and returned to the Talbot. In the entrance hall of the Memorial Hall the stench of the men's toilets was overpowering. There was a little paper sign on the door opposite that said 'Ladies and Disabled'.

Inside the Talbot, things were hotting up. Nothing had changed since my last visit in the early seventies. The regulars were all in: farmers in flat hats and checked shirts. I met John Jones, one of the oldest farmers in the area, and he told me lots of hilarious stories about winning a trip to America because he was bald. John and his brother farmed 2500 acres

around Soar y Mynydd, with about 2500 sheep. The nearest village was Rhandirmwyn, half an hour's drive away. John and his brother were both in their sixties, unmarried and child-less – who would continue after them? They still used horses to round up their flocks on the hillsides. I asked him if he found his life lonely – he looked incredulous. 'It's a wonderful life,' he replied with great dignity. In the old days, young lads had come up from Tregaron to help with the shearing and harvesting. Not any more.

The atmosphere was livening up, after several rounds, and John kept squeezing me round the waist – I hoped he wasn't trying to tempt me into a life involving rounding up 2500 sheep in all weathers.

At this point, John's friend Dafydd presented me with a stick he'd carved, to take me on the rest of my journey. Made of antler, it had taken three days to create. It was the most beautiful present I could imagine. I said goodbye to them and went and had dinner in the Talbot's restaurant: simple hearty fare, starting off with vegetable broth with bits of mutton in it, which was peppery and delicious, followed by lamb chops. I didn't like to ask whether they'd come from any of John Jones' flock!

DAY 35
Nantymaen to Teifi Pools

It was a clear blue sky, with no wind, I started walking from the lonely telephone box at the crossroads at Nantymaen. I met Asa, who'd been a shepherd most of his working life and up here for about 20 years. He was a very well-spoken, tall, middle-class Englishman, in his sixties; I didn't like to ask why he was a shepherd but I was fascinated. He has driven sheep hundreds of miles through Scotland and Sunderland and round here, and now he looks after about 1000 sheep on a hill near Nantymaen with his dog, Lass. We talked about the Beast of Bont, a mysterious wild cat or puma that's been killing sheep. The locals know it's a wild cat because of the way the teeth go into the fleece, and because of rather grizzly details, like the way it leaves the guts in a pile by the carcass. Over the last two years about 30 sheep have been killed in this way on the 1000 acres where Asa tends his flock.

According to Asa, the wild cat lives in the forest, and climbs up trees when cornered. If I got lost I should use a whistle, and he presented me with a fine specimen he'd made from a piece of ram's horn – flat, with a hole in it. I stuck it in my mouth and all that came out was a load of dribble. He managed to play a tune on his! So I started my walk to the Cistercian ruins at Strata Florida, attempting to whistle, walk and dribble simultaneously.

The track I was following ended just after the deserted Nantymaen farm. Then it became boggy, contouring round a hill covered in sheep. Asa had agreed with me that forestry was ruining this area. First of all, it's planted too high up. When it's planted over the brow of a hill it destroys the natural landscape, turning the soft velvety edges of these hills

into hard, dark green lines. It all looks identical. Then, when the 30-year-old trees are being harvested, the resulting landscape is very unattractive. Sure, it brings a few jobs to the area, but not enough, in my opinion, to justify such large-scale desecration of the landscape. As for the acid rain, I knew all about it. Every time it rained, my face stung, no matter what cream I slapped on.

I climbed Garn Gron (1706 feet), which was slightly off the path, but I just did it as I hadn't climbed a peak for a few days! A shame there was no one there to take my photo, with not a cloud in the sky. I rested the camera on a boulder and hoped for the best. The last time I did that, the wind turned it round and I wasn't in the picture!

I came down from the trig point, headed north, crossed over a couple of streams and climbed a hill to get a better view. Then I saw a gate on my right, on which I could dimly make out a blue and white way mark. I went into the forest, now heading north on a path that was often blocked by fallen trees. Climbing slightly, and crossing quite a few streams, I passed a ruined farmhouse. The ferns rustled and I was on my guard for the Beast of Bont, whistle at the ready!

Eventually the path became an old drovers' road, and I followed it to the ruin of Talwrn. I turned west over a stream and then north, down through fields and trees, until I came to a brand-new footbridge. Then I discovered, to my horror, that the path ahead to Strata Florida had become a stream! And when I looked closely at the directions, there were the fatal words: 'path along stream'. How could I hold a map in front of my face for two hours and not read three words?

I emerged quite cross and flustered on the road right by Strata Florida Abbey, where I met Fred, who runs the gift shop. He told me that only 10 people doing the Cambrian Way had come through in the last year, and there had only been one woman in three years!

In the graveyard next to the abbey I saw the grave of a local cooper who'd had an accident, when making a barrel, in which his leg had been cut off. The leg was buried, but he then went to America and died there, so his body's in one continent and his right leg in another. There's also the grave of a tramp, who used to come to the valley selling *Old Moore's Almanac*. One day in 1929 he set off along the road that I would be walking, but the weather took a turn for the worse and a few weeks later his body was found. The locals clubbed together and paid for a gravestone in the churchyard which reads:

'Unknown. Died in a snowstorm by Teifi Pools, February 1929. He died upon the hillside drear, alone where the snow was deep. By strangers he was carried here, where princes also sleep.'

In the graveyard was an impressive yew tree, said to be 1400 years old, and under it lies the body of one of Wales' most famous poets, the bawdy bard Dafydd ap Gwilym, a fourteenth-century contemporary of Chaucer's, who travelled widely and wrote reams of verse about unrequited love and rampant lust.

Strata Florida (established in 1164) was the richest Cistercian monastery in Wales, but the last monk left in 1539. The ruins are not so extensive or impressive as those at Easby or Fountains, or any of the great abbeys in Yorkshire, but the setting is sensational, beside the Teifi River, nestling on the edge of the foothills between Tregaron and the mountains.

I started to walk along the dead end road that goes east from Strata Florida towards the Teifi Pools. It's a lovely little road, with ferns on one side and a steep hill on the right. A brook runs along the north side of it, and every now and then a squirrel popped out of the bushes and ran across the road.

The road climbed west up a valley and on either side the hills gradually became more rocky and flinty-looking, shimmering in the late afternoon sun. The road went over a little stream and then climbed up to Tyncwm farm. At this point on the right there was a very unexpected sight: a pretty chapel with coloured bricks over the arched windows. But it was in a really bad state of disrepair: all the windows were smashed and it was boarded up – miles from anywhere. I couldn't imagine who had ever used it or visited it. I turned left and walked through a farmyard.

The path climbed north-west, with the river on the left, up a very beautiful valley. Waterfalls cascaded down the hills on my left. It was a long haul up, but worth it. Gradually the path flattened out and became grassier.

I climbed one more hill, and there, in one of the most beautiful spots you could imagine, were the Teifi Pools, a collection of absolutely exquisite blue (well, actually they're brown water, but blue when they reflect the sky) pools, sitting extremely high up, amongst rocky outcrops that were lit up by the late afternoon sun. But at the end of the one we approached first, from the south, was quite the ugliest dam I have ever seen. All over Wales there are beautiful, castellated dams; grand dams, resembling castles and houses, but this one was two slabs of concrete with a bright blue painted pipe in the middle, and a lifebuoy.

I remembered that the other pools were higher up, so I climbed another 75 feet and was rewarded with the sight of two further pools, both at different levels, and a little fishing hut. There is where Jimmy Carter allegedly comes to fish, although I didn't know if this was the actual hut the ex-president had sat in. I decided to follow the ridge going north, and immediately waded into a really deep bog and went in up to my knees. But I didn't care. I sat on a rock and changed my socks, while a large hawk circled overhead.

Eventually I rejoined the main road and turned left. After about 300 yards, you can look back and see one of the most beautiful sights in the whole of Wales: the pools laid out, with the little rocky hillocks around them, like pieces of jewellery set with opals, in the evening sun.

I could have waited another hour until the sun had set behind them and made them all pink – it was the most perfect summer evening – if only I hadn't been so hungry. But I'm sorry to report that I dragged myself away to supper.

During the last few days I'd probably done some of the hardest walking since I'd walked in the Himalayas a few years ago. It's nothing to do with altitude, or climbing or dropping; it's to do with endurance and how you hold your mind together while you're walking without any tracks at all, just over rough terrain; how you keep going when the mist comes down and you can't see where you are; how you keep going when you've walked 6 miles and you've got another 5 to go and it's pouring with rain, and your boots are full of water and you've just put a clean pair of socks on, and they're wet through, too. I was going to walk today with my friend Janet. She's one of my best friends – I couldn't have done it alone, and I wouldn't have wanted to do it with a warden or a guide. You need a friend there to talk to, to laugh at each other falling into the streams and the bogs.

That's a kind of preface to today's walk really, because it was much harder than I expected it to be. And, as I continued, I realized that, because I'd already been long distances, I had no reserves of energy or mental strength, and I was extremely tired after the first three hours.

During the drive up, the sun had shone and shone and the sky had cleared of cloud. But, as we started to walk at 12 o'clock, I noticed clouds gathering ominously right overhead. We were on a high, bleak plateau, with lots of tiny hills, limestone outcrops and little lakes. It's an alpine, glacial landscape. In between these little protuberances are bogs and no footpaths.

The first thing we had to do was to strike north-west from the road and find a little farm building marked on the map as 'Claerddu'. That building was not visible until we were almost upon it, and the minute I saw it I remembered it from 25 years earlier. Made of stone, with the slate roof recently repaired, it sits in a little cleft between two breaks in the rocks.

We crossed over a stream and got our first taste of the bog that was to come. It seemed simplest to try and follow the higher ground, climbing a series of grassy knolls, up several hundreds of feet, rising and falling on a switch-back. There was no path whatsoever, but the heather wasn't too high underfoot, and the grass was relatively easy to walk on. Now the wind really whipped up, a mist started swirling around, and visibility was cut right down. At this point I realized the walk was going to take much longer than the four hours I'd allowed. I'd told everyone gaily that I would meet them in the hotel at Devil's Bridge for tea at 4 o'clock. No chance.

We plodded on, against the wind. We couldn't see the lakes to our north to take a bearing because they were higher than we were, something that *The Cambrian Way* book doesn't mention. Also, if the visibility is poor, this is not a section of the walk to do by yourself or without a guide because there are simply no way marks after the lakes.

We climbed up, and eventually Llyn Fyrddon Fach appeared on our left. We were in

exactly the right position to skirt it. It would have been a beautiful sight if the mist had lifted. I got momentary glimpses, but the wind was whipping off it and the rain was beating against me. My leggings were soaked and my feet were getting pretty wet too, so I put a nylon poncho on over my Gore-Tex jacket in the hope of keeping warmer.

We dropped down slightly to a boggy plain and passed the second lake on our left, Llyn Fyrddon Fawr. Thankfully, for about a mile, there was a footpath that ran along the eastern side of it.

Now we were supposed to head for a trig point Domen Milwyn (1817 feet). Well, all I can tell you is that it's about a mile beyond the end of the reservoir in a north-easterly direction, but there is a series of rounded hills, all more or less the same height, and it's extremely difficult to locate. We walked across deep bog, headed uphill, got to where we thought the trig point was, and couldn't find it. Maybe we headed too far east. In the howling gale and rain, God gave us a sign! It's not often you ask for a sign, but sometimes you get one. And there, on top of the hill, was a standing stone. It turned out not to be the cairn for Domen Milwyn but another one marked on the map a quarter of a mile to the east. We dropped down the hill a little and headed slightly west in the hope of locating a river. There was no footpath anywhere in this area: odd sheep tracks, but mostly just deep bog. We passed outcrops of rocks and some drier, grassy areas, but it was a godforsaken spot, that was for sure. I truly could not imagine farming or living in this inhospitable environment.

The mist lifted enough to see a stream. We made our way up through very wet, reedy ground, and – surprise, surprise – found the ruin that's mentioned in *The Cambrian Way* book. It was 2 o'clock. We'd been walking for two hours and were shattered and wet through. So we clung to the eastern end of the ruin, sat down on the grass, and decided to have lunch, out of the wind and the rain. We took off our nylon ponchos and hung them on a tree to dry. I took off my really wet leggings, stood in my knickers, shivering, and then put my waterproof trousers on. Having taken off my soaking wet socks, I put on dry ones and put my feet back into the wet boots. But at least they were going to be dry for an hour.

I ate about five sandwiches, I was so hungry. Funnily enough, I wasn't that thirsty, but I was already mentally extremely tired. It's a strain trying to read a map when you're on a broad moorland with hills that all look identical.

We followed a track above the stream in a westerly direction for about half a mile, and got a bit confused. After a few false starts, we went over the brow of a hill and had to drop down extremely steeply. We could see Cwmystwyth ahead of us in the mist, and the hills facing us to the north. We dropped hundreds of feet down a grassy slope (terrified that we were going to slip in the pouring rain and straining our knees to get a grip) to the river at the bottom.

We made our way through Cwmystwyth, a hamlet of holiday houses and farms, until we reached a school building which had been turned into a pleasant house. There we took

A bizarre sign in a field outside Devil's Bridge.

a path northwards by a stream, passing a house with a giant teepee in the front garden. Next we had to climb over a little tributary to the stream, wade through a lot of mud and go round the back of someone's garden. Then, horror of horrors, we had to traverse a very, very boggy field, going from tussock to tussock, to a stile, where I nearly fell.

To the north was a large stretch of woodland which had recently been cut down, leaving a bare, ugly patch. We turned right and then left, heading west along a forestry track. To our north and on our right were the most beautiful high trees, probably about 150 feet tall, looking exquisite: to our left, devastation, where the plantation had been cut down. After 100 yards or so, we crossed a footbridge and then followed a decent track out of the woods which passed a poor-looking farm. The concrete on the outside of the house was cracked, the windows all needed painting, there was an oil lamp in one of the windows and an ancient Land Rover outside.

We were high above the valley now, almost as high as where we'd come down from the clouds before lunch. The only trouble was, we were on our second set of ridges and we had no energy left. We contoured along through more forestry plantation on a decent track, eventually coming to a picnic site with tables. We were shattered. It was 4 o'clock, we still had 2 miles to go to Devil's Bridge, and the weather was cold, windy and grey. We sat down at one of the picnic benches, grateful to rest our legs.

On our table we laid out the remains of our meagre provisions. They were: one fruit and nut bar, three custard creams, a carton of orange juice and half a bottle of water. We demolished the lot. We had no more dry clothes to put on and our second set of socks were wet through.

At the end of the car park was a beautiful stone arch. A sign announced: 'The old masonry arch you see spanning the B4574 was erected by Thomas Johnes in 1810, to mark the Golden Jubilee of George III's succession to the throne, and it is here in Myhern that Johnes also carried out his pioneering work on a forest in the hills in the years from 1780 to 1830'.

We passed under the arch, on a minor road that passed between Devil's Bridge and Cwmystwyth, and after 100 yards turned off to the left and carried on in the same direction along a pleasant wide forestry track. We followed this for a mile or so, keeping to the top edge of the forestry plantation, and then through a forest which was incredibly beautiful. It was very dark, with shafts of late afternoon grey light filtering through, and the mist steaming off the puddles.

We emerged to find a herd of nosy, black bullocks who could have given us trouble, but we saw them off. Then we had a crazy horse to contend with. It was a large, black animal standing far higher than me. It came galloping up and immediately threw up its legs and started attacking us. It was terrifying. Janet leapt over the fence straight away, and I followed her. The horse charged up to the fence, hit it, backed up, threw its back legs up, and then pelted to the other end of the field. It was an extremely disturbed animal and I wondered whether this was too dangerous a path for walkers, especially children, to use.

Shaken, we reached a B road high above Devil's Bridge. We walked about 100 yards down it and then turned off to our right, after a little school building. We lost the path again, but just cut down the hillside in the direction of the hotel, where we could see the Land Rover far below us. It was nearly 6 o'clock – we were two hours late. Most annoyingly, the café with the cream tea had closed at 5 o'clock, like every café in England and Wales. So I drank some rather horrible lukewarm black coffee from a Thermos, ate a couple of sponge cakes from the shop, and tried to pretend I was in a café. The delights of Devil's Bridge, with its railway and waterfalls, would have to wait for another day.

I'd gone through every emotion in the last hour: fatigue, rage, despair and fear. I'd been

terrified by the horse and the bullocks when I was very tired. And, when you're tired, you do lose your way.

Anyway, I put it all behind me, got into the Land Rover, took my trousers off, put some sweat pants on, took off my wet socks and put a pair of old trainers on. Then I put on a warm waistcoat to try and hold some warmth in my body. I'd taken my *Cambrian Way* book out of my pocket so many times that my Gore-Tex jacket was covered in tiny white bits of page, and the map itself had a hole worn right through it. I put it on the hotel bedroom radiator to dry, a sad sight.

I decided to make a little detour at Devil's Bridge and pop down to see the falls, because I used to come here as a child with my mum, and then I came again in my twenties, so I wanted to see if it had changed.

> **DAY 37**
> *Devil's Bridge to*
> *Dyffryn Castell*

The Rheidol Valley is steep and spectacular, and the gorge is a tourist attraction. The area used to be full of holiday homes, but these days most of the residents live here full-time: lecturers from the huge university campus at Aberystwyth; artists and writers; people who've retired and fallen in love with the scenery. At the point where the Rheidol and Mynach rivers meet there are three bridges stacked one on top of the other. The original, lowest, one was probably built by the monks from Strata Florida around 1075. When lead mining was at its peak in the eighteenth century, another arch was built on top and finally a road bridge on top of that in 1901. The legend — about why it's called Devil's Bridge — is a quite common tale in Wales. The Devil heard that a bridge was required across the chasm formed by the River Mynach, and offered to build one in return for the soul of the first living creature to cross the finished bridge. However, the first creature across was a dog chasing a round loaf of bread, so the Devil was outwitted.

At the entrance to Mynach Falls I paid 50p for a copy of a certificate which declared: 'Judith Chalmers and the *Wish You Were Here* crew have visited the world-renowned Devil's Bridge, Mid-Wales'.

Next stop was the Vale of Rheidol Steam Railway, back up on the main road, heading west out of the village. It takes an hour on these little trains to travel the 11¾ miles to Aberystwyth. Built in 1902 to service the lead mines and timber trade, the line was run by British Rail until 1989 but is now privately owned. Sadly, I didn't have time for the train journey, but I admired the gleaming paintwork of the *Owain Glyndwr*. In the little café, tourists were drinking coffee and awaiting departure time. The car park was packed with railway enthusiasts. This little line takes about 40,000 passengers a year and has three engines.

Dragging myself away from the Thomas the Tank Engine memorabilia, I walked along the road past the post office, heading west out of the village. After the last house, a

bungalow, I turned right by a footpath sign. I went across a field, entered some woods, and then dropped down to the railway tracks. I was very high up at this point and could see the gorge dropping away to my right and rising up on the other side of the valley. A series of tracks passed through a beautiful oak forest, heading westwards, zig-zagging down, sometimes crossing the railway track, and entering a nature reserve on the other side. This somewhat lackadaisical route didn't really bother me, as it was extraordinarily peaceful and beautiful. Inside the forest I had a carpet of brown leaves to walk on, and every now and then an interesting mushroom to investigate. Eventually I crossed the track one last time and dropped drastically down towards the river below, the sound of which became an increasing roar. This was about a mile below the falls, but the river still had an urgency and life of its own.

I found a wooden footbridge and crossed the river. Above and below was a series of rock pools which must have been delightful to swim in during the summer. Unfortunately the water had a rather ugly white scum on it. Perhaps a camper had tipped washing-up liquid into the river, higher up. On the other side of the bridge was a tarmac road, which I crossed, before taking a tiny track that rose up very steeply. I'd already seen, on the way downstream, a disused mine. Now I was to climb a 1:2 path to rise above it.

After 100 feet or so, the path crossed a couple of tram tracks, obviously from the quarry. These were soft, gentle, broad grassy tracks. If only they'd been my route, but of course they weren't. I got hotter and hotter, toiling my way up, the chill wind completely forgotten. I took off my fleece. Eventually I got to a T-junction, turned right, eastwards, and after a few hundred yards emerged at the head of the quarry. At this point there were a few ruined buildings. From a pool of bright mustard-yellow water coloured by the oxides in the stone, a little yellow stream ran across my path and tipped down the hillside.

I stood there sweating and gasping, drinking from my bottle of water. Then I looked across – I could hear the sound of the steam train. It was directly opposite me on the other side of the valley. I heard a little poo-pooing noise, the sound of the train toiling up the valley; after about two minutes it came into view.

It was pulling three carriages, and it really didn't seem to be travelling much faster than I'd walked. After another few minutes it emerged in the clearing on the other side of the gorge. By the time the train had passed, I'd got my breath back and resumed my climb uphill. I climbed round and above the end of the ruined mine buildings, and then up through woods, which soon stopped being beautiful oaks and gave way to dreary pines. At the end of it, I turned north over some rocks that were covered in pink heather, now sadly past its best. Once over a stile, I emerged into pastureland. I was at the top!

I crossed the meadow and ahead of me were real rocky outcrops, bare stones; it looked exactly like the slightly lunar landscape around Strata Florida. If you didn't know there was a gorge behind you, you'd have no idea how high up you were.

To my right was a disused school building which looked pretty grotty. Over the top of a stone wall I could see some urns: I was by a cemetery. I skirted round these buildings and a youth hostel, and emerged, after a very soggy 25 yards in which I managed to get both feet completely wet, onto a narrow road. Here I turned right. There was a lot of debris about, including a wrecked car. What a shame that such a beautiful spot looked like a rubbish dump.

I continued along the road, heading north-east. After the rubbish next to the youth hostel, I was surprised to see, on my left, an expensive-looking, newly built bungalow, complete with leaded windows and a swanky XJS Jaguar in the driveway. Someone had pots of money!

I carried on up this road, passing another beautifully restored farmhouse, which had views to the south, right over the gorge and the mountains beyond. I took a sheep path and headed over pastureland on the northern edge of the mountains, encountering some bad bog at the bottom.

Having found a stile, I walked across fields to a small stream, where suddenly, whoever's in charge of paths in the area had built a smart new stile and a new bridge over the stream. I crossed the stream and went up through a gate onto the A44, which was distressingly busy. Then I turned right in front of the George Borrow Hotel: the beer garden with all its empty picnic tables was a sad sight, with not a car in the car park.

After the hotel there was a forestry plantation on my right. The branches of the trees pushed me further into the road than I would have liked, and two huge lorries en route to Aberystwyth nearly forced me off – it was a frightening experience.

Just before the junction with the road to Devil's Bridge was a terraced house, painted white, with signs stuck all over it, proclaiming it as the home of the real Welsh dragon. And, sure enough, along the front white wall were stuck lots of bright red, plaster-of-Paris, Welsh dragons. Apparently you could go in and buy them. I laughed out loud at the incongruity of it!

I turned right on the A4120 and, by a bend in the road, I took a track heading east. On the edge of a forestry plantation I sat on a slope and ate lunch. Then I had a wonderful find: some huge field mushrooms sitting right by the path, the size of table tennis bats. I photographed them and took six, carefully stowing them in my rucksack.

After this, I walked along the B4343, still heading east, slightly south of the horrible A44. Eventually my road curved up to the A44 by a disused old mine, and I had another nasty couple of hundred yards until I got to the Dyffryn Castell Inn. Just before it, I saw a bizarre sign that said 'Interesting bar meals'. Well that's a first in my book!

At this point I decided to leave the ascent of Plynlimon for another day: according to my maps, the path started on the far side of the pub. I planned to visit Llanidloes instead, a few miles down the road. It was the most beautiful Victorian and early Georgian town,

'Unique' and 'original' Welsh Dragons for sale on the A44 near Dyffryn Castell.

with two or three main streets and a fine market building in the middle, an impressive Victorian town hall, and side streets of pretty brick, terraced Victorian houses. In the tea shop I ate a toasted teacake and read a leaflet about making rocking horses – one was in the window. I realized, when I saw the Laura Ashley shop, that this was the home of that organization.

After a walk round the town, we were driven back to Aberystwyth. On the way we passed a huge Elvis sign that had just been graffittied on one of the rocks. So I took a picture of Iwan, my driver, standing on it, playing an air guitar made out of a log. Then it was back for a huge dinner, a lot of sorting out of the maps, and an early night.

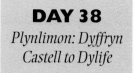

When I woke up there was a clear blue sky and a cold wind. It was very warm as I left the hotel, but I was glad I had my leggings on. I got to the Dyffryn Castell pub and met Donald Hoare, a local walker who was going to accompany me. He had on a wonderful pair of ancient plus-fours that he'd had specially made, and a very small and battered rucksack (like all walkers, he'd obviously had it for years). And he told me that he had owned the same knitted balaclava hat since the early fifties. I recognized all that only too well. Donald lived in the converted schoolhouse I'd walked past outside Cwmystwyth.

The route up Plynlimon was marked on the map as starting right by the pub, but there were no signs for a footpath. We climbed over a gate, walked through a fenced piece of land with a wooden garden shed in it, climbed over another fence, and followed the stream up.

After 50 yards we were absolutely sure we were on the footpath because we could see its outline. We followed the stream up for a mile, keeping old fencing on our right. Then we came to a flat area, bore slightly north-west, and started a really steep climb (probably about 800 feet) up the steep foothills of Plynlimon to the top of the escarpment. Way below, we could see cars toiling along the dreary A44, getting smaller and smaller.

We followed several sheep paths over a series of hillocks, occasionally stumbling across boggy bits and being careful not to drop down into steep and very eroded slopes. After about half an hour, we saw the edge of a forestry plantation.

Plynlimon is really more than one mountain. It is the highest point in Mid-Wales (2467 feet) but, more importantly, it forms a wilderness area of about 80 square miles, with few roads, the large Nant-y-moch Reservoir to the west, five shapeless peaks and a lake – Llyn Lygad Rheidol. George Borrow said, 'It does not look like much of a hill,' but climbed it all the same. Well, we were following in his footsteps, plodding up this large grassy fell, enjoying spectacular views and a fine day. The area is also the source of many rivers, including the Rheidol, the Severn and the Wye.

So we headed north-west, skirting around deep forestry, until we met a fence coming in from the right, and then took an almost northerly route over undulating grassy ground. The track was indistinguishable in places and clearer in others. We simply kept the fence on our left all the way to Plynlimon, where there was a stile over a fence and a trig point. The top was pretty flat and featureless, though there were a couple of stone pens which we were very happy to rest inside in order to get out of the wind. It was extremely hot, but the wind was icy. It was an unbelievably clear day to be on top of Plynlimon, which is famous for attracting a lot of mist.

After I'd taken some photos from the trig point (from which you can see at least 20 miles in every direction), we headed east, climbed to Pumlumon Fawr, and then turned north to Pen Pumlumon Lygad-bychen. While circling the lake, Llyn Lygad Rheidol, we

Having lunch with a local walker, Donald Hoare, on the slopes of Plynlimon.

passed the Glyndwr Stone, which marks the site of the first battle fought by nationalist Owain Glyndwr to create an independent Wales.

I would have loved to have spent time on this bleak, grassy group of peaks, but two factors destroyed any reverie I might have had: gale force winds and incessant aircraft. Not more than five minutes passed all day without a jet making its way overhead.

To the east lay a forestry plantation, and, as the summits broadened out, it was harder to appreciate the magnificent drops to the north of the main summit. At the end of a fence we continued in the same northerly direction. Then we saw two small pools about a mile away and headed for them. The path was generally pretty clear; to be honest, it wasn't difficult walking at all.

The pools were limpid and still, reflecting the clear, blue sky. And the boggy grass around them was an extraordinary combination of colours: bright rusty red, orange, yellow, bright

green. Around the pools were several large slates that looked like tombstones, with 'WWW 1865' carved on them. Of course, sadly, they weren't tombstones for the World Wide Web Site or the Internet; they were marking the boundary of the water catchment area.

After the pools we made for Carn fawr. This little peak is not really clear, but we headed north over the brow of the hill. The trek there was the best part of the whole walk, for my money. We were now in a totally isolated valley, with no paths, no walkers; even the jet planes which had plagued us all day seemed to have stopped. Thank goodness for Donald's company – he helped me to find the right way down.

The going was tough here: down through deep heather, bilberry bushes and bog, with no paths. We had to negotiate our way carefully. But it was spectacular, better than any summit, to be in such a vast valley floor with nothing around but the odd hawk or sheep and complete silence except for the squelch of our boots.

We climbed up onto a dirt track and walked round a tranquil lake which had lily pads all around the edges and a little boathouse at one end. Having crossed a bridge, we turned a corner and there was a ruined farmhouse, which had once been the centre of a magnificent estate. Now it had no roof, no windows; next to it was a new barn. A very lonely spot – we were truly in Mid-Wales.

George Borrow had ascended Plynlimon with a local shepherd as his guide: 'A tall athletic fellow, dressed in brown coat, round bull hat, corduroy trousers, linen leggings.' They drank from the sources of all the rivers and then returned to the Dyffryn Castell pub for ale and a meal. Donald had been my guide; I had enjoyed his sprightly company and now said goodbye.

From the ruined farmhouse, I looked for a track to head north-east up a hillside, towards the settlement of Dylife. Well, my problems started straight away. No sooner had I left the track than I walked straight into a bog and went in almost up to my knees. I managed to stagger across the stream and then up the opposite hillside, where I immediately changed my socks.

After crossing a flat boggy plain, I headed east and picked up a stream on my right. Eventually I came to an isolated barn and some farm buildings, dropped right down, and crossed a river coming in from the north over a footbridge. Then I climbed in a north-easterly direction, over a series of grassy hills. The river was thundering down to my right and I could see a series of disused lead and silver mines. The whole place had an indescribably melancholy atmosphere; it just felt about the loneliest place you could ever imagine working in.

I skirted round some more trees on a very muddy track, crossed over a river and then hugged it all the way into Dylife. Above me was a series of houses. Outside one was a sign that said 'Panic Puppet Theatre' – it seemed so incongruous.

Around me were mountains that seemed to hold memories of everything that had gone before. To the right the stream flowed through a series of spoil heaps from the mines, and there were ruins of buildings and caves. I came up a track to a road, crossed over it by a phone box, and entered the Star Inn, an old building, with some mountain bikes resting by the door and a couple of cars in the car park.

The Star Inn was a jolly place, run by two English women: Sue (a Londoner) and Claire (a Scouser). Despite being in such a remote area, they had six walkers staying that night. Aled, a local farmer, explained to me that only 100 years ago there would have been 2000 people living in Dylife; in those days, it was a thriving mining community. Miners used to walk up to 20 miles to get there by daybreak on a Monday morning to sign on for a week's work, then they'd sleep in shifts. Now it was a ghost town and the community was down to 35.

In the bar I met ex-Python Terry Jones, his wife Alison, and their dog Mitch. They'd walked up the hill from their cottage nearby – they were regulars. At first they used to stay in a friend's cottage, then they rented it, and finally bought it.

Terry is a highly intelligent fellow, with an open, friendly and relaxed manner. He and his wife have been coming up to this area for over 20 years. He was born in Colwyn Bay in North Wales (the son of a bank clerk), but his parents were English. Terry says he feels very Welsh, particularly when he's in Wales, and talked very eloquently about what was special about the area: 'You get a feeling of freedom in this part of the world, which is absolutely unique, and I don't think there's any other part of the world where you can actually go anywhere you want to up on the mountains. We walked over here this afternoon, and you can go anywhere, you can climb any mountain, you can go in any direction…'

Of course Terry was taking a romantic view. Mark my words, if any farmers see walkers not on a footpath, there's no predicting how they will react, although Aled seemed very pro-ramblers. His family were originally tin miners from Cornwall, and came to the area to work in the lead mines, turning to farming when the lead industry declined. Nowadays farming couldn't be their only source of income: he and his wife need the money from walkers, and he said the Welsh locals would have to accept that leisure and tourism would be part of their way of life in the future. Over the last 20 years almost everybody Welsh had moved out to the towns, and incomers – some Welsh, some English – had moved in to take their places. They'd restored the farmhouses and some had stayed and started little businesses. I thought Aled's was a very sane and interesting point of view, because so much twaddle is written about preserving the rural way of life; you have to accept that the way the countryside is used, and who lives in it, changes like everything else.

And on that sensible note (with Terry admitting he harboured a secret desire to be crowned King of Wales – I *think* he was joking), I left them to their pints and headed to Aberystwyth and dinner.

decided to walk this long and isolated stretch with my friend Janet. We started early one morning by the Star Inn. Above the pub was the graveyard and a ruined church. We turned north up a dirt track, and continued in a vaguely northerly direction. Then we went through a gate and round a barn, in which two farmers were sitting with their sheepdogs. We said hello, but they didn't answer. Not as friendly as Aled – or perhaps they didn't wish to speak English? Then it was through another gate, where we headed north, still up the track, until it dropped down over a stream. Now, according to *The Cambrian Way*, we had to find an undefined path by the stream and head north-west. Well, that was a laugh! We climbed up through the heather and bilberries but we couldn't find the track.

As we passed through a couple of fenced fields, we began to see the biggest mushrooms ever. They were sprouting up everywhere, like strange white protuberances: balls of all different sizes – plates, saucers, dinner plates! It was hilarious – we just laughed and laughed. There was a fresh wind and a remarkable feeling of openness and spaciousness. We felt like the only people for 10 miles, and, apart from the two farmers we'd seen in the barn way back, we probably *were!* It was obvious that hardly anyone ever walked here. Most of the gates were tied, and the paths were through bracken and heather, and very hard to follow.

At a kind of summit we followed a track and looked north. We could see miles ahead, and make out Cadair Idris and, closer, Moelfre. By now it was very grey and cloudy, with a little patch of blue sky, and we imagined that Snowdon was the far peak we could see maybe 20 or 30 miles away. Anyway, the broad, grassy track we were now on dropped down from our high plateau. Then it curved slightly around to

Mushrooms as big as berets!

our right and a steep hill rose up, with even bigger mushrooms. We lay on the ground with our heads next to them and photographed each other, laughing hysterically. Thank goodness there were no other walkers or farmers about. They would have thought we were nuts – especially when I made Janet wear a particularly big flat mushroom as a beret for an 'art' study!

A solitary tree in a lonely valley near Maesteg.

Then we zig-zagged through a wood and up over a hill. There's something so totally irritating about walking in forestry plantations, where little way mark posts have been put up every now and then, and you know that you're zig-zagging up and down in order to go only a few hundred yards, because that's the way they've decided you're going to go.

The light was completely different in the wood. These trees were 30 or 40 years old and you couldn't see through them – it was pitch dark. At one point we walked through on a narrower path and felt completely enclosed by the stillness and silence. Under the trees were some of the largest ceps I'd ever seen. We left the forest through a narrow gate, then walked over the brow of the hill and skirted another mountain called Moelfre. We headed east and then followed a wire fence through the moor, where, irritatingly, a new shooting track had just been cut by farmers to the south of us.

We were walking a ridge from west to east and we could see for miles. Having passed an old reservoir at one of the highest points, the track started to curve north-west. We looked forward and could see Moel Eiddew to our north; we were now at the pass of Bwlch Glynmynydd.

We were very tired. It had been quite hard walking – about 8 miles so far. Our track curved down and met a road, and this was when our troubles started. According to a diagram and the map, we were supposed to take a footpath directly opposite. We missed it. We took a path but it soon disappeared, and we found ourselves lost in a forestry plantation – so badly lost that we were crawling on our hands and knees. We went from laughing earlier at all the huge mushrooms to now being really frightened. I knew from the map that we had to head north to get out of it, but what I didn't know was that we were too far east, so when we got to the northern edge of the forest, the land just dropped away, sheer. We went a little way round the outside of it and realized it was extremely dangerous.

It was really hard to walk over ground which had been turned into a series of furrows for pine trees. It was very slippery and overgrown, and we made slow progress. We re-entered the forest, and walked down an avenue, putting our coats over our heads so the branches didn't scratch our faces. Finally we saw a light at the end of what seemed like an endless tunnel of trees. We walked towards it and found ourselves in a clearing, carried on and got to the edge of the wood. There we found a track and then a gate that was marked on the map.

The path we took bore no relation to the map; I think the maps were inaccurate and that the forest had been planted over existing paths. Anyway, to cut a long story short, we took a track that undulated round various hills, finally dropping to a ruin. Here, thank God, a decent stone track took us west, following a river; then the track ran out. After this we skirted a headland and found the road at Maesteg. It was about 2 miles long, dropping gradually to Commins Coch. Soon we could hear the River Twymyn to our right and the sound of cars travelling along the busy A470.

On our left we passed a small stone cottage. It was about 6 o'clock and the door was open. An old man sat having his tea, watching television. But he was listening to The Prodigy – rave music belted out through the windows of the house. He was obviously stone deaf.

Now, according to the map, we had to take a footpath on our right, down to the river, to get into Commins Coch. We crossed over, went down a field and found that the footpath had been blocked up. So we climbed over a gate and walked down through a driveway to the road.

I looked back and a sign said: 'Danger. Private Property. Keep Out. Rottweilers at large'. What a load of old garbage: it was simply someone's driveway and they objected to it being a footpath. We were at the junction of the A470 and our little B road, which went under it to the rest of the village.

We were exhausted, but had rucksacks full of delicious mushrooms, even if our limbs were scratched from our exploits in the evil forestry plantation.

DAY 40
Commins Coch to Dinas Mawddwy

When I woke up I mused how, on a long-distance walk like this one, you are totally unaware of man-made boundaries like county lines. I was on a journey through clearly defined land masses, from one mountain range to another, via long rivers, wide grassy ridges and bleak, windswept moorland and bog. Ahead might lie the peaks of Snowdonia, but for the moment I was in the under-populated and unspoilt rural landscape of Mid-Wales, far from the tourist honeypots of the Brecon Beacons or Snowdon. This area was a long way from anywhere: forgotten by the government power-brokers in Cardiff and the middle classes in Llandudno and the Conwy Valley. The railway didn't even bother to stop in the little hamlet of Commins Coch and the busy A470 bisected the place. Round here lived hard-core proponents of alternative living, with their recycling bins and fish ponds (there was a large Centre for Alternative Technology down the road to the west). But mainly people got on with the thankless task of sheep farming, offering bed and breakfast to the occasional walker to supplement their income.

I started the day by the sign that said 'Rottweilers at large', went under the A470 and climbed up through the village, travelling north along a narrow lane. I was very stiff from the day before, so I made pretty slow progress. The air was still muggy, with no wind whatsoever. Clouds filled the sky, which was uniformly grey; it looked almost thundery.

I followed this pretty lane, climbing up and heading north-east, past a farm that was for sale. After a while I went onto Glyndwr's Way, an enclosed lane that was muddy underfoot with hawthorn trees almost making a tunnel overhead. I headed east, then cut up north-

Opposite: Discussing the plight of sheep farmers with the Reverend Michael Balchin.

west along another lane, where, at a farm called Tynllwyn, I met the Reverend Michael Balchin, a vicar who had become a farmer and was having his sheep dipped. He was over six feet tall, ramrod-straight, with white hair and a wiry build, wearing a green rubber jacket and wellingtons. He had driven his sheep up there to use his friend Derek's sheep dip.

Michael used to be a parish priest on the edge of Exmoor, and then, 10 or so years ago, he'd decided to start again as a farmer. He told me it was tough, and he and his wife had worked out that they end up earning 25p an hour each for all their effort.

The sheep about to be dipped looked like healthy, white, rounded animals in peak condition, yet Michael told me that their wool was used for carpets – it simply wasn't as fine a quality as Australian wool, which was preferred for clothing. And no one ate mutton any more, so they were basically breeding carpet tiles for the world!

I left Michael pushing his sheep through the dip, making sure their heads went under at least twice to fight the sheep scab that starts around their ears. The sheep were hating it! I found out later that the farm I had passed down the road with the 'For Sale' board was Michael's. He told me it had been very, very hard to sell and he was planning to retire and buy a house in the area. He really enjoyed living here, but the farming was just too tough.

I headed east, through one of Derek's fields, up a steep slope, and I could see wind farm turbines just over the brow of the hill. After I'd climbed up several hundred feet, I was really panting. It was pathetic – after all the slogging I'd done the day before. Then I picked up a road, followed it up to the brow of the hill and cut across in a northerly direction to the very top. The wind farm turbines hadn't been moving when I'd been down in the bottom of the valley, but from nowhere a gust or two seemed to spring up, and they whirred into action. It was one of the eeriest moments of my life – following this deserted road along the top of the Mynydd y Cemais ridge, passing 24 turbines all slowly whirring away. It sounded as if the blades were almost tearing through the air. I thought they were a welcome addition to this ridge, which was perfectly flat and boring on top. At least they gave it a feature.

This was the first wind farm in Wales when it opened in 1992 (now there are 10). The 24 turbines were connected to gearboxes that drove a generator; the land was rented from local farmers for a good rate (another source of income), and their sheep munched happily away around this controversial development. Local opinion seemed to be split – the farmers liked the money but the trendy incomers didn't want their view spoilt. To my mind, they were no more of an eyesore than evil dark green forestry plantations! However, all these turbines only made enough electricity for 4500 households a year, according the maintenance man I chatted to, and they did cover a large swathe of landscape and were visible for miles: I'd first spotted them when climbing out of Dylife the day before.

At the end of the wind farm, I skirted along the edge of a forestry plantation and headed north. From now on, the route took an irritating zig-zag around a bog – it was pretty wet even on the edge – and then it joined up with a path and led north-east over another ridge. At the top of the hill I was supposed to head north-west down the hill, find a ruin at Bryn Glas, and then follow a track north. I followed the river bed down and found what I thought was the right ruin, but then I had a disagreement with John, the director, about what path to take. Unfortunately I let John's word prevail. We immediately took the wrong path and headed due east, crossing a river and ending up on a B road going in completely the wrong direction.

When we finally got to the road I realized the mistake we'd made, and turned west, walking up farm tracks, until we rejoined the official route. I suppose it was only a detour of a mile and a half, but it was all uphill – another little cross to bear. I wearily wound my way west, contouring round a hill and passing through a couple of farmyards. Pheasants and partridges bred in these woods scurried across the little-used track.

Finally I emerged at the roundabout at Mallwyd, crossed over it and took a B road opposite that followed the meandering River Dovey, about half a mile away from the main road. I was in a new and more dramatic landscape now. Mountains, not fells, rose up steeply on either side of the river, signalling the start of my approach to the spectacular peak of Cadair Idris. Exciting Welsh legends tell of how, around the year 1550, this area was terrorized by a particularly vicious gang of red-haired bandits. The local population used to put scythes and sickles up their chimneys to prevent them from breaking into their houses that way. The bandits robbed settlements and rustled cattle and sheep in broad daylight, before returning to their dens in the mountains.

I went over the main road and walked between rows of restored mill workers' cottages, with Victorian Gothic windows. Some were still in the process of being done up. It seemed a happy place, with children playing on their bicycles, well-tended front gardens, and an air of community.

Then I took the footpath back up the main road and cut down again to Dinas Mawddwy. This village had no heart, no post office, and one pub; it seemed dead as a doornail. By the Red Lion, I turned left and went up to the main road, to my hotel nearby.

How the landscape had changed since I'd left Llandovery. These mountains had steep sides and exposed areas of shale. Here the road was cut through, rather than undulating over, hills. On my way out of the village I noticed a small sign that said, 'Hand Made Welsh Furniture'. I peered through and saw a dresser, just like the one in my granny's house when I was a child.

Overleaf: Passing the wind farm with its 24 prominent turbines on the eerie and deserted road at the top of Mynydd y Cemais.

I started off at 12 o'clock exactly today – zig-zagging up through a wood in which forestry workers were busy chopping down trees right across the path, so it was quite hard to follow. They recognized me and cheerfully directed me on my way. After climbing a few hundred feet, I joined a forestry road and skirted north-west on it, then I made the big mistake of turning up from it and going along some steps. After rising another 75 feet I realized I was going nowhere – it was simply steps to a manhole cover, and I was hemmed in by barbed wire on two sides. I slid back down, rejoined the forestry road, looked up and there, 25 yards further along it, was another footpath sign: how annoying. I now had to climb hundreds of feet on an extremely narrow footpath, zig-zagging up through bracken, heather and young rhododendrons. It was the first time I'd seen them on this walk – some were in flower and there were a lot of fresh new shoots. The path seemed little used. In many places trees had been cut down to open it up more, but it was very slippery and I had to be extremely attentive.

Then the path entered the forestry plantation, after which I crossed over a stile, headed west, skirted along the top edge of the forest, and contoured around the mountain of Foel Dinas, being careful not to lose any height. I then came to a fence and realized I needed to be about 100 feet higher up. The gradient was about 1:2, but I climbed up another 200 feet to make sure that when I met the ridge, around the corner, I wouldn't have to climb up to it along shale. The path was curving south-west, away from the main road. It then met the east–west ridge of Bwlch Siglen, which I crossed along the edge of the forestry plantation. Earlier, there hadn't been a cloud in the sky, but now it was getting cloudier and cloudier.

To the north of the ridge was a series of rocky crags, down which cascaded waterfalls hundreds of feet high. Bwlch Siglen was probably one of the most beautiful ridges I'd seen on the walk so far. I continued climbing up, keeping the forestry on my left, but heading towards the crags of Maesglase (as far above and behind them as I could).

I ate my lunch above the crags, in a little grassy hollow by a stream, but the wind soon got to me; I could only really stop for 15 minutes. I headed north along the rest of the ridge, climbing up to Maesglase (2211 feet). At this point, the sun came out. I was almost at the summit, facing north, looking at mountain after mountain (Snowdonia in all its glory), but they were still slightly misty. Clouds cast beautiful shadows on the wooded hills; below me were the grassy spurs of the mountain, and at the bottom of them, fields lined with oak trees, and little white farms dotted around the bottom of the valley. To the south lay a long, bare, grassy ridge, about the same height as me, with an old wire fence silhouetted on the skyline.

My only companions were sheep, a hawk that flew out of the forest, and hundreds of ugly, fat, round, dark brown, furry caterpillars. I resisted the impulse to tread on them, even though they popped up underfoot approximately every 20 yards.

The best thing about this part of the walk was that the path was extremely narrow and under-used, with no sign of erosion, and I couldn't see thousands of footsteps there ahead of me. (That had been one of the big disappointments of Plynlimon and many of the other mountains I'd walked.) In fact, climbing up to the ridge, the path was so narrow that the left side of my left foot started aching from gripping the slope.

Now I dropped down from the summit, walked alongside a fence, climbed over a ladder stile, and headed south-west over a second ridge. I stopped to put some suntan lotion on my face, and suddenly heard the unmistakable sound of a chain saw. Below me, to the south, lay a half-demolished forestry plantation, with someone busily at work. I skirted round and stood at Craig Portas, on the edge of a big, rocky bowl. To the north and east of me were sheer drops, wonderfully modelled in the late afternoon sun.

After I'd climbed across the ridge, I had my first low moment of the day: I realized I had to head further up to reach the summit of Cribin Fawr (2162 feet), involving a long, slow haul northwards. I got to the top but it meant going through some big peat hags. For the first time I could see Cadair Idris in front of me. It stood away to the west in the late afternoon light, surrounded in a blue haze. It was much higher than the summit I was on, and I realized the enormity of the climb that lay ahead.

My legs were exhausted by the time I got to the top of Cribin Fawr. The peat hags were enormous and involved lots of climbing up and down; due to the long drought, it was quite possible to walk across some of the boggy bits without my feet going in.

After this I went over a stile and followed a fence on my right. I could see my next summit, which was Waun-oer. Irritatingly, it was about the same height as Cribin Fawr, but it involved a hike down a ridge and then up some rocky protuberances.

I dropped down, hugging the fence (which was a good idea). Below me was a large forestry plantation, and an ugly new forestry road had been cut into the south side of Waun-oer a few hundred feet below; it looked like a fresh wound. I went over another little stile, and then began the climb up through the rocks, sometimes on all fours. Although I was tired, I didn't mind a really steep slope because at least I was gaining height quickly and, as I'd eaten all my lunch, my rucksack wasn't that heavy. The main problem was the wind blowing in from the south. As I got higher up the ridge, I was nearly knocked sideways against the fence by a particularly strong gust. I put on my jacket and my hat with ear flaps, and tied it firmly down. Thank goodness there was no one around to see how stupid I looked!

First of all there was what looked like a radio mast or a weather station, and then I saw the trig point (2198 feet) for Waun-oer behind the fence. I climbed over to it; the sun was blazing, but the wind was icy. I hugged the trig point for a minute to prove I was there, then climbed back over the fence and had a rather long hike, with the fence on my right and a forestry plantation on my left, for at least 2 miles. Cadair Idris lay ahead of me the entire time, like a beacon – the Holy Grail that I had to achieve next!

Finally there was a stile, and I turned to the north and dropped down on a path that became more and more indistinct. I crossed over numerous streams, keeping some crags on my right, then over a very old path by some stone walls. After this, my path cut between two crags to drop down to the road, and became blue shale. The final section, from the stile down to Hotel Minffordd, involved a terrifying walk along a road full of lorries carrying logs, and cars determined to turn it into a race track.

My path now dropped down from the road to the valley floor: it was a steep, v-shaped valley, with the eastern flank of Cadair Idris on my right. Following a stream down a couple of miles, I found the sound of the traffic intrusive after my day's peace and solitude. After a campsite I rejoined the 'racetrack' and was extremely glad to reach Hotel Minffordd, with Tal-y-Llyn lake ahead in the setting sun. Hotel Minffordd had a restaurant but it was firmly closed – a shame as I'd been dreaming of a gin and tonic all the way down from the stile!

It had been an exhilarating but tough walk. I was sure elsewhere in Britain it must have been 85 degrees, but on top of those mountains it was about 50. Out of the wind it was really warm, but the wind was Arctic. Once again I could see the damage the afforestation was doing to the area: it's OK when the forest is young and looks relatively fresh, but large areas I'd walked through today had been hacked down, creating great ugly scars on the landscape. Nevertheless, some of the walk had been through a secret part of the mountains, far from any roads, and I'd seen some beautiful valleys, without a house, road or track in them; so it had been a rewarding five hours.

DAY 42
Cadar Idris to Barmouth

Today Janet and I climbed Cadair Idris. I had already tried to do so the day before but, when I got to Hotel Minffordd, the cloud was down to about 100 feet: I couldn't even see above the forestry, so I'd abandoned it. Last night I still felt the pressure of this walk really strongly. I woke up at 3 o'clock in the morning going over the route again in my head. When you climb a mountain, you need to establish a steady pace and not stop, because every time you stop you get cold and your legs get stiff.

The afternoon when I'd walked from Dinas Mawddwy, I'd looked across and Cadair Idris had risen up without a cloud on it, looking majestic, the long ridge up to it and the broad shoulder hiding the lake. Since then Cadair Idris had not been out of cloud: it seemed to exist in its own micro-climate. Guides told me that the mountain was in cloud four days out of five, but I wanted to wait for the perfect day.

Anyway, to cut a long story short, I woke up at 7, felt a bit stiff, tried to think positively, looked out of the window and saw the cloud. After breakfast we drove round to the Hotel Minffordd car park, to be met by Jack Grass, our guide, and the porters who were going to carry up the filming equipment. We were now in the Snowdonia National Park: its

boundary was just south of Dinas Mawddwy and I'd be staying in the National Park all the way to Conwy, except for a little trip into Barmouth.

Janet and I have walked together for 25 years. She's a good listener, long-suffering, with a great sense of humour: the perfect walking companion. We've trekked together in the Himalayas, in Ireland, the Canary Islands and the Pyrenees. She has a pretty laid-back attitude to life, whereas I'm the first to admit I have a bit of a temper and am prone to sulk. We planned to climb up the Minffordd path, which is about 3 miles to the summit – the shortest and steepest route, involving about 2850 feet of ascent. Janet was immaculately clad in high-tech lightweight kit, whereas I was sporting a 15-year-old T-shirt and leggings with moth holes in them. We thus represented both extremes of the outdoor pursuits clothing debate. My boots cost £35, and hers most definitely did not.

From where we started, the cloud was high above the trees and the broad shoulder of Cadair Idris. Although we couldn't see the peak itself, the lake was well out of cloud.

So we started our ascent, up a stepped narrow path through a forest. Then we followed a river, heading north, until we left the bubbling stream and the forest below and entered a broad, grassy area, where we curved away to the west and continued to rise. You couldn't see the lake, Llyn Cau; it was hidden above us in a wonderful rocky amphi-theatre. At this point we could see above us the top of the ridge that we were going to climb, but the peak of Cadair Idris (2928 feet) was in cloud. As we toiled up the slope above the lake, the cloud began to come down surprisingly quickly. The drizzle really set in and we had to put on our waterproofs.

We met a team of young men who were repairing the path, paving it and building a series of steps. One brave soul was even camping up there in a tent! Although everybody had told me that Cadair Idris was one of the least-climbed mountains in Wales, it was perfectly clear that this path was pretty over-climbed. I'd read an article by Simon Jenkins in *The Times,* bemoaning the erosion of Cadair Idris, which he described as 'the loveliest peak in Wales'. Jenkins allowed that walkers cause erosion, but also talked of the drastic change in the mountain vegetation over the last few decades. Heather and bilberries have turned into grass and he blames over-grazing by sheep as farmers collect subsidies and the landscape is literally eaten away.

Anyway, we curved around and up, carefully climbing the loose shale. Then the going got much easier. It was still about 1:3 but this route would give us the longest ridge walk at altitude – and the best views.

Our guide, Jack Grass, was a cheery fellow in his sixties who used to run an outward bound centre and had climbed this mountain over 500 times. He regaled us with stories about the history of the mountain, the birds he'd seen recently, the flora and fauna, the geology; in fact he never drew breath. But we didn't mind – he was a mine of information and obviously loved the mountain so much.

Previous page: Jack Grass points the way to the top of Cadair Idris.
Above: Two Janets, soaked through and trying to get some shelter from the awful weather.

When we had finished climbing to the west around the lake, we continued around the rocky amphitheatre that encircles it and headed north, still rising, following cairns. In some places the path was extremely rocky. We went over a ladder stile and continued to rise to the peak of Craig Cwm Amarch (2595 feet), then dropped down onto the saddle briefly, before making the final ascent, heading north, and then finally north-east up to the top of Cadair Idris.

It was a shame that we couldn't see more than 100 yards through the swirling mist. Occasionally the lake came into view, but basically on the final ascent the rain was pelting

down and we were freezing cold, so we just pressed on to get to the trig point. It hadn't taken us that long to climb up, and, to be honest, it wasn't at all dangerous, although I could see that if people were stupid enough to get close to the steep drop down to the lake in high winds it might be another matter.

The final ascent was not as bad a gradient as I'd encountered elsewhere; only the high winds made it a little unpleasant. We passed the ruins of a café built in the eighteenth century by a guide from Dolgellau, Richard Pugh, where we could clearly see a stove, a really incongruous sight in the mist and rain. After the trig point we walked a few yards and then saw a shelter: a cosy little place with a bench outside, which, of course, no one was sitting on because it was freezing. Inside, it was snug and warm, with a bench all the way round and nails on the beams to hang your clothes to dry off.

We sat and drank our tea and coffee and got up a good old steam. Jack told me that one fanatic had spent Christmas in this shelter. He'd gone up there for three days with all his own food, put up decorations and had a really good celebration. I can only assume he was some kind of masochist because I can't imagine it would be very warm at night. I went outside and took some blurry snaps in the swirling cloud, remembering all the Welsh legends about kings being killed by Saxons and giants.

From the summit we headed down a slope, westwards. The first 200 metres were somewhat steep, but the pony path was clearly marked, and even in the wind and rain we were able to follow it. We gradually descended, bearing north-west, to where a lot of tracks converged. At this point we headed off sharply north, still following the pony path. This was about the easiest mountain descent I'd had in weeks, even though Cadair Idris was the highest peak of my journey so far. As I've said so often, let the macho men tick off summits on their lists and charts; it's the totality of the walk that interests me!

We passed through a bog where plastic mesh had been laid with stone on the top to try and hold the ground more firmly in place. It had worked and was not as unpleasant as walking across bog; on the other hand, walking on plastic netting does feel a bit unnatural.

Suddenly we walked out of the cloud and could see north, across the valleys in front of us, and to the west, Barmouth and the sea. The green grass of the valleys below us was sensational, especially after walking all day on grey rock with just a few patches of bright green lichen.

At a gate in a wall, we headed north, following a track down a pretty steep slope – we had to watch ourselves on the grass. Eventually we emerged in a lane, and to our right was a little sign that said 'Teas', so we went down a track to a farm called Tynyceunant. There, Mrs Jones made Janet and me tea for £1.20 each, and we ate her delicious mixed fruit cake, the recipe for which we managed to prise out of her. It seemed to involve a cup of sugar, half a pound of butter, a load of mixed fruit and her secret ingredients (a pinch of mixed spice and some bicarbonate of soda).

While we walked, Janet and I reminisced about our return to Kathmandu after three weeks of tent life; we went into the smartest hotel and asked for a really nice room. When I got into the lift I said 'Excuse me' to a dusty, red-coloured person who was in there. Then I realized it was me – I hadn't had a mirror for three weeks and I was covered in dust and absolutely filthy! Our first gin and tonic in Kathmandu was the best in years – especially after weeks of black tea, tea with butter (ugh!) and alcohol made from potatoes, rice and corn on the cob.

Back in Wales, we walked west for over a mile along the tiny road, the mountain rising above us on our left. At a cattle grid we took a track which led up towards a farm, across the slope of the valley, and went through a farmyard where a barking dog ran round us in circles. I had heard that a lot of farmers in the area were very hostile to people walking the Cambrian Way, so I was feeling a bit nervous at this stage.

Anyway, we went on over various stiles, and climbed up a track on the hill past the farm. After a mile, a woman emerged from the stone farmhouse below, got in a Land Rover and belted up the track behind us. Janet and I felt extremely anxious. What was she doing? Was she going to object that we were walking the Cambrian Way and stop us? She caught up with us and so did her dog, which had been following. She jumped out of the Land Rover and rushed towards me: 'Please, please can I have your autograph? I heard you were walking this way and I really want it for my daughter.' We just laughed with relief, I signed the piece of paper and we had a little chat. Then we continued, skirting round the mountain that had hidden our view of the lake, and going across the valley floor which had rust-coloured grass in the really boggy patches. A lot of the land here was owned by the National Trust, and they'd been out signposting everything.

Ahead of us lay one of the most beautiful lakes I'd ever seen. Llynnau Gregennen has an island in the middle of it and has apparently featured in lots of car advertisements. To the north, a pretty hill rose up, with an Iron Age fort and some interesting archaeological ruins on it. We skirted round the northern edge of the lake, on a well-defined track through the heather, and then got to the car park where we met the crew. Now, depressingly, the cloud was dropping down and, although the lake itself wasn't going to vanish in mist, Cadair Idris certainly had.

After the car park we took a signposted track to head east over a series of fields, in the direction of Arthog, only pausing to pick field mushrooms. At the end of the track we crossed a stream which we followed as it cascaded down the hillside to the Arthog Waterfalls through a wood of old oak trees; it was extremely beautiful.

On the road at Arthog we turned right and then immediately left, following a raised

Opposite: Making our way down from the rocks of Cadair Idris. Breaking free of the clouds at last, we could appreciate the green of the valleys spread out before us.

path across a field to a series of mud flats – a nature reserve. Signs announced a whole succession of trails and nature walks. And the spectacular sight of Barmouth and its estuary lay ahead of us, with mountains dropping into the water: more like a lake in Italy or Switzerland than an estuary in Mid-Wales.

We were now on a grassy meadow, where sheep munched away happily; it was edged with reeds and, every now and then, a little hillock with pine trees. We headed north to the sand and then emerged by an incongruous Victorian red-brick terrace of houses facing Mawddach Estuary.

To the west, lay the wonderfully romantic, long, wooden, pedestrian and railway bridge spanning the mouth of the estuary. The railway arrived in 1866 (it's 1 mile across the bridge or 11 miles by road around the estuary). British Rail tried to close the line in 1971, but 800 written objections kept it open. From April to September it costs 50p to cross the bridge on foot and the toll house sits at the Barmouth end. In 1980, the wooden bridge was threatened by the toredo marine worm (which can grow up to 12 inches in length). Quite simply, the worms were boring into the timbers and now 80 of the piles have been replaced and protected with casings of glass.

We skirted round the back of the houses and went through an oak forest, which was the final headland before the bridge. We then crossed some mud flats and climbed up on the bridge itself. The tide was out, there was miles of mud and sand, and seagulls swooped about overhead. As we walked across the wooden bridge, it was like something from *Twin Peaks*. It made an indelible impression on me – undeniably thrilling and sexy: I could imagine bodies being washed up, assignations being fulfilled, people jumping from trains…

The estuary at Barmouth is surely one of the great undiscovered and un-fanfared wonders of Wales. Around it are magnificent, well-proportioned Victorian villas standing in elegant gardens. It is framed by mud flats, water meadows where sheep graze, and garlanded by mountains. The sand flats were gold and coppery coloured – and apparently gold-panning still goes on in the upper reaches of the river.

In front of us, Barmouth looked comfortably Victorian. There was one house apart from all the others, sitting on the very edge of the estuary. It had a tower with a clock in it – my dream house! I imagined a Victorian writer of Gothic novels living there and being inspired by the mist rolling off the mountains and the steam rising from the mud flats in the summer. Then I imagined myself living there, Gatsby-like, waiting for Mr Right to cross the bridge…

Barmouth itself seemed to consist of rows of grey stone houses, formed in neat terraces up the steep hillside above it, rather like a painting by Lowry. We entered the town and turned left along a front, which, if it hadn't been in Wales and had had a bit more money spent on doing the houses up, could have been the Cap d'Antibes. Anyway, it wasn't, it was

Barmouth. Lots of businesses were for sale, restaurants had closed down, there was a Woolworths and a Spar grocers in the High Street, two fish and chip shops (the Carousel and the Dolphin), and a pub, the Barmouth Arms (where we were later to go and hear a band playing blue grass – no matter how incongruous that sounds).

The town was overshadowed by the gigantic church of St John's, built halfway up the cliff: a magnificent structure. Frances Sarah Perrins (married to James Dyson Perrins, the son of the founder of Lea and Perrins) apparently decided the town needed a status symbol, and donated three-quarters of the money to build it. However, the church was constructed on a narrow ledge on the cliff above the town, and when the tower collapsed in 1891 Mrs Perrins came to the rescue once more. The building, complete now with a plaque by the lectern in memory of the late Mr Perrins, was finally finished in 1893.

Dotted around the town was a whole series of chapels, most of which had been turned into theatres, bargain shops and antique shops. One was now the Dragon Theatre, another was Chapel Antiques, another was Discount World (not to mention The Price Is Right) and one a garage.

Barmouth and its estuary certainly attracted Victorian gentry, with its sea-bathing and pleasure steamers running to and from Liverpool. A hundred years ago, Victorian hill walkers and mountaineers flocked here and used local guides to climb the Rhinogs and Cadair Idris. Everyone who was anyone, from Wilberforce and Ruskin to Tennyson, Darwin and Gladstone, visited the area. Apart from Mrs Perrins, the flour magnate Arthur MacDougall and the Cardiff tycoon Solomon Andrews both bought land here.

Now Barmouth's fortunes have declined: caravanners and coach trippers have replaced the Victorian middle classes, and the season has shrunk to a few weeks a year. By giving permission for huge caravan sites along the coast on the northern edge of the town, Barmouth signed its own death warrant. These revoltingly ugly, serried ranks of white boxes (yes, I *loathe* caravans) are not only visually repulsive, but also form little camps, with their own shops, bars and entertainment.

That night we repaired to the recently renovated Barmouth Hotel in the main street to meet Geoff Reynolds, a locally based banjo maker, who not only sells his instruments all over the world, but travels widely, playing in festivals. His band usually played here on Wednesdays to an audience of about 30. In the other bar, the patrons were more interested in the international football on the television. The band played everything from Celtic music to blue grass – all thoroughly catchy and enjoyable. Geoff said it was hard to get the locals out in the evening, which surprised me, as Barmouth didn't exactly offer a cornucopia of entertainment delights. He said it was a depressed area and the locals really counted their pennies.

Overleaf: Entering Barmouth across the wooden bridge which spans the estuary.

It was dark when we left the pub at 9.15, and Barmouth was already preparing for bed. I could see why blue grass music was so popular in Wales – I'd certainly walked across a lot of prairie over the last few weeks, although whether I'd felt lonesome or not was another matter, with the crew always a few paces behind!

DAY 43
Barmouth to Cwm Nantcol

Of all the walking in Wales, no other section excited me as much as the prospect of traversing the Rhinogs, the range that stretches from Barmouth and the Mawddach Estuary in the south to the Vale of Ffestiniog in the north – about 13 miles from point to point but a real endurance test in terms of terrain. I decided to split the range into two (only a superhuman would try to do it all in one day!) and come down at the pass between the two most famous peaks – Rhinog Fach and Rhinog Fawr – on an old drovers' path. From here I would head east until I could be picked up by the Land Rover. I was to walk with Rhodri Evans, a genial, bearded chap who was the Warden for the Rhinogs, a National Nature Reserve. (Rhodri also kept bees and did martial arts!)

My *Cambrian Way* guide was thrillingly cautious, describing this section as 'the most demanding, most rewarding and most controversial part' of the whole route, and adding: 'The traverse should not be undertaken unless the walker is capable of moving safely over difficult terrain…good navigational ability is essential and one must be prepared to take much longer than the distances suggest will be necessary'.

The Rhinogs are probably named after the Welsh for 'threshold' and they do form a formidable barrier between the land and the sea. Some writers have suggested that they may have taken their name from the Welsh word *rhiniol,* meaning 'secret and mysterious, or otherworldly'. As I had approached them from the south, I had no preconceived notions cluttering my mind. I was up for it, however difficult it might be. I didn't intend to give up!

I ate a delicious pair of kippers at the Penmaenuchaf Hall Hotel near Dolgellau: I was staying in a pretty room with a sloping roof and a fine view across Barmouth and the estuary. Rhinogs' Day One dawned grey, with odd bits of blue, but nothing to write home about. I set out from Barmouth, with the sea on my right, and walked past guest houses and hotels, until I came to a set of steps marked 'footpath'. I climbed up steeply, past people's gardens and kitchen windows, and was soon rewarded with fine views of the estuary and the dreamy bridge. Clouds were already massing on Cadair Idris on the other shore.

I met Rhodri, who was waiting where the footpath met a B road, and at 10 o'clock we struck off. We headed west, straight up to the crest of the hill and its radio mast, admiring the wonderful views of the estuary and the mountain ranges to the south. The weather was getting worse, however. Any scraps of blue sky had disappeared and the grey clouds seemed lower and more threatening.

We then headed north-east over a series of stiles, annoyingly dropping down slightly as we passed through fields, before turning left again and climbing due north, heading for the top of the ridge. Here we found a cairn and then had a thoroughly enjoyable tramp along the ridge, keeping a wall on our right. But the wind really started to pick up, so I put all my gear on – fleece, jacket, thick padded hat. Soon the rain was bucketing down, so I added my waterproof trousers, gloves and nylon poncho. The ground dropped steeply away on the other side of the wall and our path became rockier and rockier. We were gradually ascending to Diffwys, which is Welsh for 'precipice'! Rhodri asked if I wanted to continue, as the weather was atrocious, but I was all for going on. We actually climbed over the wall and hugged it to try and get out of the piercing wind coming from the west – the only trouble was, we were picking our way along a narrow rocky path between large boulders with a sheer drop on our right. It was extremely dangerous and our progress was slow (not helped by the fact that I had to keep wiping the rain off my glasses every five minutes to be able to see where I was going).

We continued along the wall till about 1.30, looking for shelter and finding none. Visibility was down to about 50 yards. Eventually we had lunch in the pouring rain, sitting with our backs to the wall – I wrapped my maps round my middle to try and block out the howling gale coming through the gaps between the stones. After 10 minutes we had to press on; it was too cold to stop. Our path followed the wall all the way along the ridge of Crib-y-rhiw – described in all the books as 'exhilarating'. My experience was a bit more primal, as the drop on my right became so precipitous that I had to climb back over the wall. I then made painfully slow progress, now with a drop on my left too, carefully picking my way between slippery boulders and muddy puddles, trying to keep my balance.

Parts of the route were, thankfully, grassy, but still slippery. We did not speak for what seemed like hours. All our attention was given to putting one foot in front of the other as we dragged ourselves up to the cairn at the summit of Y Llethr, a steeper lump at the edge of the ridge, which had a flat, grassy top. Now we had a steep drop over grass and then rocks to a pass, with Llyn Hywel on our left and the smaller Llyn y Bi on our right. At this point we could have struck off to the right, to the summit of Rhinog Fach, a couple of hundred feet above, but as the cloud was so low (we were now unable to see 20 yards ahead, let alone the summit), we decided to forgo this optional extra and take a terrifying rock path down to the Llyn Hywel. This path suddenly appeared out of the mist, dank and gloomy, like something from an Edgar Allan Poe horror film.

I slithered and slid down the rocks to the water's edge – you could not imagine a bleaker, more godforsaken place! To my dismay, we had to clamber over giant boulders and smooth slabs of rock around the perimeter of the lake. We found a path from its north-west shore and then dropped steeply down a narrow, indistinct rocky path, northwards to our pass. This descent was just as trying as the one to the lake, and took a good hour. Finally

we were at the junction with the path up from Cwm Nantcol, and we turned east, crossing a stream and walking between Rhinog Fach and Rhinog Fawr, which both rose up majestically, but disappeared into cloud after 100 feet or so. I felt as if I'd been pummelled all over with a wet towel; my knees were like jelly from all the steep descents and my fingernails were broken and full of dirt because I'd taken my gloves off to hold onto the rocks.

Gradually the pass widened out and we followed a well-defined path on the northern edge of the valley by a stream, dropping down into a forestry plantation through some huge pools of mud (the last thing I needed). Here we picked up a track out of the forest and eventually, after about half an hour's walk, emerged on the other side of the fir trees to see the Land Rover. Hoorah! It was 5 p.m. – it had taken seven hours to walk about 10 miles through the mountains. I drank some hot coffee and ate a huge sticky bun with white icing and a cherry on the top. It tasted brilliant. I didn't have any dry clothes left to put on, but we dropped Rhodri back at his car and went to the hotel where John, the director, was sitting by the fire, poring over maps.

'I wish you'd filmed today,' I moaned pathetically 'I want people to see what I went through.'

When he didn't rise to the bait I added, 'And that crew will never be able to climb up the rest of the range with all their equipment. I think we need a mountaineering crew.'

'Well, it's too late to change things now,' he countered. I flounced off to my room to peel off my wet layers.

I then lay in a hot bath drinking cup after cup of tea. My brain was wired, my ears battered by hours of wind and my face was bright red. I looked as if I'd scoured it with a brillo pad. I know how I felt when I staggered into supper an hour later – superior! I'd just been through the toughest walk of my life – worse than the Himalayas – and I was very proud of myself. I had learnt something valuable today that would serve me for the rest of my life: I hadn't given up.

DAY 44
Rhinogs to Maentwrog

Two days later, we drove back to the forest where I'd stumbled down from the first day of walking in the Rhinogs a battered, sodden wreck. Now it was a beautiful sunny day and, as I drove north up the A470 from Barmouth, I could clearly see the route I had taken in thick cloud earlier in the week. The range stood there like a forbidding wall, with the long flat ridge leading to the peak of Y Llethr (the highest point in the Rhinogs, but probably the least spectacular), with the rocky pinnacle of Rhinog Fach next to it. We got out of the Land Rovers and everyone put on enough kit for an SAS training exercise. I knew that half of it would be coming off as we toiled up the rocky slopes of Rhinog Fawr.

My route lay across this rock pavement in the final section of the Rhinogs.

We started by retracing our steps through the forest and up to the pass. On the way, Rhodri told me that the conditions we'd endured the other day were the worst he'd ever encountered in that section of the Rhinogs. I knew it had been tough, but felt that perhaps he was flattering me – after all they must get really bad snow, ice and blizzards in the winter. Our path to the foot of Rhinog Fawr – Blwch Drws Ardudwy – had been used for hundreds of years by the sheep farmers of Dinas Mawddwy and Dolgellau to drive their sheep to the winter pastures of Harlech and Dyffryn Ardudwy.

Our first climb was to be up a barely defined path, if you could call it that, to the summit of Rhinog Fawr (allegedly the rockiest mountain in Wales, apart from Tryfan). The

Janet and I are ecstatic that we managed to climb right through the gruelling Rhinogs range.

Rhinogs are hard Cambrian rocks: fragmented gritstone, with heather, mosses and bilberries growing in its nooks and crannies. We started the ascent and the path, such as it was, soon vanished. I clambered up the rock, pulling myself up by my bare hands where necessary.

At one point there was a brief respite, when we rested on a flat shelf; the cameraman and director lit up cigarettes and everyone stood panting, lost in their own exertion; all you could feel was your own heartbeat. The blissful view across the forested plain below was a welcome diversion from the physical discomfort.

There is no set way to climb this mountain: for the final part of the climb we all struck out and scraped and scrambled our way up as best we could. The summit (2362 feet) and the trig point were great seats from which to admire Snowdonia in front of us.

I started descending by scrambling down a much-eroded slope, heading west, slipping and sliding over loose rocks, until I came to a wall. Then I turned north, towards the tiny but perfect lake of Llyn Du, which sat on the edge of another drop, like a tear-shaped

mirror. Having walked around the lake, I went down between rocks to the pass of Bwlch Tyddiad. Here I followed an ancient paved pathway between banks of rocks on either side – the Roman Steps. This route is not Roman but certainly medieval; one theory is that it was built as an alternative supply route to the sea at the end of the thirteenth century, when Edward I assumed control of the area and rebuilt Harlech Castle.

On my way down I noticed a large yellow slug with a death-wish slowly crawling across a large flat slab on the path. This was like venturing into the fast lane of the M1, for the Roman Steps were fairly bustling with visitors walking up from the car park below. I felt so sorry for Mr Slug, I flicked him to the safety of a nearby bilberry bush with my walking stick. I was obviously undergoing a personality change as a result of walking over 450 miles, and turning into a nicer person!

Cwm Bychan was a restful spot between the mountains; a good place to have lunch sitting by the stream. Then Rhodri and I set out to climb Clip, the first hill in the final northern section. There was no clear path, so we headed up the grassy slope from the car park and then entered a nightmare section of waist-high bracken and big rocks. The final scramble to the top took nearly two hours and was one of the nastiest bits of climbing I've ever done. All my nails were now broken and full of dirt, my arms covered in scratches. The perfect sunny day compensated somewhat – but the biggest reward was the view from the flat pavement on the top. It was only 1937 feet, but it could have been Mont Blanc for the effort involved. I lay flat on my back, recovering slowly. Then I drank some hot tea, ate some chocolate, admired the views down to the coast and took lots of photographs. My good humour returned as I realized that, although traversing this northern section would involve scrambling up and down rock pavements with gullies between, a visual feast of rock formations and tiny lakes lay ahead.

Over the next two hours we picked our way through the lunar landscape, heading from cairn to cairn in a northerly direction. Moel Ysgyfarnogod (2044 feet) had a grassy summit and a trig point and I met the crew there: they'd got a lift up on a quad bike with a local farmer. The next summit was Foel Penolau – directly opposite with a flat, rocky pavement on top and cliffs on all sides.

By dropping down a grassy gully to the north-east, we skirted round these walls of rock until we found a way to scramble up. The areas of rock pavement in this part of the Rhinogs are unique: split, with deep vertical cracks, and spotted with orange and yellow lichen. Centuries of erosion from wind and rain left small boulders marooned on the smooth surface, like discarded giant footballs. It was a volcanic landscape walked by few people. We climbed down from it and then up one final top, Moel y Gyrafolen, covered in heather and bracken. But where was the path down? According to my *Cambrian Way* guidebook, we had to look for a path down to the north-west and head for a stile. We slid and slithered down a small sheep path, falling over several times, grabbing onto rocks and bracken to slow

ourselves down. It was frightening – thrilling but requiring total concentration to avoid disaster. We inched our way down, then followed a stream until we came to a well-defined path leading through a broad grassy pass east towards Lake Trawsfynydd. Passing through some gates, we re-entered civilization and the domesticity of farmland after our brush with lunar madness and rock world.

At the bottom of the path I went down a narrow, old cart track, opened a gate and emerged onto a road by the farm. I said goodbye to Rhodri and decided to press on to Maentwrog alone. Lake Trawsfynydd lay in front of me, with the nuclear power station rising up like two concrete blocks (not looking at all like the Welsh castle that Sir Basil Spence claimed he had in mind when he designed it in 1962).

The lake is in fact a reservoir, created in 1924 to supply the power station 2 miles away at Maentwrog. Many locals are worried about pollution – claiming that the lake contains radioactive waste. Magnox (who own and run the station) want to turn the lake into a leisure centre – one possibility in an area of high unemployment. In 1994 the film *First Knight*, a version of the Arthurian legend starring Richard Gere and Sean Connery, was shot here, and a big fibreglass and plywood version of Camelot was built on the shores of the reservoir. The film was panned by the critics but loved by locals – 600 of them got jobs as extras at £40 a day.

I walked a little way down the road by the lake and then picked up an extremely old cart track, with hawthorn trees forming a canopy overhead and old, low, stone walls on either side. After a while the track rose up slightly above the lake and crossed a bracken-covered headland. This got extremely boggy. Then I reached a stone channel containing water being funnelled into the lake.

I crossed the dam on a concrete road to the pumping station, which was on my right. I followed this road along; on the left a stream dropped down to a valley. By a forestry plantation I saw an amusing sign which said: 'Beware. Footpaths ahead'. Taking a laddered stile on my left, I headed into the forestry along a well-defined track between mature trees.

After half a mile or so, this was crossed by a large forestry track, and it was here that I went wrong. My guidebook told me to look for pylons above, but it had clearly been written before the forest had grown as large as it is now. All I could see was the tops of fir trees; it was growing dark and I was getting extremely cross and tired.

Having walked east along this track for about half a mile, I got the compass out and realized I'd gone wrong. I retraced my steps, in a thoroughly bad mood. Why, oh why so many times on this walk were there footpath signs into forestry plantations, and then none whatsoever within them? By now I was getting a bit jittery, as I could hear gunshots about quarter of a mile away in the forest. Someone was out getting rabbits.

I continued for a few hundred yards, emerged into a field, and lo and behold, there were the bloody pylons I'd been told to look out for! I crossed under them and passed through

a series of fields. Dusk was coming in pretty quickly now. I went over some stiles, found a house on my left, skirted round it, went through a gate onto their driveway and walked down it, until I met the road at Bryn Tirion. The sunset was magnificent: the stormy sky varying shades of pink, with lots of grey clouds and blue between.

I then followed a very pretty B road through isolated farms, in the direction of Maentwrog. I was dying to pick some sloes to make sloe gin, and outside the farmer's house I saw three bushes laden with them. He came out of the house as a lady drove up and delivered a parcel to him, and when I saw how poor his house was and how old he was, I didn't think I could pinch his sloes for my gin.

So I continued, curving through a most beautiful, old oak forest until my road was joined by another from the left, and it became wider. I passed some pretty grand houses on the way to the village of Maentwrog, and I noticed that the village itself had some very well-built, large stone houses. It was interestingly situated, descending a hill, with magnificent views down the estuary to the west. At the Grapes pub I called it a day!

Today my route would take me up from the valley floor of the Vale of Ffestiniog, past a power station and up to the peaks of Moelwyn Mawr and Cnicht, the latter being described as the Welsh Matterhorn – more because of the outline of its summit rather than its height (only 2265 feet but a grand mountain all the same). I'd pass through a remote valley and a deserted slate quarry – a menu of varied visual delights guaranteed to please any walker. So *why* did I have such a troubled night?

DAY 45
Maentwrog to Croesor

My knees were really hurting. I got out of bed at 3 in the morning and did some yoga and stretching exercises, then I put on my track suit and rolled round on my orange plastic acupressure balls on the floor. Eventually I went back to sleep at 5 and was woken by the alarm at 7. Feeling really grizzly, I went downstairs and ate a kipper for breakfast. The sky looked grey and threatening.

I couldn't face walking in continual rain, so I had a protracted telephone conversation with John Ellis Roberts, my guide, about the weather. He thought, on balance, it would be showery, so I arranged to start walking with him by Llyn Stwlan at the start of the ascent to Moelwyn Mawr. I planned to knock off the lower part of the walk by myself.

At Maentwrog I had a cup of coffee in the Grapes, then started walking along the road over the Dwyryd River, turning right along a small road before the main road climbed the hill on the far side of the valley. I took a signposted path that rose up through woodland (part of the Coed Maentwrog Nature Reserve). I went past a house on my left (what a fantastic position it had, facing south over the valley with cows grazing in the luxuriant green meadows below) and then over a little railway line – the Ffestiniog Railway. Heading east, as

I climbed ever higher, I criss-crossed over the line, passing the deserted station of Dduallt, where the line circled back on itself. Eventually I emerged from the woods and picked up a wide track, which climbed over a hill (at this point the railway was in a tunnel below me), to emerge at the southern end of the Tanygrisiau Reservoir.

There I crossed over the line and followed a path above it, along the side of the valley. My path now rose even higher to cross a stream by a wooden bridge near a ruin. Hearing rustling above me, I turned and saw a wild goat about 10 yards away. It had the most enormous handlebar horns – they must have been almost 3 feet across from end to end. The animal's coat was long, silkier than a sheep's and very unkempt. This monarch of the moors seemed totally unfazed by my presence and continued to munch some leaves on a branch that was overhanging the stream. Finally, as I approached, it loped off: a formidable encounter.

Now I faced a steep climb up past some disused mines on a series of paths that were hard to find. I could see the retaining wall of Llyn Stwlan high above me as I toiled slowly up the slope. At the dam I went over to the car park.

John Ellis Roberts was a tall guy with a strong face, grey hair and a likeable manner. He was very positive, a man of few words, and I liked him enormously from the start. He seemed rather shy at first, but warmed up after a bit. He was definitely someone who took control of the situation, which is what you need in the mountains.

Moelwyn Mawr, our first summit, was in cloud. We crossed back over the dam and a pumping station swirled in and out of the mist – very, very atmospheric. On the far side, we followed the bank round and then struck up, heading along a narrow, indistinct path, aiming for a ridge high above. We climbed up, first through grass and then through boulders, heading directly north. The summit was 2527 feet.

As we got onto the ridge an exciting thing happened: the clouds separated and seemed to blow up from below, then past us. We looked to the west and could see the coast – Harlech and the Rhinogs all became visible and then invisible. It was absolutely magical: probably one of the best weather moments of the entire trip. I took lots of photographs and just roared with laughter at the way the clouds swirled about. One minute we were in sunshine and the next in cloud. It had been pretty warm walking up. The lake lay in a steep-sided bowl of rock and grass, with the crew and their Land Rover tiny below us.

Our final ascent to the peak involved quite a lot of scrambling up very eroded rocky paths. Having achieved the peak (and this one was a top experience, well worth the climb), we turned north-east, descending from the rocks, and climbed down the grassy, broad flank of the mountain to the north of the reservoir. After that, we crossed a remarkable landscape, heading north through a series of old slate quarries. First of all we saw piles of spoil, then ruined buildings, then whole roads made of slate, then whole mountains of it. It was a

Looking back at Moelwyn Mawr with cloud swirling about us.

vista of purple, each flat expanse of stone embellished with green lichen. As we went down, we saw some places where the slate off-cuts were so thin that they were like leaves piled against each other, the ends forming intricate geometric patterns.

We were now on a large valley floor, with the ridge leading up to Cnicht forming the northern edge. This was an area of bog and many lakes. I'd heard stories that, during the last war, the paintings from the Royal Collection had been stored somewhere in a cave in this bleak, deserted landscape. We dropped down a track made up of tiny pieces of waste slate to a fine archway set in the wall of a ruin. This was Rhosydd Quarry, which opened in 1852 and at its peak had 200 workers. It closed during the First World War, reopened in 1919 but closed again in 1930. One last attempt to make it pay took place in 1947, but it was finally dismantled in 1948.

We sat on a slate bench outside a shelter to eat our sandwiches before a rain cloud disgorged its contents. We were opposite two terraces of ruined houses: they had been quarry offices, and workers had once walked miles to get here every day. It looked a

bit like an eerie version of Coronation Street, miles from anywhere. Some of my Welsh ancestors had worked in the slate quarries at Bethesda, and I tried to imagine what it must have been like to lift these huge slabs and cut them by hand. It seemed that licences had been granted for quarrying to resume near Rhosydd, meaning an end to the eerie calm that existed at present.

Gradually we climbed northwards, heading for the ridge of Cnicht. There were lots of little lakes and John told me that not all of them were natural. Many had been made by the quarry owners to store water, which they would then divert and use to run water wheels and to turn the quarry machinery. This part of our route, it seemed, was often used by outward bound and navigation courses. In this desolate landscape you can't navigate by looking at the lakes and relating them to a map because the water table is constantly changing and the lakes change shape – they shrink or get bigger, or the islands disappear. You have to navigate by compass to understand where you are, especially as the cloud can come down at any time and the path is virtually non-existent.

As we picked our way across this rather intimidating and desolate environment, I started to feel a bit downcast at the thought of another climb, but John gave me a really good tip. If you look at the size of the sheep on the ridge opposite, you'll realize it's much nearer than you think. Funnily enough, no one had ever said this to me before. From then it was a long slog south-west up to the summit of Cnicht, first on a broad, green grassy path, but finally climbing through a most exciting series of pinnacles. Here the route got narrower and narrower and we went over a series of lower summits until we finally reached the main one, which was an outcrop of pointed rocks probably about 12 foot square. A terrific top! I gave a big cheer and took lots of pictures. The views on all sides were breathtaking. I could see right across Snowdonia, although the top was in cloud, and to the south, the Rhinogs, and Moelwyn Mawr that we'd just climbed, which was now completely covered in cloud.

When you see Cnicht from the village of Croesor below, it looks like a monumentally steep mountain to climb. The steep descent from the summit is actually about 100 yards long. I headed down slightly to the left, and came to no harm whatsoever. I must admit, though, that it's not a summit I would recommend either climbing or descending from in high winds and rain, as the rock can be incredibly slippery.

Then, gradually, we started coming down a broader and broader flank of the mountain. We got to a wall on our right and skirted round a rocky outcrop. Then we kept to the centre of a broad, green bulge in front of us, came to a ladder stile and carried on heading in the same south-westerly direction, until we got to a path on our left which took us down into the village of Croesor.

From the reservoir to Croesor had taken just under four hours, so I had acquitted myself well. It was a switchback of a walk and the presence of that ghostly slate village in the

On the rocky summit of Cnicht with Porthmadog estuary behind.

middle was an added bonus. I thought about it afterwards and it reminded me of those dead mining towns in Arizona and Nevada, near Death Valley.

Instead of dry desert, this part of Wales is often like a wet desert where nothing grows. There is simply grass, bog, rock and sheep. I thought how many Americans I knew would have loved to have done the walk I'd done today. It was spectacular – every bit as good as Monument Valley, Arizona. The slate village was just like a giant piece of Barbara Hepworth sculpture. It was humbling really: the thought of hundreds, probably thousands, of men toiling with these great lumps of slate, breaking them by hand and carrying them round with no assistance. It was a lot of toil for an industry that seemed so troubled. And now slate floors are all the rage once more…

DAY 46
Croesor to Bethania to Beddgelert

I walked through Croesor – it was Sunday morning and people were in chapel – and continued up from the village to where I'd come down from Cnicht, following a wide track down a pretty valley: to the north was Yr Arddu, a very rocky mountain. The path wound its way west, curving round the bottom of the mountain on an old drover's track. It joined a tiny road and crossed a bridge, then went up through some woods. Eventually I dropped down into the little village of Nantmor. A sign announced that there was line dancing in Beddgelert – was there no escape?

My path briefly joined the A4085, which was full of Sunday drivers out summit-spotting. Then, at the car park at the far end of the village I walked up onto a disused railway line and followed it above the river, north through the Aberglaslyn Pass, all the way up the valley to Beddgelert. I went through one long tunnel first and then a series of shorter ones. Unfortunately I didn't have a torch. Some people came the other way with lights, which was handy because I'd never have seen them in the dark. I could hear their whispered conversations and the sound of water dripping through the ceiling.

When the film *The Inn of the Sixth Happiness,* starring Ingrid Bergman, was shot here, the Great Wall of China was built in Nantmor and the Aberglaslyn Pass became the Yellow River. Apparently 100 Chinese children came from London to be extras; the local kids who appeared got a guinea each and the adults two guineas. I was now in rhododendron country – they sprouted everywhere. But, although tourists come to see them in bloom, it seems the National Trust and the National Park are determined to eradicate this pest of the shrub world. They've spread like weeds, thriving on the acid soil, since they were introduced 200 years ago; nothing grows under them and they poison plant-eating mammals and insects. So four 'rhododendron bashers' are employed in Nantmor in a futile attempt to stop their progress!

The railway track I so enjoyed walking along is currently the centre of massive controversy. Once run by the Welsh Highland Railway, there are now plans to reopen it. In 1922 it was the longest narrow gauge railway in Wales, running from Porthmadog to Dinas Junction near Caernarfon. It always lost money and eventually closed in 1937. Now the Ffestiniog Railway wants to reopen this section and have the whole route operating by the year 2005. A public enquiry started in December 1997 to debate the issue: ramblers and the National Park were objecting.

I met plenty of other people coming in the opposite direction, many clad in gear more suitable for an ascent of the Matterhorn than a couple of miles of almost level gravel! After a few more tunnels that were no more than extended arches, there was a bridge over the river to my left that had a large 'Closed' sign on it. The crew took no notice, of course, and walked over it, just as everybody else seemed to be doing.

On my right the mountains rose up very steeply. I followed the river across a meadow

into Beddgelert, crossed a stream, turned left and found myself in the centre. There were hanging baskets everywhere – it was a total tourist trap, no doubt about that, but none the worse for it. I bought loads of postcards in the newsagent's and stopped in a café for tea.

The fascinating thing about Beddgelert's premiere position in the league of Welsh tourist attractions is that its popularity is entirely founded on a lie. And it's a really good example of early marketing to tourists. This village sits at the meeting point of the rivers Glaslyn and Colwyn, a stone's throw from Snowdon and its attendant scenic splendours. Early Victorian climbers and walkers used to come here for healthy holidays. But in 1800, David Pritchard, the landlord of the Royal Goat Hotel, had a brilliant idea. Why not build a grave for Gelert, the dog at the centre of the story every Welsh schoolchild knows, which goes as follows.

Llewelyn the Great had a faithful dog, Gelert, who accompanied him on all his hunting trips, but one day stayed at home while his master hunted. A wolf came into the prince's home and, seeing the prince's son in his cradle, he made for him, only to be intercepted by Gelert. In the fight that followed the wolf was killed, Gelert was wounded and covered with blood, and the cradle was overturned, the blankets falling on the bloodstained floor. Llewelyn returned and was horrified to be greeted by the bloodied dog and was convinced it had killed his son. He stabbed his dog, whose dying yell woke the baby asleep under the blankets. Only then was the wolf's body found and Llewelyn realized how faithful the dog had been.

The myth – Beddgelert or Gelert's grave.

In Welsh, *bedd* means 'grave', so David Pritchard passed off the new grave of Gelert as Beddgelert – and ever since people have come from all over the world to stare at a plot of earth under a tree where nothing whatsoever is buried! The 'grave' sits in a meadow just by the river. When I walked past, reverential Japanese were photographing each other by it and the place was teeming with visitors.

I retraced my steps, crossed the river in front of a very pretty house and followed the river once again, heading east in the direction of Bethania, towards the lake of Llyn Dinas about 2 miles away. High above me to the south, on the slopes of Moel y Dyniewyd, was the Sygun Copper Mine. Working until 1903, it was reopened in 1986 by a mining enthusiast as a tourist attraction – now it gets over 50,000 visitors a year. A large Welsh flag was flying outside. Opposite the mine was the wooded hill of Dinas Emrys, the site of an ancient fortress where Merlin is supposed to have left treasure in a cave. It was a fine, sunny afternoon and I reached the edge of the lake, the water still and perfectly blue. On the far side a steady stream of cars passed along the A498 – there were a lot of visitors, considering it was late September.

At the far end of the lake I walked over water meadows and then along the edge of a wood, finally crossing a bridge. I passed a little farm with chickens outside and arrived on the main road by the post office in the tiny hamlet of Bethania, named after its chapel.

There used to be so many workers in the slate quarries and copper mines that Bethania was extended in 1867. Now it's just somewhere people park their cars and school minibuses before they climb Snowdon. The car park at the end of the village was full: people were returning from their walks – it was 6.30 – and a festive atmosphere prevailed. I was surrounded by noisy teenagers in Nike trainers and matching hats – there wouldn't be much privacy on the remainder of my route.

DAY 47
Snowdon

We assembled in the car park at Bethania. I was to walk with Sam Roberts, the National Park Warden for Snowdon, who I'd already seen on television extolling the beauty of his mountain. Sam was passionate about the landscape and determined that people should respect this special part of Wales. I was looking forward to my climb, although I knew I would find it crowded after the lonely adventures of the Rhinogs. And this despite the fact that the route I was to take was one of the least popular because it involved the greatest ascent (about 3387 feet). Most people walked the Horseshoe Route using the Miners' and Pyg Tracks up from the Pen-y-Pass car park, starting at 1168 feet! Snowdon, because it has a little railway all the way to the top, is the most visited mountain in England and Wales as well as being the highest (at 3560 feet).

Of the 500,000 people who come here each year, about one-third take the easy option and travel up on the train, which started operating in 1896. There are six different routes to the summit, the first recorded ascent of which was by a botanist, Thomas Johnson, in 1639. The Welsh name of the summit is Yr Wyddfa, which means 'the tomb or tumulus'. According to legend, the summit of Snowdon is the tomb of Rhita Gawr, a fierce king-killing giant who dressed himself in a cloak made of kings' beards. Rhita was eventually slain by King Arthur.

Sam and I set out on the Watkin Path, named after Sir Edward Watkin, a railway tycoon, entrepreneur, dreamer, pioneer of the Channel Tunnel and Liberal MP. In 1892 he invited William Gladstone, then 83 years old and just elected prime minister for the fourth time, to perform the opening ceremony. Gladstone addressed a crowd of 2000 people on 'The Land Question in Wales'. A roofed and carpeted platform held the guests and the crowd sang Welsh hymns in the rain. The path started off as a broad track, first passing through trees and then following a stream up on our right, past a series of waterfalls. We rose up through the grassy valley floor and came to a large boulder, in which is set a slate tablet commemorating Gladstone's visit. Then we followed the old tramway path to the disused slate quarry at Hafod-y-llyn. Here the ruins of the manager's house, the workers' dormitory building and the workshops were all still visible.

Now Sam and I struck out for the ridge, heading west and rising to the pass of Bwlch Cwm Llan. We toiled up through the bog of the valley floor, through tufts and tussocks of grass. But, as the ground rose more steeply, the final few hundred yards of the ascent was on a narrow trail through scree and loose rocks.

Four overweight, middle-aged businessmen in very new walking kit were coming down, looking smug. They recognized me and asked what I was doing. They were clearly on one of those executive-bonding exercises and all looked a bit red and sweaty (more used to walking from their company cars to the lift than scrambling down a mountain). I am always reminded of Germaine Greer's witty remark when someone asked if she gardened to relax and she replied: 'Why should I take my worries and anxieties out on plants? I garden because I like it!' And so I wonder why beautiful mountains should have to deal with the male menopause and executive stress. I want people to walk because they love it too, not because it's some desperate form of therapy! Well, I've got that off my chest.

Now we were on Allt Maenderyn and ascending a rocky ridge, wider at first, but with clear signs of erosion. The clouds, which had seemed so high above us, were closing in. Even though this route was supposed to be unpopular, there was a steady stream of walkers coming in the opposite direction. The drops were thrillingly steep on both sides, but the views gradually vanished in mist. I was climbing ever upward, sometimes scrambling a bit, lost in my private world of effort, hearing only the sound of my own breathing and dealing with the steady drip of my nose.

Another ridge joined our path from the left – the Lechog Route – and there was a 100-yard section with sheer drops on either side of a ridge only a yard or so wide winding through large boulders. I was wrapped in cloud and battling with a high wind so I slowly and painstakingly picked my way upwards through the rocks, feeling very definitely 50. I knew I was almost there when the ugly sight of the café hove into view.

Snowdon is a fine mountain, demeaned by the eyesore that sits on top of it. Allegedly designed by the architect of Portmeirion, Clough Williams Ellis, it must be the product of

Above: On the lower slopes of Snowdon.
Opposite: Sam reveals his bright pink socks for the camera.

one of his off days. The first refreshment hut was erected here in 1837, so Snowdon has always been a mountain for the people – not a secretive, lonely spot, but somewhere tourists could sit and enjoy. Originally there were plans for a hotel here, but they were scaled down, and the present monstrosity dates from 1936. At the moment there's an impasse in the debate about what should replace this café: the Snowdonia Preservation Society don't want anything, and the National Park have put forward two sets of plans.

It seems to me that as long as people come up by rail, you might as well accept that it's a tourist honeypot and provide better facilities for both walkers and rail users. At the moment there are large signs inside the café forbidding users to consume their own food. I asked permission to eat my smoked salmon sandwiches with their tea, as it was blowing a gale on the tiny concrete terrace outside. The cairn was just past the café – with the toilets forming the main feature of my view! On the cairn lay a lot of rotting flowers and notes in memory of Princess Diana, just adding to the general air of squalor. Apart from the wind, the most intrusive sound was that of the café's generator.

I'd had a low moment just before the summit, when the blistering pace I'd set on the early part of the ridge had slowed to a crawl. But when I got up to the café and chatted to a group of walkers from Manchester, I felt pretty happy – they made me roar with laughter by displaying the bizarre selection of food and drink they'd carted up in their rucksacks. One young man gave me a jam tart

from a large packet and another was brandishing a huge bottle of tonic water. They'd got up early and driven from Manchester for a day's outing. I really enjoy the companionship and laughs you get from meeting people on mountain tops – everyone is drunk on the experience of the climb!

I said a little prayer, and sure enough the clouds lifted briefly and I got a tantalizing view of Anglesey and the coast, then it vanished in thick swirling mist. My path down followed the track of the railway for a short distance to a large stone monolith at Bwlch-glas. Here I took the Pyg Track down. (Another option was to go via the very exposed Crib Goch ridge and join this track lower down, but there was no point – Crib Goch was in thick cloud and there was a howling wind.) The first part of my route zig-zagged down and had been restored in places. Below, the blue expanse of Glaslyn appeared and disappeared in cloud. This section, east of Snowdon, was once the site of extensive copper mining.

Our track slowly descended, keeping high above Glaslyn and then Llyn Llydaw, now a reservoir. We passed a third, smaller pool of water, Llyn Teyfrn, before descending on restored stone steps to the bustling car park. Here some extremely aggressive sheep tried to eat my left-over food. They were completely tame!

Here also Sam revealed he was wearing bright pink socks! He'd bought a whole lot cheap 10 years ago and was still wearing them – very dashing. The whole trip up had taken two and a half hours and about one and a half hours down. I had a slightly dissatisfied feeling – maybe I should have stuck it out and clambered over Crib Goch for a bit of a thrill on the way down. Or maybe I was just unsettled by the sheer volume of people – I'd spent so much time alone over the past few months. I thanked Sam, took a picture of his socks for posterity, and went down the road to the Pen-y-Gwyrd Hotel for tea.

This large stone building was constructed in 1810 on the site of a Roman camp. It has always been extremely popular with mountaineers and hikers, and was used as a training base for the 1953 Everest Expedition. The smoke room – a wood-panelled cosy bar – is full of wonderful memorabilia and historic photographs, including a ceiling signed by the team. The Everest Expedition members still hold their reunions here every five years.

I met Jane Pullee, the present owner. Her parents had run the hotel since 1935 and she remembered all the planning meetings for Everest from her childhood. The team members had only the weekends to get to know each other, and used to try out the oxygen bottles clambering up and down on the chairs! They held down other jobs during the week.

In a glass case in the bar Jane showed me John Hunt's string vest and the Sherpas' pay-book (where they signed using thumbprints). There were silk gloves to keep the climbers' hands warm and a straw boater. Jane said she gets tourists who arrive asking to see her 'relics'.

Looking at these thin mementoes made me feel somewhat humble. I'd moaned on about the inadequacies of my jacket in the Rhinogs. The highest I'd ever climbed was 16,000 feet in the Himalayas a few years ago. Then I was sick as a dog from the altitude. My little jaunt up Snowdon today seemed a bit toytown when I looked at the photos in the smoke room taken on that Everest Expedition. Imagine climbing the highest mountain in the world wearing a string vest!

After Snowdon I felt mentally exhausted. I'd just spent too long walking day after day, so I decided to take a week off before I contemplated my last three days, which involved climbing the Glyders, then up Carnedd Llewelyn, over the hills to Drum, and the final day into Conwy, which I'd done so many times as a child. I just didn't want to end my walk feeling too tired. Also, the muscles around my right knee were beginning to give me a few problems. I only had to go down a few hundred yards and they were starting to ache. So I took advantage of a friend's hospitality and flew to the South of France, to a house high above Nice. There I lay by a swimming pool to try to improve my sun tan, although I couldn't imagine why – when I went back to England there was no way it was going to be exposed in late October!

> **DAY 48**
> *The Glyders: Pen-y-Pass to Ogwen*

Back in London, refreshed, I caught the train to Llandudno, changing at Crewe. Then I boarded what seemed like a pathetically small train with about three carriages. An announcement revealed that there was no engine, but one was on its way from the diesel yard. After about 20 minutes it was fastened on to our very dirty train and we got underway to another apology that there wasn't a buffet car owing to 'operating difficulties'. Anyone who's ever travelled from Crewe via Chester to Llandudno Junction will know it is one of the most godforsaken sections of the railway network (once British Rail, now part of the Virgin empire). We passed acres of closed-down caravan sites in Colwyn Bay, Rhyl and Abergele, eventually trundling into Llandudno Junction about 20 minutes late, just before 7 p.m. I picked up my car and crawled along in the darkness behind a lot of very slow

Opposite: Looking back at Snowdon from the Glyders; a lot sunnier than the day I climbed it!

drivers, up the Conwy Valley, via Betws-y-Coed and Capel Curig, arriving at the Pen-y-Gwryd Hotel at 8.

John Ellis Roberts, my guide, came and had dinner and we went over the route through the Glyders. It would take about four hours to walk and there were going to be lots of interesting rock formations. My only worry was that, if it was windy once we were on the exposed peaks, it would be hard to hang around for long or have much to say. John and I pored over Walter Poucher's book *The Welsh Peaks*, looking at all his photographs of the mountains I had climbed. Poucher was a wonderful climber and landscape photographer, whose books are still the definitive guides to the mountains of Britain.

I spent a tormented night tossing and turning because the cameraman, who I'd never worked with before, had left a message to say he wasn't going to cross the Scottish border until 8.45 that night, which meant he couldn't possibly get to the hotel until at least 1 or 2 a.m. at the earliest. I got up about four times, walked around the room and scratched my head endlessly – my eczema had returned. All my Welsh relatives were supposed to meet me in a tea shop in Conwy on the last day of filming, and they'd been thrown into confusion by the time being changed, and were also completely worried about having to say anything in front of a camera.

Eventually I went into breakfast and met the cameraman and the soundman. It was all a bit much for me, first thing in the morning, when I'm definitely not at my sociable best.

The good thing was that the weather was absolutely perfect – not a cloud in the sky. When we arrived at Pen-y-Pass, the car park was already full and it was only 10 o'clock in the morning. The path up to the Glyders starts right by the youth hostel. You go through a gate and a garden at the side, then over a stile. I thought it was hilarious. What if it had been someone's house? They would have had hundreds of people tramping through their garden every day.

The path climbed up through boulders and flattened out occasionally, heading for a rounded lower summit just above the road. Glyder Fawr was 3279 feet and I reckoned it would take two hours to climb up to it. First you skirt up through pastureland, with the occasional boulder and patch of bog. Then you head to the south-west of Llyn Cwmffynnon and the mountain rises up ahead of you.

John Roberts pointed to an outcrop of white stones high above and told me to aim for that. So I picked my way up the path and when I got towards the first ridge, I could see three outcrops of rock; John told me the summit lay behind the furthest right-hand lump I could see.

This was one of those climbs where your body gets hotter and hotter but your head stays cold because the wind is so fierce. It was dazzlingly bright, and the best thing as I climbed up was the view to my south. When I stopped for a breather I could see all the peaks I'd climbed in the last two weeks; I hadn't seen them at the time because I'd climbed

them in such appalling weather. Snowdon looked absolutely fantastic – like a glittering piece of jewellery. In front of it was Crib Goch, and then, as I climbed higher, I could see the Rhinogs behind it, and even Cadair Idris which had never been out of the cloud the whole time I'd tried to climb it.

The haul up to the summit involved some rock climbing and some careful negotiation through scree; it was a toil and it did take a couple of hours. The summit itself consisted of a clump of rocks – and there were some people already on it. Two boys, who I'd passed on the way up, passed me again because I had to keep doing things over and over for the film crew, and I got cross because I didn't want them to think that I was unfit. It was my competitive streak coming out.

Anyway, the summit area was extremely exciting because of the way the eroded rock stood straight up in points. Then we crossed a spectacular ridge. It dropped away steeply on the north and the views to the south were fantastic. It was one of those walks where all the best peaks are behind you, unfortunately.

We picked our way across the slightly undulating ridge eastwards, carefully avoiding loose stones. Then we dropped briefly onto a broader, grassy shoulder before reaching the extraordinary rock formations known as 'Theatre of the Winds'. Rock upon rock lay stacked up on end like a pile of crazy signposts or exotic sculptures that had been exploded by the elements. We climbed up about 50 feet of rock, exhilarated by the clear blue sky and the thrilling panorama of peaks on all sides. Then I realized why the marines used this place for training in the Second World War – coming down was about five times harder than going up!

We sat just below the rocks and had our lunch out of the freezing wind, and I could feel the sun really burning my skin. I wished I'd packed some suntan lotion. It sounds extraordinary, as it was freezing cold at the same time.

The summit was like an adventure playground: there were so many rocks to climb. Even though I was tired and my knees were killing me, it was exhilarating. It was like being in a rock Disneyland. I really enjoyed it.

I also met a group of brave young men who were walking on top of the mountain in shorts – they'd driven over from Liverpool for a day's hike, leaving at 6 a.m. They turned out to be policemen – they must have been the only glamorous coppers in Merseyside! I was impressed.

Just before the summit of Glyder Fach (2362 feet) was the famous cantilever rock, shaped like a diving board. I stood on the very end of it and tried to imagine myself as a goddess of the wind – but I probably looked like another red-faced, windswept, old boot with delusions of grandeur. After that I was so high on the magnificence of the scenery that I didn't even mind the endless school parties of teenagers marching up with backpacks. Then we dropped down through a scree to the south of the ridge

Tryfan lay ahead of us. I wanted to come down this way until John told me I'd be absolutely potty, as it was one of the steepest and rockiest summits to come down from. Instead we went east until we picked up the Miners' Track, and then headed north-west, back on ourselves. Having skirted round the northern slopes of Glyder Fach, we had to climb up slightly to a stone wall on the ridge that connected Tryfan with Glyder Fach. Once we got to the wall and toiled over the stile, it was a steep descent on a much-eroded path, which had been restored in places. Where they've restored it is like a series of steps and you have to watch yourself every second of the way. By now my legs were incredibly tired and slightly wobbly.

All the land in this area, now owned by the National Trust, was once part of the vast Penrhyn Estate. I'd recently visited the extraordinary Victorian Gothic Penrhyn Castle near Bangor, a home of palatial proportions, now open to the public. The Pennant family were landed English gentry whose fortunes came from sugar, but by the nineteenth century their main income was from the slate quarry at Bethesda. In 1900 the entire workforce went on strike for three years to gain union recognition, against Lord Penrhyn's wishes. In the meantime, the strikers went to work at the copper mines near Snowdon, walking up this path, over the Glyders and up to the miners' huts on Snowdon every Sunday. They stayed there until work ended the following Saturday afternoon. When the strike failed, many of the miners didn't get their jobs back.

We dropped down to the lake, Llyn Idwal. The land around it was Wales' first National Nature Reserve. It sits in this beautiful glacial valley which now gets half a million visitors a year. Just to show you how busy this path is, there are two ladder stiles side by side into the car park. Thank goodness there was a café (it's been run by the Johnstone family from Bethesda for 40 years, and was started by their grandmother as a tea shack). I drank two enormous cups of tea, one after the other, and ate a huge fruit slice. The car park was in shadow, as was Llyn Ogwen, because it was now 5 o'clock in the afternoon.

Anne and John Nuttall, who've written a series of books listing and surveying every mountain in England and Wales, had been waiting for me since 3.30. (Climbing mountains with a film crew takes twice as long as climbing them by yourself.) I talked to them about their amazing feat of cataloguing every mountain over 2000 feet in England and Wales, then publishing books of routes and a wall chart so that the totally anally retentive can tick them all off. They have discovered 62 new mountains over 2000 feet and deleted 38 from existing lists. And they've climbed them all!

Anne and John were a charming couple, if somewhat eccentric (they love camping out summer and winter). They've even got an Internet site, so people can communicate with

Opposite: One of the extraordinary rock formations known as 'Theatre of the Winds'.
Overleaf: The famous cantilever rock near the summit of Glyder Fach.

Descending Glyder Fach and heading for the Miners' Track.

them! I thought it was so funny that something as primal and physical as hiking or rambling could be on the Internet.

So, instead of being like Chris Smith and bagging 'Munroes', I can now tick off 'Nuttalls' if I wish and compare my visit with those of other devotees via my laptop. Somehow I don't think I will, although I've bought their book on the mountains of Wales and very useful it is too. According to Anne and John, there are still peaks to be discovered and logged – their work is not yet done!

I said goodbye to them. By now it was almost 6 and I was brain dead.

Last night there were some very jolly advertising people in the Pen-y-Gwryd Hotel who'd gone up Snowdon on the train to shoot stills for a poster campaign for a bank. They'd taken 14 rolls of film to get one shot of the landscape, over which a computer was going to superimpose a bungee jumper. When I told them I'd walked all the way here from Cardiff

they were, frankly, incredulous. A trip up Snowdon on a train and a 400-yard walk had exhausted them! They'd started their dinner with champagne, moved on to red wine, gone on to port, progressed to Armagnac and, when I went to bed, were calling for more brandy and double vodkas… Apparently they were drinking away until 2 in the morning.

I got up at 8, having slept like a log between white cotton sheets (my favourite bedding, guaranteed to produce the best dreams). I went down to a huge breakfast. The ad men appeared in various stages of hangovers and DTs, still thinking they could keep a fried egg down. I just laughed.

I left the hotel at about 9.30 and drove to Llyn Ogwen to meet John Roberts. We met at the café in the car park at the end of the lake, then took a path round the far side of the water. I was a bit disappointed to discover that Llyn Ogwen is in fact only 6 feet deep. It's one of those magical lakes that I visited many times as a child. I used to imagine it to be bottomless, full of Loch Ness-style monsters, or at least King Arthur's sword, Excalibur, and some Welsh treasure. Now I'd found out that I could not only swim across it but probably walk across it, it seemed rather shallow and insignificant.

Anyway, John and I took the path and headed east along the north side of the lake, scrambling over rocks en route. First thing in the morning I am very stiff, even if I do some warm-up and stretching exercises, and I was frightened of slipping and hurting my back, so we made pretty slow progress. At the far end of the lake we saw a stile ahead of us, but we turned in front of it and climbed steeply uphill for a mile, with a stream on our right. Ahead of us lay a lake called Bryn Mawr, cupped in a rocky hollow.

When we'd set out from the café, I'd seen some hardy walkers striking up in a northerly direction and climbing up an incredibly steep rockface to reach our goal, the peak of Pen yr Ole Wen (3211 feet). I was really glad we weren't doing that; not because I couldn't have climbed it, but because it seemed a particularly macho and unrewarding way of approaching the mountain. There was so much more variety in our route, traversing the slopes to the north of the lake and then heading up along a stream, passing delightful little waterfalls en route.

We saw a lake above us, turned west and climbed up a very steep path that wound its way up through rock. At one point I literally had to climb up on all fours to reach the summit of Pen yr Ole Wen (which means 'top of the white light'). The views were magnificent to the south: Tryfan rising up in front, behind it the Glyders, and then Snowdon, its top in cloud. I felt a real sense of pride in having climbed them all. To my east I could see the flat expanse of Anglesey, but ahead lay an exhilarating trek of 4½ miles at over 3000 feet

through the Carneddau range. Our day would end at the peak of Drum, which I'd walked up to from Llanfairfechan so many times as a child, . Now I'd be walking on peaks I'd gazed at 40 years ago but never dreamt I'd climb.

From Pen yr Ole Wen we headed north towards Carnedd Dafydd. This wasn't too bad: we were on a path that led north-east along a ridge. Then I looked down to the lake of Bryn Mawr and realized how very cold the wind was. The weather had been forecast as being warm today, and it probably *was* warm along the coast. Isn't it irritating when you're walking, and you can see for miles but the sun's always on the other mountains? It was that kind of day – grey overhead but sunny on Snowdon, or grey overhead but sunny on Tryfan.

I'd worn a jacket when I went round the lakes to keep warm, but took it off as I toiled up to the first summit. Then I encountered an Arctic wind of unbelievable ferocity, coming from the south-east at about 25 miles an hour. Whatever heat I had built up vanished immediately. I put on all the clothes I had, including a thick woolly hat and gloves. I didn't care what I looked like – my nose was a steady drip. Now we walked north-easterly along a path that was flat for a while, and then climbed towards the summit of Carnedd Dafydd on a well-defined path, passing quite a lot of people.

We kept a steady pace upwards, levelling onto a gradual slope, and then faced another climb over an undulating ridge, rising all the time. The heavy wind blasting across my face from the east meant I had to have my hood up, and I was walking on a path of very small stones which were very loose, so I had to watch my feet. There were white and honey-coloured stones, bleached by people's feet, wind and rain.

The summit of Carnedd Dafydd was a bit of a disappointment (flat with stone windbreaks), but so many summits are. Then we followed the path to Carnedd Llewelyn by walking along the edge of an exciting ridge which dropped sheer away to the north. A series of steep cliffs, called the Black Ladders, rose up vertically for 900 feet – obviously great for climbing. The path was pretty level and we made good progress, contouring round the edge of the ridge. I took lots of photographs. The cloud kept lifting and we could see all the way to Anglesey, Bangor and Bethesda in the north. When I looked back – miracle of miracles – I could actually see Cadair Idris 30 miles away in the Rhinogs, and even Trawsfynydd Lake, like a little golden patch of water on the horizon. It was probably the longest view I'd had in the whole of my Welsh journey.

We reached Carnedd Llewelyn (3485 feet) where there was a group of exposed stones standing up on their ends, looking like tombstones, and, after climbing Llewelyn, the path carried on and we climbed up Foel Grach – a long, slow haul up to a cairn at 3202 feet. The southern slope was very eroded, so the path zig-zagged its way through soil that was free of any vegetation. Every now and then we'd see a few bilberry leaves poking out between rocks, but basically the landscape was loose rocks on bare, meagre earth.

Slightly over from the cairn we found a shelter, where we were very pleased to get out

of the wind and eat our lunch. There were a couple of men in there and one of them was well into his sixties. They were old friends – one lived in Flint and one lived in Pwllheli and they'd met up for the day to go walking.

We came down from Foel Grach and then went on to Garnedd Uchaf (again, a point of eroded rocks). We were on an easy path now; it was boggy in places and had been filled in with stones, but we could see that the peaks ahead were just rounded lumps.

The wonderful views constantly repaid the effort of coping with the wind. A little way down from the next summit of Foel-Fras (3091 feet) we met the people we'd had lunch with in the shelter and took each other's photographs. Now it was a relatively easy dip, down and up, onto the summit of Drum (2526 feet), where we ended the day's walking. The Land Rover had come up the National Trust track to pick me up and take me back. All I had to do now was walk from Drum to Conwy.

It was a poignant moment for me, walking onto the summit of Drum. I'd last been there about 38 years ago. I had walked up with my mother from Llanfairfechan. In those days, the track up to the summit of Drum seemed very lonely and frightening for someone of my age. I had looked across and seen Foel-Fras and thought it possibly the most horrible and forbidding peak I could ever imagine. The lake beneath us, Llyn Afon, had seemed black and terrifying; I had nightmares about it for years afterwards. The outline of Foel-Fras on that summer's day – with bad weather approaching – was indelibly etched on my mind. We had turned and rushed back to Llanfairfechan, and tea at my *nain's*.

I'd drawn and painted my memory of that landscape so many times as a teenager in art classes. In those days, in the 1950s, there was some kind of hut and a radar transmitter by the cairn on top of Drum (they're not there any more). When my mother and I were walking up there, a Land Rover had appeared on the track from nowhere, then turned round and gone back again; we'd found its sudden appearance and disappearance frightening. Perhaps my mother had transferred her fears to me. It seemed funny now that I'd walked all the way up there from Llyn Ogwen. Drum was actually the smallest of all the peaks and the least forbidding. The northern edge of the Carneddau range was just a series of large grassy hills, softer and gentler than their rocky relatives at the southern edge of the range.

To the east lay the Conwy Valley, a lush patchwork of fields and farms, while to the north lay Penmaenmawr. I realized that from now on it would be downhill to Conwy on the final day of my walk. I was sad that the walk was coming to an end, but I could see my goal beckoning, and civilization, with its tea shops, holiday homes and pubs, was only a short distance away. The Carneddau had been my last bit of wild, remote Wales. It was only 45 minutes down a bumpy track to Aber and the gruesome A55 – truly a road that has decimated the majestic coastline of North Wales, splitting villages in two and whisking day-trippers right by them in a series of tunnels and underpasses. Of course, by the sea all was sunny and warm – but my bright red, wind-burned face was testimony to the gale I'd walked through.

DAY 50
Drum to Conwy

It's Saturday night, 25 October, 9 p.m. and I've done it. And I expect you're wondering how I feel? Well, the answer is: mentally and physically shattered. I'm not out celebrating, I'm not drinking a bottle of champagne, I'm not in a hot bath: I'm wearing a pair of old black sweat pants and a nice baggy T-shirt with no underwear, lying here on my hotel bed on a pile of pillows, drinking a gin and tonic and thanking God I don't have to chat to anyone, look interested in anyone, comb my hair or, best of all, I don't have to walk up a hill or read a map.

It was sunny and bright today, and that, combined with a strong, cold wind, has given me a bad migraine. But I might also have a migraine out of relief that I've finally finished. After all, at the beginning I never thought I would. I secretly didn't think I'd manage to climb all these mountains, and I have. It's taken a lot more out of me than I thought it would. Physically, I suppose I'm in good condition, although last night I woke up every two hours with cramp in my legs.

When I started walking this morning I was feeling very tired – I'd probably had about four hours' sleep. I started off feeling shattered, but, thank goodness, it turned out to be the most perfect day. I looked out of the hotel window at 7.30 and it was dark. By 8 it was light and the lawn in front of the hotel was covered in frost, so thick it looked like snow.

We drove along the A55 and turned up through Aber, still a lovely, unspoilt little village despite the horrible road that now thunders through it, to the car park at the top of the village, where we were met by Elvin from the National Trust. He took us up on the track to Drum. I'm a very bad passenger in Land Rovers on these rutted tracks, so I had to keep closing my eyes, especially as the sun was coming up and seemed to be beaming straight into my brain.

It took about half an hour to inch our way up to the top of Drum, where I'd finished the walk yesterday. Foel-Fras was dappled in the sunlight, and just below us three wild ponies were grazing quietly. Up here it was cold and bright – all the puddles were frozen with thick ice. I had on a long-sleeved vest, a long-sleeved fleece shirt, a fleece waistcoat, a fleece jacket, gloves and a hat, *and* a hood. It was that cold.

As I came down from Drum, it was pretty wet, but, thankfully, the bog was frozen. I didn't want to step on it in case it cracked and I got my feet wet early on. So I kept the fence to my left and went right down to the Roman road at the bottom of the valley. To my left lay Aber and then Llanfairfechan. I could see the granite quarries where my grandfather had worked, and the little rounded hill of Dinas and its three streams where I'd spent so much time as a child. Over on my west I could see the Menai Straits and, the biggest eyesore of all, the horrible block of flats between Beaumaris and Menai, as white and ugly as Sizewell B Power Station. How they ever got planning permission I just can't imagine.

My next gripe was that the beautiful valley between Drum and the next mountain, Tal y Fan, was crossed by a double set of pylons, rising in parallel lines from Aber across to the

Conwy Valley. Why, oh why couldn't this power line be buried? I'll tell you why: because this is a poor part of Wales and for some reason people thought, well, it's on the edge of a National Park, let's just have these power lines going across the landscape. It would cost too much to put them underground.

The flat, grassy plateau below was where I used to come every summer with my mother to pick bilberries. I was on my hands and knees for hours on end, with a jam jar that took ages to fill. It would probably take twice as long now because of the over-grazing. Below me was Bwlch y Ddeufaen (the 'pass of the two stones'). And I could make out the giant monoliths on either side of the track that crossed my route.

I dropped to the valley floor and had a cup of coffee before making the ascent of Tal y Fan. It is only 2001 feet, but after all the walking I'd done, it was a summit I could have done without. Having toiled up the slopes embarrassingly slowly, keeping the wall on my right, I clambered over boulders and got to what I thought was the top, but of course it wasn't. Like many mountains, it had a fake peak. The actual summit was a big pile of rocks, with a trig point about half a mile further on. It was a glorious, sunny day, getting warmer all the time. Ahead of me lay Llandudno looking all glamorous and glittery, with The Orme a pretty good substitute for Cap Ferrat!

I dropped down off the mountaintop, heading north to an old slate quarry. I couldn't see any clear path, although there was one on the map; it just seemed quicker to head for where I could see some tips. There, by a standing stone, Maen Penddu, I picked up the quarry road and followed it through bracken, keeping walls on my right, north-east and then north.

After another 25 minutes' walking, I came to a junction where a road came in from the right. We were desperately trying to get to Conwy in daylight and do a lot of filming, and didn't want to lose any time. The director started moaning that we were late, so I left the crew and told them I would see them at the Sychnant Pass in 45 minutes – they thought it was at least one and a half hours away. I crossed the bracken, headed west, picked up a wide, grassy path and went north until I saw a plantation that I knew from the map I had to keep two fields above. Fairy Glen dropped steeply away to my left, but I found a sheep path that was pretty well-walked, and followed it north.

Having curved round above Fairy Glen, I joined the B road at Sychnant Pass and met up with the crew. I'd run as much as I could and speed-walked. Having started the day so cold, I was now sweating like mad. I'd taken off most of my clothes and just had my long-sleeved vest on. After I'd drunk half a bottle of water and eaten a couple of sandwiches I went up an asphalted road onto Conwy Mountain; the road suddenly ended and became a well-defined path. Conwy was an easy mountain to climb, thank goodness – a bit like a roller coaster, a long up-and-down grassy ridge.

Llandudno was getting closer all the time. I waved to my mum: I knew she couldn't see me but I waved anyway. Below me, for the first time, I heard the hideous roar of the A55

as it entered the tunnel below. The shoreline was blighted by an ugly caravan site: why on earth do we give these things planning permission when this is such a special piece of coast?

I sat and mused on all this on a nice, flat rock on top of Conwy Mountain, eating another one of my sandwiches and basking in the sun, when up ran a man whose age I couldn't immediately guess (he seemed in his seventies), wearing a very battered National Park Warden sweatshirt. He announced himself as John Lloyd Roberts from Llanfairfechan who'd been at school with my mum and knew Aunty Phyllis and Aunty Vi, and he'd run all the way up from the car park to say hello. Well, I was really touched. He was a lovely, lively old man. He wished me luck and said he was thrilled to see me. Then I bade him goodbye and followed the ridge all the way down into Conwy.

As I came down off the mountain, I turned between two houses into the outskirts of the town. A black Labrador sat outside a house staring at me. Some schoolgirls walked down the road together. It was a lovely balmy afternoon and everybody was out enjoying the sun. A man was hoovering his car, another was clipping something in his front garden. I paused on the railway bridge as a train thundered underneath. At the far side of the bridge, I turned right along the Bangor Road into Conwy itself, under some trees that were already shedding their leaves. At the medieval gates in the city walls, the cars were coming through thick and fast and I negotiated my way between them.

Then I climbed up onto the town walls and walked along them down to the quayside. I think Conwy is a most beautiful town; the walled part is so perfectly preserved. It was one of the towns fortified by Edward I, and its castle was built by the top architect of the day, James of St George. Edward constructed other castles at Caernarfon, Harlech and Beaumaris to keep the Welsh in their place. Earlier, the Welsh had used Conwy as a defensive barrier against the English. Then Edward I conquered the town and moved the monastery to establish his castle. The walls and castle were built simultaneously to protect the new chartered town founded in 1284. It took 1500 men five years from 1283 to build this elegant castle – and then it would have been lime-washed white.

I walked along the quayside: because it was half-term it was full of holiday-makers. Two little boys ran up and said they recognized me because I'd been on *Shooting Stars*. Well, there's fame for you! They asked me to give their love to Vic Reeves. I walked past the smallest house in Britain. After the castle this is Conwy's biggest (ha, ha) tourist attraction: 6 feet wide and 10 feet high and occupied up to 1900. The last resident was a fisherman, Robert Jones, who was 6 feet 3 inches tall.

In 1900 the council decided that the house was unfit for human habitation and should be demolished. But the local newspaper decided there might be a story in it, and the

Opposite: The very last leg – the descent down to Conwy.

editor and the owner toured Britain, measuring rival small houses in Ambleside, Cornwall, Devon and Bayswater Road, London. They claimed their house was proved the smallest and opened it as a tourist attraction. The current owner, Margaret Williams, is Robert Jones's grand-daughter and the women staff, always dressed in red cape and tall black hats, are all related and 'Jackdaws' (born within the town walls).

Ahead of me was Thomas Telford's elegant suspension bridge, a triumph of Victorian engineering, with its towers echoing the castle; and behind it, the railway bridge, built by Robert Stephenson in 1846. In 1991 the bypass under the estuary was opened. This has taken traffic away from the town but, some would say, has also robbed it of life, particularly when a huge Tesco store was built on the opposite bank, just outside Deganwy.

It is important that towns like Conwy retain a living heart and don't end up as bits of theme-park Britain – tourist traps that are dead out of season, when their marinas are closed up and the cafés shut. There were worrying signs that it was starting to happen here. Towns have to have variety within them to work for residents as well as holiday-makers. Over the water, Llandudno had managed it but Conwy seemed to be struggling.

I carried on past the aquarium and shops selling fleeces and fishing nets, made my way past the restaurant boat up to the castle, and climbed up to the King's Tower. This was the end of my journey and I was completely shattered. I could barely manage a smile. I was happy inside, but so very tired.

Then it was time to walk down the street and have tea with my Welsh relatives – my Aunty Vi, my Uncle Ray, my Aunty Phyllis, my cousin John, my Aunty Lilly and my mother. They were all waiting in the Clarence Tea Room, had already eaten about three cakes each and drunk several pots of tea, and were chatting away in Welsh until I arrived, then switched to English. We had a good laugh. I pulled my mum's leg about the sloe gin she and I had made the other week, and we sat there chatting about nothing much. It was a good end to the walk, seeing all the relatives again. Uncle Ray is English, but apparently he tried to speak Welsh before I got there. There was a big debate about whether the Galleon in Conwy or my favourite, Enoch's in Llandudno Junction, were the best fish and chip shops in the area.

The day finally ended with a visit to the line dancing in Llandudno. In an upstairs room next to the British Legion there were people of all shapes and sizes in western outfits with stetsons, fringed blouses, plaid shirts, cowboy boots, glitter, what can I say? Wild Wales embraces the Wild West. Since Dungeness I'd walked about 516 miles, climbed over 61,000 feet in Wales alone, and discovered one important fact: the people I'd met all harboured their own hopes, aspirations and fears, but put on 'Hooked on Country' and a very large proportion of them would form a line and robotically snap into action, clicking their fingers and whirling about – fantasy cowhands of the twenty-first century.

Opposite: My walk's end. Looking out from Conwy castle which forms part of the ancient walls of the town.

Postscript

I'm sitting in my kitchen in Clerkenwell in the City of London on a rainy Friday morning in late November. I finished walking about three weeks ago and my legs are still stiff. I'm thinking: why is it that, on a walk like the one I've completed, all the most difficult things never seem to get filmed? Is the real physicality of the walk going to come across in the series? It seems that the cameraman was always there when I was near a road but never there when I was struggling. Are the mud, the bogs and the rain – the hours down the forest tracks that suddenly became water-logged – all going to be apparent? Yes, the crew walked up some mountains, and they were really brave and strong, but I was walking a long, hard route day after day, and I must have gained a completely different view of the walk than the one they filmed.

Last Saturday I walked 10 miles above Littondale in Yorkshire and felt the air flowing back into my lungs. A long walk empties out your head – lets you do a lot of mental unpacking. I'll be out again with my faithful rucksack before too long. Silence and solitude were the most precious rewards of my coast-to-coast trek, and I was never happier than when I was slowly plodding through some godforsaken bit of bog in unfashionable, uninhabited, undeveloped Mid-Wales!

Places and People

Page numbers referring to illustrations appear in bold type

Aber 218
Abergavenny 110, 111, 114
Aberglaslyn Pass 200
Albery, Nick 11, 36-9, **37**
Allt Maenderyn 203
Alresford 50-1, 58-9
Amberley 37-9; Castle 39, **39**
Andover 53, 56, 57
Arthog 182
Ashburnham Forge 23, **24**
Atkinson, Ted 93

Bailey, Bill 11, 85-90, **86-7**
Baker, Julian 74, 75
Balchin, Rev. Michael **169**, 170
Barmouth 181, 184-8; bridge 184, **186-7**
Barton Stacey 52
Battle 21-3
Beacon Hill 41, 44
Beckington 75
Becton 40-1
Beddgelert 200, 201, **201**
Bethania 202
Bignor 40
Black Ladders 216; Mountain 136-7; Mountains 11, 100, 116-28, **119**, **121**
Blaenau 138
Bleadon 96; Hill 93
Blorenge 110
Booth, Sharon 27-8
Borrow, George 140-1, 161, 163
Botolphs 31-2
Bradford-on-Avon 70-2
Brecon Beacons 11, 100, 127-38, **129**, **131**, 142, 168
Bristol Channel 11, 84
Bruce Tunnel 62
Bryn Glas 171; Mawr 215, 216
Buckland Dinham 75
Bulls Green 76, **77**
Burges, William 101, 104
Burton, Darryl 122-7, 138-41
Bush, John 148, 171
Bute, Marquis of 101, 104
Butser Hill 47
Bwlch Cwm Llan 203; Giedd 137; -glas 205; Glynmynydd 167; Siglen 174; Tyddiad 193; y Ddenfaen 219

Cadair Idris 165, 171, 175-81, **178-9**, **183**, 209, 216
Caen Hill 69
Camber Sands 14, **16**, 17
Cambrian Way 11, 100, 136, 142, 153, 154, 165, 188, 193
Canals, Brecon 106; Brecon and Usk 123; Glamorganshire 102; Kennet and Avon 11, 60-70, **66**; Monmouthshire and Brecon 110
Capel-y-ffin 116-17
Cardiff **98-9**, 100-2
Carn Fawr 163; y Defaid 110
Carneddau 216-17; Dafydd 216; Llewelyn 216
Carson, Polly 64-5, 67
Castell Coch 101-4, **103**

Chanctonbury Ring 36
Channel to Channel 11, 24, 26, 78
Chantry 76
Chartist Cave 126
Cheddar 84, 85; Gorge 11, **86-7**, 88-90
Chiddingly 25
Chilbolton 53, **54-5**
Chutes, the 57-8; Causeway 57, 59; Forest 57
Clip 193
Cnicht 195, 197, 198, **199**
Cocking 40, 41
Collins, Keith 13, **14**
Commins Coch 167-8
Conholt 58
Conroy, Jim 24-5
Conwy 100, 208, 217, 219-22, **220**, **223**
Cowbeech 24-5
Cow Down 53
Craig Cwm Amarch 180; Portas 175; y Fan Ddu 128
Cranmore Wood/Tower 76
Cribin Fawr 175
Cribyn 130
Crickhowell 122-6, **124-5**
Cristea, Janet 30, 40, 153-6, 165-8, 176-88, **178-9**, **192**
Croesor 198, 200
Croft, Robert 132-6, **135**
Crofton 60, 62
Crook Peak 91
Crystal, Vicky 72
Cwm Bychan 193
Cymystwyth 154-5

Davies, Dafydd **149**, 150
Denge Marsh 14, 17
Devil's Bridge 153, 157; Dyke 31, **33**; Jumps 41
Devizes 63, 67, 68
Dial Carreg 116
Diffwys 189
Dinas Emrys 202; Mawddwy 171, 176
Dinas Nature Reserve 145
Ditchling Beacon 30
Docherty, Jim 78-9
Domen Milwyn 154
Downend 76
Draycott 85
Drum 216-18
Dungeness **12**, 13-14
Dyffryn Castell 159
Dylife 163-5

Ebbor Gorge 80, 81, 84
Evans, Rhodri 188-94; Wayne 127-30, 136-8

Fairy Glen 219
Fan Fawr 132; Foel 137; Gyhirych 133-5, **135**; Llia 132; Nedd, 133, 134
Farrant, Jenny 20-1
Ffestiniog, Vale of 188, 195; railway 195-6, 200
Fforest Fawr 133

Foel Dinas 174; Fras 217, 218; Grach 216; Penolau 193
Forest Coal Pit 112, 115
Fosbury fort 59
French, Michael 51

Garn Gron 151
Garnedd Uchaf 217
Garn-wen 110, 116
Gill, Eric 117
Girvan, John 67-8, **68**
Glaslyn 201, 205
Glyders 207-11; Fach 209, 211, **212-14**, 215; Fawr 208-9; 'Theatre of the Winds' 209, **210**
Glyndwr, Owain 162
Goodridge, H.E. 73
Grass, Jack 176-81, **178-9**
Great Elm 75
Gun Hill 25
Gwilym, Dafydd ap 151

Hafod-y-llyn 203
Hale, Gareth 39, **39**
Hanbury, Richard 108, 109
Harewood Forest 53
Hey, Stan 70-1
Hoare, Donald 161-3, **162**
Honeystreet 64-5
Hooker, Andy 73

Irving, Mike 51

Jarman, Derek 13
Jenkins, Simon 177
Johnson, Thomas 202
Jones, John 149-50, **149**; Robert 222; Terry/Alison 164

Kilmeston 50
Knight, Derrick 21-3, 22

Landor, Walter Savage 116
Lane, Hilary 27-9
Laughton Common 26
Lewes 27-9
Lewis, Donna 11, 100-2, **102**
Llandovery 139-44, **142**
Llandudno 207, 219-22
Llanfairfechan 10, 100, 112, 141, 217, 218
Llangattock 123
Llanidloes 159-60
Llanthony Priory 116
Llewelyn, Bernard 143-4
Llyn Afon 217; Cau 177; Cwm-ffynnon 208; Dinas 202; Du 192-3; e Fan-Fawr 137; Fyrddon Fach 153-4, Fawr 154; Hywel 189; Idwal 211; Llydaw 205; Lygad Rheidol 161; Ogwen 211, 215; Stwlan 195, 196; Teyrn 205; y Bi 189; y Fan Fach 136-8
Llynnau Gregennen 182
Lullington 74, 74
Lydd 14

Machen 105
Maen Llia 132-3; Penddu 219

Maentwrog 194, 195
Maesglase 174
Maesteg **166**, 167
Mallwyd 171
Marlborough 63-4
Marten 60
Mawddach estuary 184
Mellingriffith Pump 102
Mendips 11, 73, 81-93, **82-3**
Moel Eiddew 167; y Dyniewyd 202; y Gyrafolen 193; Ysgyfarnogod 193
Moelfre 165, 167
Moelwyn Mawr 195-6, **197**
Myddfai 139
Mynach Falls 157
Mynydd Llysiau 120
Mynydd y Cemais 170, **172-3**

Nantmor 200
Nantymaen 150
Nuttall, Anne/John 211, 214

Offa's Dyke 116, 118
Oxdrove Way 51

Pace, Norman 39, **39**
Paynter, Reg 60, 62
Pen Allt-mawr 120; Cerrig-calch 120; Pumlumon Lygad-bychen 161; y Fan 127-30, **129**, **131**; y-Pass 208; yr Ole Wen 215
Perrins, Frances Sarah 185
Pevsner, Nicholas 79, 80
Pewsey 63, 64, 68; Vale of 11, 62-3
Picws Du 137
Plumpton Plain 30
Plynlimon 161-3, **162**
Pontypool 108-10; Park 108
Presley, Reg 53, 56-7, **56**, 65
Priddy 84
Pritchard, David 201
Pugh, Richard 181
Pumlumon Fawr 161

Queen Elizabeth Country Pk 46

Reeves, Vic 11, 17-18, **18**
Rennie, John 62
Reynolds, Geoff 185
Rhandirmwyn 150
Rheidol Valley 157; railway 57-8
Rhosydd Quarry 197-8
Rhynogs 100, 188-95, **191**, **192**, 209; Fach 189, 190; Fawr 190-2
Richard de Clare 116
Ringmer 26-8
Rippon, Shirley 115-16
Risca 106
Roberts, John Ellis 195, 196, 208-11, 215; John Lloyd 221; Sam 202-5, **205**
Robson, Russell 44-6, **45**
Rode 73-4
Roman camp 138-9; Steps 193
Rye 18-19

Scott, Gilbert 76
Seaton, Caroline 38-9

Semington 69
Shepton Mallet 77-8, 80
Shipham 90-1
Smith, Chris 11, 144-8, **147**
Snowdon 100, 168, 202-7, **204**, **206**, 209, 211, 215, 216;
Snowdonia 11, 101, 174, 176
Somerset Levels **82-3**, 91, 93
Soronson, Peter, 66
South Downs 11, 29-48, **33-5**, **42-3**, **61**
Stephenson, Robert 222
Steyning Bowl 32, 36
Stowell Park Bridge 64, **65**
Strata Florida 150-2
Sugar Loaf 110-12, **112-13**
Sutton Scotney 52
Sychant Pass 219
Sygun Copper Mine 202

Table Mountain 120-1, **124**, 126
Taff Trail 102, **102**
Tal y Fan 218-19
Tal-y-Llyn 176
Tangley 57
Tanygrisian Reservoir 196
Taruschio, Franco/Anne 114
Tegdown Hill 47
Teifi Pools 151, 152
Telford, Thomas 222
Thomas, Alan 122-3, 126-7; Ed 111-12, **112**
Tidcombe 59
Torpantau Pass 127
Trawsfynydd Lake 194, 216
Tregaron 100, 148-50
Tryfan 211, 215, 216
Twmbarlwm 106-7, **107**
Twmpa 117, 118, **119**
Ty'n-y-cornel 146, 148

Uppark 44

Ward, Alan 132, 133, 136-8
Warnford 48-50, **49**
Watkin, Sir Edward 203
Waun-oer 175
Waun Fach 119, 120
Wavering Down 91, **92**
Wayfarer's Walk 50, 51
Weald 23-4, **24**
Wells 78-80, **79**
Welsh Peaks (Poucher) 208
West Mendip Way 89-93, 96
Weston-super-Mare 93-7, **94-5**
Wether Down 48
Whatley 76
Wherwell 53
Wilcot 64
Williams Ellis, Clough 203
Wilton 60
Winchelsea 19-20
Winchester Hill 48
Winscombe Drove 90-1
Wishart, Maureen Lehane 75-6
Wookey Hole 81
Wyatt, Thomas 74

Y Llethyr 189, 190